THE FIGHT OVER DIGITAL RIGHTS

In the political fight over copyright, internet advocacy has reshaped the playing field. This was shown most dramatically in the 2012 "SOPA blackout," when the largest online protest in history stopped two copyright bills in their tracks. For those not already familiar with the debate, this protest seemingly came out of nowhere, yet it was the culmination of an intellectual and political evolution more than a decade in the making.

This book examines the debate over digital copyright, from the late 1980s through early 2012, and the new tools of political communication involved in the advocacy around the issue. Drawing on methods from legal studies, political science, and communication, it explores the rise of a coalition seeking more limited copyright, as well as how these early-adopting, technology-savvy policy advocates used online communication to shock the world. It compares key bills, congressional debates, and offline and online media coverage using quantitative and qualitative methods to create a study that is rigorously researched yet also accessible to a general audience.

Bill D. Herman is an Assistant Professor in the Department of Film and Media Studies at Hunter College, City University of New York. He earned a Ph.D. from the Annenberg School for Communication, University of Pennsylvania, in 2009. His work has appeared in journals such as *Yale Journal of Law & Technology*, *Journal of Computer-Mediated Communication*, *Communication Law & Policy*, and *Federal Communication Law Journal*.

The Fight over Digital Rights

THE POLITICS OF COPYRIGHT AND TECHNOLOGY

Bill D. Herman

Hunter College, CUNY

CAMBRIDGE
UNIVERSITY PRESS

CAMBRIDGE
UNIVERSITY PRESS

32 Avenue of the Americas, New York NY 10013-2473, USA

Cambridge University Press is part of the University of Cambridge.

It furthers the University's mission by disseminating knowledge in the pursuit of education, learning, and research at the highest international levels of excellence.

www.cambridge.org
Information on this title: www.cambridge.org/9781107015975

First published 2013
Reprinted 2013

A catalog record for this publication is available from the British Library.

Library of Congress Cataloging in Publication data
Herman, Bill D., 1977–
The fight over digital rights : the politics of copyright and technology / Bill D. Herman.
   p.   cm.
Includes bibliographical references and index.
ISBN 978-1-107-01597-5 (hardback)
   1. Copyright and electronic data processing – United States.   2. Copyright – United States – Electronic information resources.   3. Fair use (Copyright) – United States.
4. Copyright infringement – United States.   5. Information networks – Law and legislation – United States.   6. Censorship – United States.   I. Title.
KF3024.E44H47   2013
346.7304´82–dc23   2012036032

ISBN 978-1-107-01597-5 Hardback

Additional resources for this publication at billyherman.com

For Tina, Mom, Bob, Trinity, and Finnegan

Contents

List of Figures

List of Tables

Preface

This study is the embodiment of an intellectual evolution more than a decade in the making. As an electronic and hip hop music DJ when I began my graduate studies in 2000, I became fascinated with remix culture, questions about creativity, and – with a nudge from Brian Ott – the socially constructed nature of authorship. The art of DJing and sampling became the locus where I began to investigate all of these questions over the course of my master of arts program in what was then the Department of Speech Communication (now Communication Studies) at Colorado State. As I progressed, I kept bumping up against questions of copyright. Was anything I was doing with my records on the weekends illegal – or, more realistically, was any of it legal? Could copyright evolve to keep up with new media technologies, in music and in other media, that had led to such a breakdown in the walls that separate individual copyrighted works? If authorship is socially constructed, and the romantic theory of authorship in particular is built on a problematically narrow view of the production of creative works, why should we allow copyright to restrict the other, equally valid means of being creative? Thankfully, for the sake of my academic progress, both Brian and my thesis advisor Denny Phillips encouraged me to save such questions of political economy for my Ph.D. program.

I began my studies at the Annenberg School for Communication at the University of Pennsylvania in 2003, intending to follow in the footsteps of Kembrew McLeod and Siva Vaidhyanathan – to add to our understanding of the system of cultural creativity, as well as of the poor fit between that system and the copyright law that governs it. While Annenberg Penn is indeed the home to first-rate qualitative work on communication cultures, it was also my first in-depth exposure to quantitative social scientific methods. I soon realized that not only do I like social scientific methods, but these could allow me to make a more unique contribution to the growing interdisciplinary area that Vaidhyanathan would dub "Critical Information Studies."[1] With several nudges from Oscar Gandy, I also began to look at the communication around copyright as a subject ripe for investigation – as a means of saying something about the political and economic forces behind copyright. This began with a quantitative study of the first two triennial rulemakings to determine exemptions to the Digital Millennium Copyright Act's (DMCA) ban on circumventing digital rights management (DRM) technologies.[2] This rulemaking is a microcosm of the broader debate over DRM and copyright, pitting the content industries and mostly sympathetic policymakers against a more diffuse, growing coalition of public interest groups, librarians, scholars, and technologists. We found hundreds of people willing to communicate a pro–fair use message via the online submission process, but only a few had the funding and time to appear in person, making the in-person hearing a much friendlier forum for the voices for stronger copyright. Moreover, we found that policymakers in Congress and the Copyright Office were strongly inclined toward the strong copyright end of the debate.

Building on what Gandy and I had found, I sought to conduct a broader study of the major debates over proposed DRM legislation. I had noticed, though, that official debates in Congress and unofficial in-person discussions were not the only places where relevant policy information was shared. As an outsider, I had still been able to learn a great deal about ongoing debates over copyright via the websites of groups such as Public Knowledge and the Electronic Frontier Foundation, internet research centers such as those at Harvard and Stanford, and scholars such as Lawrence Lessig. Although they provide far less detailed coverage, mainstream news sources, such as daily newspapers, are a particularly important source of coverage for nonspecialists. For instance, in helping him organize a 2004 conference on copyright as an obstacle to research,[3] I saw firsthand that this was how Annenberg Professor Joseph Turow had learned of many of the stories around copyright – stories that echoed

---

[1] Vaidhyanathan, "Afterword: Critical Information Studies."

[2] Herman and Gandy, "Catch 1201."

[3] The conference, held in June 2004, was titled "Knowledge Held Hostage: Scholarly Versus Corporate Rights in the Digital Age." For a brief recap, see Tom Zeller Jr., "Permissions on Digital Media Drives Scholars to Lawbooks," *New York Times*, June 14, 2004, http://www.nytimes.com/2004/06/14/business/technology-permissions-on-digital-media-drives-scholars-to-lawbooks.html.

his own accidental interest in this area of law.[4] Combined, then, the very formal medium of congressional hearings, the still-stately outlet of major newspapers, and the totally unregulated online debate seemed like the most natural place to examine the debate over DRM. From 2006 to 2009, I did exactly this, and the resulting dissertation – supervised by Professor Michael X. Delli Carpini – became the basis for this book.

There are many perils to writing a book that is largely about the internet – print is not interactive, concerns about cost constrain the sharing of relevant documents and data, and the internet will surely change a good deal in the time between manuscript submission and when the book is in readers' hands. For all these reasons, I have created a companion website for the book, to be hosted on my personal site: billyherman.com. Of particular interest, readers will find interactive, full-color versions of the maps of the online copyright debate. With these, readers (or, in this context, users) can click on the circles representing individual websites to see how they relate to other sites in the map, zoom in or out, and click on site names to go to those sites. I have also included items that will be of particular interest to specific audiences. For social scientists, I have provided my complete dissertation, which contains much more methodological and statistical discussion than is provided here. I have also provided my complete dataset in SPSS and CSV formats, as well as additional graphs and charts to delve further into specific outcomes. For legal researchers, I am also placing copies of all of the congressional hearings in question on the book's website. In the case of older hearings, this may potentially save a future researcher from duplicating some of the hours I spent at the library's microfiche machine. I would love to provide complete sets of newspaper articles and web documents as well, although ironically, copyright concerns limit me from doing so. Readers who are interested in particular documents for their own research,

---

[4] Turow, not a scholar who had previously studied copyright, became interested once he encountered a staggeringly labyrinthine and expensive process to get permission to use brief clips of TV representations of doctors in a multimedia project that, by any reasonable analysis, made only fair use of the clips – and thus should have required no permissions or payments at all. Entitled "Prime Time Doctors: Why Should You Care?," the work was a multimedia essay on DVD, distributed to approximately 20,000 first-year U.S. medical students by the Robert Wood Johnson Foundation each summer from 2003 to 2008. Newspaper coverage had tipped Turow off to the fact that he was not alone – that even scarier stories had also led people such as Princeton computer scientist Edward Felten and then–Swarthmore undergraduate Nelson Pavlosky to become interested in copyright. This inspired him to organize the conference.

however, are encouraged to contact me. My website will always have my current contact information.

This book is intended to be readable for a general audience yet of interest to experts and those working in the field. I have done my best to write for those who may have little or no training in communication studies, political science, or copyright law – yet hopefully with enough rigor, theoretical grounding, and detail to satisfy those with expert training in one or more of these areas. I realize that I will not have succeeded on either count, let alone both, to the total satisfaction of all readers. In terms of readability for those who are not experts in one or more relevant areas, where I have unwittingly assumed too much background knowledge, I hope the cited literature can provide answers, and the materials on the companion website may provide the additional details and explanations a reader may need. If all else fails, please e-mail me; in addition to replying, I may post an explanation on the companion website that can assist other readers. In terms of pure readability, I have pushed a lot of the more detailed discussions into the footnotes, and I have substantially streamlined my citations, including a bibliography of all scholarly works, as well as the statutes and cases I discuss. Likewise, to maximize the use value of the bibliography for other researchers, full citations for other materials – bills, congressional hearings, news stories, and websites – are found in the first note of the chapter in which each item is used, or they are identified in sufficient detail in the text.

In terms of my effort to be rigorous and detailed enough to satisfy experts and practitioners alike, this book will surely be less than totally satisfactory to many readers. There are undoubtedly areas where I have overlooked important details, failed to cite or make proper use of important prior literature, made claims that belie my long time in the academy and very short time in the trenches, and generally failed to write the book that others may have wanted. I accept this as one of the perils of conducting a study such as this, and I look forward to learning more by way of criticism.

This book would not have been possible without the generosity and support of the countless people who have helped me along the way. I can never repay the debts owed to Oscar Gandy and Michael X. Delli Carpini for their support of and patience with me during my time at Penn, both leading up to and during my dissertation writing process. I also thank Bob Hornik for making the time to help me make sound methodological decisions and appropriate use of statistics, even though the study is very far indeed from his areas of interest. Thanks to all of the faculty at Penn and CSU who helped turn me into the scholar I have become. In addition to those already named, the late Ed Baker deserves mention as having played a particularly vital role in shaping my work; being published by the same press that published his seminal works is an honor that I will always cherish.

My graduate school classmates at Penn and CSU have been some of the most amazing colleagues and friends one could hope for – too many to name – and I thank them for being there for me through the highs and lows of life. Thanks as well to the staff at each school, and in particular, Bev Henry. Additional thanks to my colleagues at Hunter College and the staff in our department and in research support offices. For helpful feedback and/or research assistance, thanks to Lokman Tsui, Lee Shaker, Tarleton Gillespie, Hector Postigo, Can Sun, Bill Rosenblatt, Peter Vardy, Joann Olivo (Hunter College Valedictorian, Spring 2011), Marisa Collins, Tina Collins, Charles Collins, Juan Medrano, and the reviewers and editorial staffs of the *Journal of Computer-Mediated Communication* and the *Yale Journal of Law and Technology*. Support for this project was provided by a Dissertation Research Fellowship generously provided by the Annenberg School, as well as a PSC-CUNY Award, jointly funded by the Professional Staff Congress and the City University of New York. Thanks as well to John Berger and everyone at Cambridge for the first-rate treatment I have received.

My family and friends have been amazingly nurturing and patient over the last six-plus years as this project has moved from conception to completion. Words cannot express my gratitude for my parents, Bob and Candy Appel; my niece, Trinity Herman; my extended family and my in-laws, especially my wife's parents, Charles and Pat Collins; and my son, Finnegan Connors. As a scholar herself, my wife Tina Collins has been more than just a supportive spouse – although she has been that and more, to a higher degree than I could possibly expect. She has also been my role model, editor, writing coach, and topical discussion group. The world is a much better place with her in it, and I am beyond lucky to have had her next to me for the last seven-plus years.

List of Abbreviations

AHRA: Audio Home Recording Act
BPDG: Broadcast Protection Discussion Group
BSA: Business Software Alliance
COICA: Combating Online Infringement and Counterfeits Act
DAT: Digital Audio Tape
DFC: Digital Future Coalition
DMCA: Digital Millennium Copyright Act
DNS: Domain Name System
DRM: Digital Rights Management
EFF: Electronic Frontier Foundation
IITF: Information Infrastructure Task Force
IP: Internet Protocol or Intellectual Property
ISP: Internet Service Provider
MPAA: Motion Picture Association of America
PIPA: PROTECT IP Act, itself an acronym for Preventing Real
          Online Threats to Economic Creativity and Theft of
          Intellectual Property Act
RIAA: Recording Industry Association of America
SC: Strong Copyright
SCMS: Serial Copy Management System
SFU: Strong Fair Use
SOPA: Stop Online Piracy Act
TLD: Top-Level Domain
USTR: United States Trade Representative
WCT: WIPO Copyright Treaty
WIPO: World Intellectual Property Organization
WPPT: WIPO Performances and Phonograms Treaty

Lightning in a Bottle

On January 18, 2012, the English language version of Wikipedia went dark. Instead of the usual homepage, visitors found an ominous warning cast against a dark gray background. The site warned:

> For over a decade, we have spent millions of hours building the largest encyclopedia in human history. Right now, the U.S. Congress is considering legislation that could fatally damage the free and open Internet. For 24 hours, to raise awareness, we are blacking out Wikipedia. Learn more.

In addition to linking users to a page with more information, the Wikipedia homepage also urged visitors to contact their elected representatives and included a box for looking up the representatives' contact information via the visitor's ZIP code. Wikipedia is the sixth most-visited site in the world, and it enjoys the same lofty ranking in the United States,[1] so this dramatic message on its homepage caught the attention of millions of people – a message that was amplified by near-universal news coverage of the blackout. Wikipedia was one of more than 115,000 sites that participated in spreading the message against this legislation.[2] Many others also blacked out their sites to illustrate the argument that the proposals, if passed, could lead to the censorship of legitimate, worthwhile content. Other sites did not go dark but instead used their homepages to further help spread the message. Most prominently, this included Google, the most-visited site in the world and in the United States. The search engine was still available, but the homepage featured a black banner over the Google logo and, under the search box, the plea that visitors "Tell Congress: Please don't censor the web!"

---

[1] Throughout this study, site rankings are reported based on rankings at Alexa.com and are current as of June 12, 2012.

[2] Fight for the Future, "January 18 Blackout."

These sites were mobilizing in an effort to stop two bills, the Stop Online Piracy Act (SOPA) in the House, and the very similar PROTECT-IP Act (PIPA) in the Senate. The goal of each bill – both of which are discussed in detail in Chapter 11 – is to shut down foreign sites that are accused of criminal copyright infringement. If a site is managed in the United States, copyright holders or prosecutors can simply pursue them for copyright infringement; for sites run by those outside the United States, however, it is not so simple. The bills were designed to get around this problem by trying to make it harder for foreign infringing sites to maintain business relationships with U.S.-based businesses, as well as make it harder for them to communicate with U.S. audiences. If the bills became law, copyright holders or administration officials could seek a court order requiring advertisers and financial services providers to sever connections with specific foreign sites. Because this would result in a list of sites that are off-limits to these domestic actors, the bills have been widely described as creating a blacklist of forbidden sites. More dramatically, the bills also would have attempted to scrub blacklisted sites from the domestic internet. This would have been accomplished in part by forbidding internet service providers (ISPs) from translating the domain names of these sites into the numeric address of the computer that is hosting the site's content, as well as preventing search engines from linking to blacklisted sites. This attempt to create an internet blacklist was viewed by many as censorship and thus profoundly un-American and against the ethos of the internet. Motivated by this view, they sought to use the internet to spread this message, and it worked beyond their wildest dreams.

On that day in January, in response to the blackouts and calls to action on sites across the internet, millions of American voters contacted Congress to demand that SOPA and PIPA be shelved. More than ten million people signed petitions in opposition, more than eight million tried to call Congress, and more than four million sent e-mails.[3] Phone lines at many congressional offices were jammed. Many members' web pages were so swamped with traffic that they went down. This day of action – often called the SOPA strike or SOPA blackout – became the "largest online protest in history."[4] This tidal wave of online action

---

[3] Ibid.
[4] Boonsri Dickinson, "The Largest Online Protest in History Started Here," *Business Insider*, January 19, 2012, http://www.businessinsider.com/largest-protest-in-history-started-here-more-than-a-billion-people-will-see-anti-sopa-messages-2012-1.

happened over proposed reforms in copyright law, a subject that just fifteen years ago was of little interest to the general public.

The members of Congress certainly took notice. Before the SOPA strike, the House and Senate bills both seemed very likely to pass. Powerful members of both parties, in both houses of Congress, were shepherding the bill through at the fastest speed they could muster, and the handful of representatives and senators who opposed the bills seemed poorly positioned to stop them. When the blackout began, the bill had nearly three times as many supporters as opponents in Congress; by the end of the day, it had nearly twice as many opponents as supporters, including several former co-sponsors who had switched their positions.[5] In the days that followed, dozens more members piled on to the opposition tally. By January 20, just two days after the strike, House and Senate leadership announced that the bills were being shelved indefinitely. The internet had spoken, and Congress had listened – both in nearly the most dramatic way possible.

With some noteworthy exceptions, the news media has not really captured the essence of the SOPA strike: who organized it, how it happened, or what it says about politics in the internet era. On all three counts, mainstream reporting generally failed to grasp the central role played by nonprofit groups. This is disappointing, especially because nonprofit information policy advocacy groups, particularly Public Knowledge and the Electronic Frontier Foundation (EFF), have regularly appeared in mainstream news outlets over the past ten years. Yet it is also explicable because of the commonly held, simplistic understanding of the copyright debate as a fight between Hollywood and Silicon Valley – that is, just another fight between corporate sectors with competing interests. In this view, copyright is used to determine the split of revenue between sectors in the digital economy, such as much of Pandora's revenue goes to record labels and songwriters and how much the webcaster gets to keep. In this view, the debate over copyright is really about who will have the upper hand during the contract negotiations that will determine which vendors can carry which media works, in which formats, and at what prices. If we take this view to its logical conclusion, disputes over digital copyright are just part of the process of dividing the spoils as the internet calcifies in its role as the ultimate for-profit entertainment medium – an on-demand

---

[5] Josh Constine, "SOPA Protests Sway Congress: 31 Opponents Yesterday, 122 Now," *TechCrunch*, January 19, 2012, http://techcrunch.com/2012/01/19/sopa-opponents-supporters/.

cable network with three thousand channels, albeit with an appendage of millions of public access shows.

The view of copyright as a fight between corporations – and the implicit view of the internet's future as inexorably ever more corporate – is woefully inadequate. For the millions who participated in the SOPA strike, the internet is and should continue to be much more than a means for delivering approved corporate media content to relatively passive audiences. These digital activists may indeed like Google and Apple much more than they like BMI and News Corporation, but they were hardly doing Google's bidding. If copyright really were a war between new and old media corporations, and Google had asked previously uninterested users to help it to win the war, user participation would have been modest to nonexistent. Instead of millions, it might have gotten tens of thousands to respond. More fundamentally, if the dispute really were primarily of interest to and between corporations, Google never would have used its homepage to reach out to voters in the first place. It would have continued its strategy of inside-the-Beltway advocacy, where it and its allies are woefully outmatched by the content industries, and something like SOPA would have passed into law.

This book is not primarily about the SOPA strike and the fallout that resulted; that would require another book, which thankfully is under development with a partial draft already available online.[6] It is about the political history of and debate over digital copyright regulations, from the late 1980s to early 2012. I do discuss the SOPA strike and related issues in some detail in Chapter 11, but that is just part of the larger story I tell. Most of the book's research and writing were completed before the strike even happened. It turns out, though, that the story of this book is what is missing from the oversimplified explanation of those remarkable events. Without setting out to do so, I have written a book that helps demystify the SOPA strike, providing the context for understanding what was otherwise a somewhat inexplicable internet revolt. I began the research for this book in 2006, believing that internet advocacy around copyright is interesting and important – both for how it was reshaping the politics of copyright and for what it says about online advocacy more generally. Six years later, events on the ground buttressed that belief, following it with quite an exclamation point. This book is not an explanation of the SOPA strike; rather, the SOPA strike

---

[6] Engage and Demand Progress, eds., *Hacking Politics.*

is a much stronger validation of this book's central claims than a scholar should have any right to expect. It just so happens that the book also offers a lot of what is missing from the collective understanding of those events.

Online advocacy has profoundly reshaped the copyright debate, and these effects were reasonably clear well before SOPA was even proposed. The impact of online advocacy in the copyright debate offers important lessons for both the future of copyright and for online advocacy more broadly. Before further developing this thesis, it is essential to begin with the basics of the copyright debate and the specific slice of that debate that I have chosen to study. It is also important to discuss some of what has already been said about political advocacy. This study incorporates an unusual combination of research strategies, including both political, historical case studies of specific debates, as well as quantitative measurements of how well each coalition was represented in Congress, in newspapers, and on the web. With such a diverse mix of research strategies in play, these will also require a brief explanation. After that, I lay out the roadmap for the rest of the book.

THE COPYRIGHT DEBATE: AN OVERVIEW AND A NARROWER FOCUS

Copyright is a government-granted monopoly on the right to reproduce, distribute, and make certain other uses of mediated works of creative expression. Copyrightable works include examples such as books (fiction or nonfiction), movies, sheet music, recorded music, paintings, drawings, and software programs. Each of these is a kind of information good – a product in which the information embedded in a physical medium has value above and beyond the value of the medium itself. A good book is worth more than the paper and ink of which it is made; the extra value is the value of the information contained in the book. The problem with information goods is that they do not obey the laws of economics that apply to most other types of goods, from a bag of sugar to a parcel of land. If I take your sugar, you no longer have it. If I squat on your land, you no longer have unfettered use of it. Yet if you write a book and I make photocopies of that book without paying you, you do not lose your copy. If the cost of photocopies at the local copy shop is lower than the retail cost of the book, the copy shop and I come out ahead, and you, the author, have lost out on a potential benefit.

What Copyright Is For

If it were not for copyright, there would be little if any basis in law to stop anybody from making endless copies of popular works, selling them cheaply, and undercutting the official versions. In this way, those who produce the very information that makes these goods more valuable than the media that contain them – legally speaking, "authors," whether the creativity in question is written or not – would have fewer financial incentives to make new works. There are many ways one can solve this problem, from charitable and government subsidies for information production (a key driver in the production of scientific knowledge) to advertisements embedded in works. Copyright law is another system for solving this problem. It allows authors (or the publishers who buy or license their works) to decide how many copies of a work will be produced, how these will be distributed, and (to a large extent) what the price will be. As in all monopolies, the monopoly of copyright gives the copyright holder the ability to set prices above the cost of producing the next unit. If my grocer tries to charge $50 for a bag of sugar, I can go elsewhere, but if Stephen King and his publisher decide that his next novel will cost about $50, only those who are willing to pay that price will get the book. Even at the much lower prices one does pay for popular novels, the cost of production and distribution is substantially lower than wholesale price – much more so than for a bag of sugar. Although a good portion of this extra difference goes to marketing and other expenses, another (hopefully substantial) portion goes to the author.

Copyright creates a space between the pricing model for sugar and the pricing model for creative works. It now costs tens or even hundreds of millions of dollars to make a major movie. For instance, it cost roughly $220 million to make the 2012 blockbuster *The Avengers*. That cost was spent to make the very first copy of the film. Compared to that investment, the cost of each subsequent copy – even the celluloid copies used in theaters – is little more than a rounding error. The same is true for the cost of an individual CD versus the cost of recording an album, the cost of an installation DVD versus the cost of creating a major (proprietary) software program, and the cost of printing a copy of a book versus the untold hours an author spent writing it. The cost of a bag of sugar is and should be about the cost to produce, distribute, and sell that specific bag of sugar, hopefully with a small profit for everyone who helped your morning coffee taste a little better. In contrast, if it is to be sold in a for-profit marketplace, the cost for a copy of a creative work has to be much higher than the cost of delivering that specific copy. Otherwise, *The Avengers* never gets made, *David Copperfield* never gets written, and the world loses out on valuable culture. In terms of why we have copyright, then, Charles Dickens and Joss Whedon are in the same boat. In terms of the ease of copying in each one's respective era, however, the differences are staggering.

Debating Copyright in the Digital Millennium

The internet is a worldwide, distributed network for transmitting copies of data – that is its very purpose. The mass adoption of the internet has thus inspired many in the public sphere to reassess the goals and ideal strategies for copyright law. On one hand, many have portrayed the internet as a profound threat to copyright because of sharply increased ease of infringement and difficulty of enforcement; to the extent that technology makes copying easier, they argue, we need to make copyright that much stronger.[7] Those who advance this position point to the hundreds of thousands of dedicated professionals who make up the cultural industries today, as well as the often high quality of their work. On the other hand, many have argued that the internet greatly accelerates the communication power of information producers whose incentives do not require copyright protection, highlighting the need for a temperate copyright system that can fuel these information producers' legal access to information inputs.[8] Those who take this stance also have their heroic examples of producers of quality works. A favorite example is the computer programmers who have built free/open source software tools such as GNU/Linux and Firefox, as well as many less well-known applications and protocols – including nearly every core technology that makes the internet go. Other favorite examples include the untold thousands of contributors to the free online encyclopedia Wikipedia, as well as the scholars and librarians who produce and curate research in the sciences and the humanities.

To some extent, this debate boils down to a debate over how best to balance the interests of a diverse set of constituencies. On one side are the companies, institutions (such as university presses), and individuals that sell copyrighted works as their primary means of generating income. This group places tremendous emphasis on the commercial markets in copyright-protected works that work well for incentivizing the production and circulation of information and culture. On the other side

---

[7] Boyle, *Public Domain*, 54–82.　　　[8] Benkler, *Wealth of Networks*, 41–58.

are the individuals, institutions (such as schools), and companies that primarily produce and disseminate culture and knowledge for incentives other than the sale of copyrighted works in the marketplace. This group generally has a net interest in less copyright protection and a wider berth for the exceptions and limitations that make their work cheaper and easier, so they will emphasize the points in the media system where copyright is unnecessary or counterproductive. Of course, it takes the whole cast of characters to create the total of our cultural and scientific heritage today – some of the best and most important of which depends on copyright-protected markets, and some of which does not.

Although nearly every sector in the information ecosystem can contribute value, however, not every sector's voice carries equal weight in Congress. Historically, the commercial media sectors have dominated the policy discussion, and policy outcomes have reflected this dominance.[9] It was in the context of this political dominance by the commercial media sectors that Congress first sought to adapt copyright law to the digital media era. In particular, those who support stronger copyright law as a response won the day repeatedly in Congress in the 1990s, racking up legislative victories such as the 1992 Audio Home Recording Act (AHRA), the 1997 No Electronic Theft Act, and the 1998 Digital Millennium Copyright Act (DMCA).[10] By the late 1990s, policymakers and media industry advocates were expressing particular concern about the possibility that the internet would enable infringement. Yet the laws they passed in response to this concern failed to stop widespread online infringement, which spiked especially with the 1999 launch of the peer-to-peer service Napster.[11] The record industry fought back with waves of litigation against infringing end users, but this did not even slow down – let alone stop – online infringement. To this day, millions still trade illicit files. In light of this continued infringement, those in the "strong copyright" (or SC) coalition – copyright holders and their political supporters – call for a response of ever-stronger copyright. On the other side, those in the "strong fair use" (or SFU) coalition oppose copyright's expansion, support a widening of copyright exceptions (such as fair use), and invoke the cause of internet freedom. Members of the SFU coalition include scholars, librarians, educators, nonprofit advocacy groups such as the

---

[9] Litman, *Digital Copyright*.
[10] To reduce note clutter, statutes and cases are generally referred to in text only and listed in the bibliography.
[11] Alderman, *Sonic Boom*.

EFF and Public Knowledge, and a few allied policymakers. Their heavy reliance on internet communication inspired this study.

Focusing In: Digital Rights Management

The copyright debate revolves around many topics, so, in conceiving this study, I chose to focus on one in particular: the regulation of digital rights management (DRM). A DRM system is an attempt to use digital technologies, such as encryption, to build a heightened degree of copyright holder control into digital media. Broadly speaking, this will generally fall within one of two business models. First, when applied to physical media, DRM is largely designed to help tether the data to the copy in a way that mirrors the experience of the analog era. For instance, the encryption on motion picture DVDs is a DRM system that keeps most users from "ripping" their DVD collection – copying the data to their computers for later replay. Thanks to the DRM, the data on the DVD are, for most users, tied to each disc. In contrast, music CDs are unencrypted, so many if not most computer users rip all their CDs; for music CDs, the data are quickly untethered from the physical copies. Thanks to a few clever users, there are also several applications to rip DVDs; users who want their movie data untethered from their discs can do so. Copyright law was amended with the goal of discouraging the distribution of such tools; the 1998 DMCA includes anticircumvention provisions[12] that, among other bans and regulations, render such software illegal.

In addition to tethering data to physical media, DRM is also used in media distribution systems that did not exist in the analog era. This includes, for instance, the market for movies streamed over the internet. If a movie-streaming service was set up simply to transmit the data to customers with no control or restrictions on how customers could then use the data, it would have a nearly impossible task finding movie studios willing to deliver enough content to make such a service attractive. So movie-streaming services build their systems so that it is reasonably difficult for end users to keep the data rather than merely watching the films. As long as the DRM system is mostly seamless, users are often more excited about new services than upset that there are limitations built in. As such services have become the norm – and as these have mostly had the DRM go reasonably smoothly – their built-in digital restrictions have become commonly accepted.

---

[12] 17 U.S.C. §§ 1201–1204.

For a period of nearly two decades – roughly 1989 to 2006 – the debate over DRM was the most significant, regularly recurring single issue in the debate over the future of copyright. For that period, members of the SC coalition generally believed that, to manage the problem of infringement via digital technologies, the best strategy would be to use yet other digital technologies and to give these limiting technologies the force of law. Their policy strategies reflected this belief. The DMCA was and remains the most politically significant embodiment of this strategy because it gives the force of law to any DRM system that copyright holders introduce into the marketplace. Other proposals sought to deal with circumstances in which copyright holders could not initially introduce restricted formats. The first was the proposal that became the 1992 AHRA, which required a specific type of DRM that limited the copying capabilities of what was then an exciting new technology: stand-alone digital audio recorders, such as digital audio tape (DAT) decks. After the DMCA, several other DRM-related proposals received some consideration, but the one that came closest to becoming law was a failed attempt to mandate a technology known as the "broadcast flag." The system sought to limit what viewers could do with recordings of digital TV broadcasts – and, in a related proposal, radio broadcasts.

One other important DRM-related proposal was discussed, but this one was advanced by the SFU coalition. They sought to reduce the reach of the DMCA's anticircumvention provisions. The DMCA prohibits most circumvention of DRM, even if the intended use is noninfringing – meaning that it would otherwise be legal under copyright law. Representative Rick Boucher (D-VA) and congressional allies proposed allowing circumvention for noninfringing purposes – such as teaching, research, and personal use – and allowing some development and sale of circumvention devices. These proposals garnered a major push from sympathetic members of Congress during the sessions from 2003 to 2006, a clear sign of the SFU coalition's increased political capital. Although these proposals were rebuffed, the SFU coalition's heavy use of internet advocacy at least gave them a fighting chance.

Along the way, and in the years since, there have been other key political developments and policy proposals. I tackle what I view as the most important of these to provide a fuller picture of the copyright debate. As promised from the outset, I tackle SOPA, PIPA, and related policy proposals. I would also be remiss not to discuss the birth and growth of Napster, the industry lawsuits and public backlash that followed, and some of the other developments that came (or at least started) between the 1998 passage of the DMCA and the start of the serious debates over the broadcast flag and DMCA reform in 2003. Nonetheless, because the debate over DRM was the most central question of digital copyright regulation for nearly two decades, the study particularly focuses on the major debates in that area. This serves to provide a more manageable topic to study, and it also sets up something much more like an apples-to-apples comparison across different time periods.

POLICY ADVOCACY, MEDIA STRATEGY, AND NEW MEDIA

On many policy issues, the online debate differs substantially from that issue's representation offline. There are good reasons to expect this outcome, especially as grounded in a broader vision of the nature of collective action, the policymaking process, the role of media strategy in policy advocacy, and the potential changes introduced by new media technologies. In light of all of these, it then becomes a great deal clearer what we can expect from online advocacy around copyright.

Collective Action: Mobilization and Free Riding

If one hopes to have any real policy influence, the first step is to identify and mobilize allies. Yet most potential activists will stay on the sidelines. Most policy outcomes will affect people whether or not they fought for the outcome, and, for a typical citizen, the odds that his or her efforts will be uniquely responsible for a given policy outcome are slim indeed. Thus, the economically rational choice is usually to free ride. This is the problem of collective action, and although it is a key hurdle for all policy activists, it is a higher hurdle for some than others; the fewer actors one needs to mobilize, the more likely one is to succeed.[13] Small groups with concentrated interests are relatively easy to identify and mobilize; for instance, the major executives in a given industry generally know each other. In contrast, mobilizing diffuse groups is far more difficult. Five people or institutions who each have a million dollars at stake will be easy to identify and mobilize, whereas a million people who each have five dollars at stake will be much harder to identify and mobilize. This is why concentrated groups tend to be better at securing policy victories than do diffuse groups, a phenomenon that is so pervasive in U.S. politics – and one that so magnifies economic privilege – that Jacob S. Hacker and

---

[13] Olson, *Logic of Collective Action*; Ostrom, "Institutional Rational Choice."

Paul Pierson identify it as the root cause of the country's gravest economic problems.[14]

Policy Subsystems, Attention, and Outcomes

Debates over policy issues tend to be fairly insular. For most of the time, on most issues, just a few people are actively communicating with policymakers; this small group is the issue's policy subsystem.[15] Humans have a bottleneck of attention, so large institutions, such as Congress and newspapers, delegate issues to subdivisions, such as committees and section editors.[16] Occasionally, an issue will burst out of these constraints and into broader attention – the front page, the House floor. When this happens, we tend "to overreact with 'alarmed discovery'" at the sudden recognition of "new or previously overlooked information."[17] This brief period of shock and tendency toward overreaction gives policy advocates a brief opportunity to reframe the issue and advance substantial changes. For example, the financial crash of 2008 led directly to the 2010 Dodd-Frank Act, implementing the most substantial financial reform since the Great Depression. Without a deluge of public attention to the issue, those who supported the reforms embodied in the bill never could have pushed its passage into law.

These windows of opportunity are only open briefly, as the public's attention is always moving from one issue to the next. As it moves through each formerly obscure issue, it opens the chance for a major shift in the politics and policy around that issue. After the public has moved on to the next issue, such changes become far less likely. This movement of attention-fueled change creates a cycle of what Frank R. Baumgartner and Bryan D. Jones refer to as "punctuated equilibriums" – long periods of relative stability interrupted by brief windows of major

---

[14] Hacker and Pierson, *Winner-Take-All Politics*. The authors describe the American political economy as a thirty-year war waged by and on behalf of the wealthiest few, leading to staggering growth in inequality, and they provide remarkably detailed evidence that this outcome is a result of domestic politics much more than apolitical economic forces such as technological development or globalization. They conclude in part:

> Where the conventional wisdom confidently declares, "It's the economy," we find, again and again, "It's the politics." And because it is domestic politics, not global economic trends, that matter most, the future is within our control. This is the very good news that this book delivers. As hard as winner-take-all politics will be to change, the economic developments that precipitated our present crisis represent political choices, not technological imperatives. (pp. 290–1)

[15] Sabatier and Weible, "Advocacy Coalition Framework."
[16] Jones and Baumgartner, *Politics of Attention*.
[17] Ibid., 52, 55.

change.[18] Here, they are importing the same idea from evolutionary biology, in which developments happen slowly for incredibly long periods of relative stability, only to be interrupted by major changes in the environment – a major asteroid crash, a sudden change in temperature – that unleash a short time of rapid changes. This is followed by a new period during which changes again happen slowly within a new set of conditions. Policy change follows a similar trajectory, only instead of asteroids and ice ages, the major driver of change is a sudden shift in attention by outsiders, including – especially – voters in general. A major event – the economy crashes, a scandal rocks a specific industry or regulatory body, and so on – dominates the headlines, and the public and policymakers respond by considering major changes.

The boom-and-bust cycle of punctuated equilibriums in the policy environment sets up clear incentives for communication strategies among different policy actors. The coalition seeking change has an obvious incentive to seek greater media attention; if it gets a large upswing in attention, it greatly increases the coalition's odds of forcing change. This incentive leads to substantial efforts at media outreach by change-seeking coalitions. Conversely, supporters of the status quo rarely seek destabilizing increases in media attention; if they are prudent, they stand ready to engage in media outreach as necessary, but such efforts are not nearly as motivated or such an important part of their political strategy. There are also other forces at work beside incentives, and that is the potential gap in coalitions' political and financial resources; these differences can be modest or staggering. Those groups with the greatest funding and political access will generally have won something close to the policy outcomes they desire, and even to the extent that they seek policy changes, they will often be more likely to seek changes within the insular world of policy subsystems rather than making a broad public appeal.[19] In contrast, groups with less capital are likely to take their case to the public even when they are seeking to preserve the status quo.

New Media and Changes in Policy Advocacy

The internet reshapes policy advocacy in several ways, most of which mitigate the problem of collective action. First, internet communication is cheaper. Everybody gains more absolute communication power, but

---

[18] Jones and Baumgartner, *Politics of Attention*, 17–20; Baumgartner and Jones, *Agendas & Instability in American Politics*, 1–24.
[19] Kingdon, *Agendas, Alternatives, and Public Policies*, 61.

this is a much greater relative gain for the poorest groups. The gains are real, but they are also limited; the low cost of online communication leads to an inflation in the number of messages directed at policymakers and the general public, thus reducing the value of each.[20] A less-recognized but perhaps equally important gain is the increased affordability of intracoalition communication, such as information sharing, message development, and agenda setting. This is the backbone for more public advocacy, and it may be even more important than the more visible changes in public strategies.[21]

The internet also makes it easier to identify and mobilize issue publics. Groups can e-mail potential activists; create websites, blogs, and social media pages; and even advertise online for relatively small sums. With every conceivable media niche finding a home online, sympathetic news sources and audiences are easy to find. Occasionally, online communication goes viral, potentially bringing still other activists into the fold. These technologies also break down the barriers between private and public communication,[22] making it much easier for citizens to communicate a coalition's message to others, recruit new members, participate in the policymaking process, and thus effectively join a coalition.

Finally, the internet helps coalitions seeking to reshape the perception of an issue and heighten its visibility for the broader public. The internet has become an important part of how more traditional news sources decide what counts as newsworthy.[23] Additionally, news outlets are increasingly relying on external sources, such as e-mail and the web, for identifying hot stories and doing background research – especially as newsroom budgets shrink.[24] All of these factors have combined to enable policy victories by underfunded coalitions on issues ranging from banking privacy[25] to broadcast ownership rules[26] and broadcast indecency.[27] In each case, an underfunded, diffuse group of citizens and nongovernmental organizations (NGOs) scored a victory against a concentrated, well-funded industry group, highlighting the potential for online communication to shape policy outcomes.

---

[20] Bimber, *Information and American Democracy*, 107.
[21] Marres, "Net-Work Is Format Work."
[22] Bimber, Flanagin, and Stohl, "Reconceptualizing Collective Action."
[23] Wallsten, "Agenda Setting and the Blogosphere."
[24] Davis, *Public Relations Democracy*.
[25] Bimber, *Information and American Democracy*, 1–4.
[26] McChesney, *Problem of the Media*, 252–97.
[27] Thierer, *Examining the FCC's Complaint-Driven Broadcast Indecency Enforcement Process*.

Coalitions in the Copyright Debate and Internet Strategies

For policy advocates, the decision on whether to devote substantial personnel resources to online communication depends on several factors. For the reasons noted above, two reasons justify online mobilization: to fight against an entrenched status quo, and to mobilize a relatively large number of potential coalition members. A third reason also applies to a subset of debates, most especially including technology policy: if one's actual or potential coalition population is more densely populated by internet enthusiasts than one's opponents. On all three counts, the SFU coalition has every reason to seek very heavy online participation, whereas the SC coalition does not.

First, on the degree of change sought, copyright law in general and DRM regulations specifically are much better reflections of the wishes of the SC coalition. The DMCA stands as a cherished SC coalition victory, and opposition has galvanized the SFU coalition. To reform the DMCA would be a major change in DRM policy, and it would require the kind of major mobilization for which lots of internet-generated attention would be helpful. In contrast, although the broadcast flag proposal was indeed an important possible change in copyright,[28] it would have only applied to digital over-the-air broadcasts and thus represented a much less substantial proposed change than DMCA reform.

Second, the SC coalition is far more concentrated. This is the simplest explanation for the century-long expansion of copyright to the benefit of copyright holders.[29] In principle, stronger copyright means higher prices and a decreased availability of information; these benefits accrue mostly to a handful of multinational media conglomerates, whereas the cost is spread thinly across the rest of the populace and other industries. Pamela Samuelson concludes, "this mix of concentrated benefits and distributed costs is likely to yield the best laws money can buy."[30] The much more diffuse SFU coalition, therefore, must seek broader public attention and sympathy.

Finally, the SFU coalition is more densely populated by internet enthusiasts. For instance, the EFF's Board of Directors has long been an all-star roster of world-famous computer engineers, internet visionaries, and cyberlaw experts. The group even sponsors hacking contests and sets

[28] Gillespie, *Wired Shut*, Chapter 7.
[29] Landes and Posner, *Political Economy of Intellectual Property Law*; Litman, *Digital Copyright.*
[30] Samuelson, "Should Economics Play a Role," 9.

up booths at hacker conventions. Although not every member of the coalition is a computer expert, other allied sectors, such as technology law scholars and librarians, also tend to be among the earliest and most enthusiastic adopters of new internet tools. In contrast, entertainment industry advocates do not necessarily see the internet as their natural place to communicate – especially when so many of them see the internet as a threat to their livelihoods. The SC coalition also includes major portions of the software industry, but this just slightly tempers the SFU coalition's substantial advantage in technology savvy – and their even stronger advantage in moral credence among the technorati.

NEW TOOLS FOR STUDYING NEW PHENOMENA

To better understand the politics of copyright in the digital era, this study incorporates a mix of research strategies. On one hand, I have undertaken a political history and case study of the advocacy around some of the key issues in digital copyright law, from 1989 through early 2012. On this count, the study is in the tradition of historical/critical works by scholars such as Jessica Litman,[31] and Siva Vaidhyanathan[32] – and, more recently, Tarleton Gillespie,[33] Peter Decherney,[34] and Patricia Aufderheide and Peter Jaszi.[35] On the other hand, I have conducted a quantitative study of the arguments around these same issues, as those arguments have been made in relevant congressional hearings, the *Washington Post* and *New York Times*, and on the web. Here, the study combines a range of methods, including content analysis methods as developed by scholars such as Klaus Krippendorff,[36] as well as using tools developed by Richard Rogers for analyzing the relationships between websites.[37] In this way, the study also seeks to build on recent work by political communication scholars trying to understand online issue advocacy – as distinct from,

---

[31] Litman, *Digital Copyright.*

[32] Vaidhyanathan, *Copyrights and Copywrongs.*

[33] Gillespie, *Wired Shut.*

[34] Decherney, *Hollywood's Copyright Wars.*

[35] Aufderheide and Jaszi, *Reclaiming Fair Use.* In addition to a fine legal and political history, the authors also provide a detailed history of the movement they have led, empowering communities that depend on fair use to create legally vetted documents that can guide their decisions. Even though they are confronted with a difficult task – to document a movement for which they deserve more credit than anybody – they provide a tactful, accurate description of their role in the process.

[36] Krippendorff, *Content Analysis.*

[37] Rogers, *Information Politics on the Web.*

though certainly not unrelated to, partisan electoral campaigns on the one hand, and social movements on the other. While one could name many scholars in this quickly growing group, a good place to start looking is at the University of California, Santa Barbara, where one can find frequent collaborators Bruce Bimber, Andrew J. Flanagin, and Cynthia Stohl.[38] Thus, this study is based on an unusual combination of research methods, deployed to achieve what I believe is a well-rounded understanding of the politics of digital copyright, especially as those politics have gone online.

A Political History

By conducting a political history, I have sought to identify and explain what I see as the most important developments in digital copyright law from 1989 to early 2012. About each policy change or proposal, I try to identify the following:

- The political, economic, and technological context for each proposed change
- The policy actors in support of and opposed to each proposal
- The details of each proposal, including important changes in successive versions, where appropriate
- An overview of some of the key arguments for and against each change, and
- The political process by which each proposal wound its way to becoming either the law of the land or another addition to the scrapheap of history

I have focused primarily on developments in the U.S. Congress because that is the primary body for political advocacy around copyright. In many policy arenas, there are local, state, and federal policies in play; this is true, for instance, for most debates about environmental policy. Likewise, in many policy debates, administrative agencies are central players in determining policy outcomes; again, environmental policy issues are often great examples, as these debates are often, to a very large extent, over agency policy. None of this is true of copyright. Since the 1976 Copyright Act, changes in copyright are exclusively the domain of the federal government. Further, there is no federal agency that oversees the

---

[38] Among many works, see: Bimber, *Information and American Democracy*; Bimber, Flanagin, and Stohl, *Collective Action in Organizations*; and Bimber, Flanagin, and Stohl, "Reconceptualizing Collective Action in the Contemporary Media Environment."

implementation of copyright. Federal agencies such as the Federal Bureau of Investigation (FBI) get involved in criminal cases, the Federal Communications Commission (FCC) played an important role in the broadcast flag debate, and the U.S. Copyright Office – technically a part of the legislative branch rather than an administrative agency – determines limited exemptions to the anticircumvention provisions of the DMCA. These each represent substantially expanded roles in copyright policymaking since the late 1990s, and I discuss these increased roles in the relevant chapters. Appointed policymakers still play a relatively minor role overall in shaping copyright, though, so this study's political history is mostly set in Congress.

For a number of reasons, this study also does not generally consider court decisions in extensive detail. First and foremost, analyzing case law is the bread and butter of legal analysis; with the high interest in digital copyright law, there is a small army of legal analysts at every level, from law review editors to towering senior scholars, at work in those fields. While I also sometimes try my hand at this kind of traditional legal analysis – even making some smaller forays in that direction in this book – there is far less need for that kind of work.

As an additional reason not to focus too much on judicial decisions, most cases involve a specific, nonpolicy conflict between private parties. This is not to dismiss the policymaking role of the "important" cases, as well as the legal strategies of many actors. For instance, some companies, institutions (the Electronic Frontier Foundation comes to mind), and even individuals have used lawsuits to try reshaping the interpretation of the law. A number of these kinds of cases deserve a great deal of legal commentary. One example is *Viacom v. YouTube*, in which Viacom was hoping for case law that would impose an increased burden on such content hosting sites to actively filter out infringing content.[39] Yet to the extent that a case is important, it is already (or soon will be) the subject of extensive legal analysis by trained lawyers. Thus, while not dismissing the regularly important role of cases or even the sometimes important

---

[39] Bill Rosenblatt, "YouTube Emails Discovered in Viacom Case: Smoking Gun or Wet Blanket?," *Copyright and Technology*, October 8, 2009, http://copyright andtechnology.com/2009/10/08/youtube-emails-discovered-in-viacom-case-smoking-gun-or-wet-blanket/. In explaining why Viacom should view this as a chance to reshape the case law, Rosenblatt argues, "Viacom should want the law changed so that services like YouTube are required to block unlicensed copyrighted material proactively, not just in response to takedown notices. . . . For example, Viacom should want vicarious liability strengthened so that services that choose not to install filtering technologies become liable."

role of agency decisions, I focus mostly on legislative proposals, straying from this focus only when agency or court involvement helps illustrate a particular issue or political development – such as when cases lead to or follow directly from legislative outcomes. This helps to keep this study's focus on areas in which it can better make a more distinct contribution to the scholarship on copyright, since the political history of copyright legislation is the subject of far less work.

In choosing topics to study, I have sought to consider the policy proposals with the most direct and clear impact on whether and how copyright shapes the future of digital media technologies. As DRM regulation has been the most important version of this debate over the last two plus decades, I focus much of my attention there. This is not the exclusive point at which copyright can regulate digital technologies, and I have also sought to discuss other issues – such as ISP liability and domain name regulation – in the time periods in which I believe they have had the most political significance. For those readers who already know a great deal about the copyright debate, it will not be difficult to identify other issues (or specific versions of broader themes) that I have neglected. The point of this part of the study is not a comprehensive political history of the copyright debate writ large over this period; rather, I focus on some of the central debates in copyright in order to explore how the political landscape in copyright has changed over time. The topics I have chosen prove more than adequate to demonstrate a real shift; the changes I identify represent nothing less than a fundamental reordering of the copyright policy subsystem.

A Quantitative Study of the Copyright Debate

In addition to a political history of the debate over digital copyright, this study also includes a quantitative study of how that debate is represented in different time periods and different media. Here, the study is closely based on my previous work,[40] and since that is freely available online, readers who want to know a great deal about my methodological choices can look there. This section in the book is therefore intended for the reader – especially the reader who is not a social scientist – who is

---

[40] Herman, "Battle over Digital Rights Management." I revisited the data and even some of the documents in preparing for this study, even making some small corrections in findings where warranted. Thus, whenever there is a conflict between the two studies in the data reported, please take the present study as definitive.

more interested in this study's results than its methods, but who would appreciate at least a summary description of how I reached them.[41]

The main tool used for this part of the study is quantitative content analysis, as developed by communication scholars such as Klaus Krippendorff.[42] There is a great deal to this method, but the goal is to develop a system for analyzing communicated messages in such a way that different people can agree on how different messages fit within the system. Ideally, any competent observer trained within the system would then apply it in a way that is reasonably close to the way it would be applied by any other trained, competent observer. In this case, that meant examining a large number of policy advocacy documents related to each of four very similar copyright policy debates, asking the same set of questions about each document. This section gives a brief description of the topics I chose to focus on, how I went about finding documents relevant to those topics, and the questions I asked about each document.

Identifying Specific Digital Rights Management Debates

The political history is not limited strictly to DRM debates, and, in some cases, I cover policy proposals with varying levels of attention. For the quantitative portion of the study, such choices would make the results much more difficult to interpret, so I have limited the study strictly to what I identify as the four major debates specifically over DRM regulation. I have also chosen to look at each over a period of four years, or two sessions of Congress. These are the debate from 1989 to 1992 over what became the AHRA, the debate from 1995 to 1998 over what became the anticircumvention provisions of the DMCA, the debate from 2003 to 2006 over proposals to scale back the DMCA, and the debate from 2003 to 2006 over proposals to impose the broadcast flag on digital broadcast receivers. Each of these four topics was specifically or implicitly the central subject of multiple relevant congressional hearings, and each was covered by multiple news stories in both the *Times* and *Post*. The four-year periods neatly capture the peak of interest in each of these topics, and the subject of each debate is a very similar question about using law and technology to limit unlicensed copying. Choosing these topics for these time periods thus makes for the clearest apples-to-apples comparisons.

---

[41] Whether or not one has training in any of these methods, all readers are welcome to contact me with questions about the methods or data used in this study. My website, billyherman.com, should always have my current contact information.

[42] Krippendorff, *Content Analysis*.

Finding Relevant Documents

Finding relevant newspaper articles and congressional documents (for convenience's sake, "offline" media) was fairly straightforward if remarkably time-consuming. The *LexisNexis* database has a complete set of all articles from the *Times* and *Post* during the relevant periods. I simply searched for all articles in the relevant time periods for which copyright was in the headline, lead paragraph, or search terms; made at least a cursory examination of each; and weeded out the majority that were not relevant to the DRM debate at hand. Similarly, *LexisNexis Congressional* indexes congressional hearings. I searched for hearings that were relevant to copyright, used the descriptions to identify those that were specific to the debate over DRM regulation, and tracked down the full transcripts online or in the local law library. Then, I treated each individual speech or written submission as a separate document, identifying those that were relevant to one of the DRM debates at hand.

By the time of the policy debates from 2003 to 2006, the web had become an important source of information and tool for advocacy, so I also studied what the most important websites in the copyright debate had to say about these proposals. Unlike well-preserved offline media, such as congressional hearings and newspaper articles, internet messages are not as systematically organized or catalogued, to say the least. Fortunately for researchers, sites cluster in groups, and members of these clusters link to each other. Because of this, hyperlinks can be used to identify clusters of related sites and each of those sites' relative online authority. This is the core insight that made Google a success, and it enables researchers to say a great deal about online content.[43] Within each topical cluster is a small set of the most authoritative sites, shown by the group's collective linking behavior to be more authoritative in much the same way that regular scholarly citations establish high scholarly authority.[44] These core websites dominate the issue space.[45] As a first step for identifying the key documents in the online copyright debate, then, this study looks at the hyperlinks between sites involved in that debate. This is a fairly straightforward process thanks to a tool called the Issue Crawler (developed by Richard Rogers and available at IssueCrawler.net). To use the crawler, one feeds it a "seed" list of related websites. The crawler then

---

[43] Barabási, *Linked*; Hindman, *Myth of Digital Democracy*; Rogers, *Information Politics on the Web*.

[44] Barabási, *Linked*.

[45] Benkler, *Wealth of Networks*; Hindman, *Myth of Digital Democracy*.

visits the seed websites, searching for hyperlinks to still other websites. The crawler produces a map of interlinked websites, and it also reports the raw number of incoming links for each site. I say a bit more about this process and discuss both types of results in Chapter 8.

The next step was identifying the relevant web pages and other documents (such as PDF or Word documents) on each website. To do this, I used targeted Google searches to search each web domain. For instance, to identify web pages related to the broadcast flag debate, as found on the EFF website, I used the following search term:

copyright (audio OR video OR radio OR broadcast) flag site:eff.org

This search and the search for DMCA reform each produced a very large number of results on several of the websites – sometimes hundreds or even thousands of results for a single search, far too many in total to examine each document individually. Fortunately, Google does a great job of putting the most relevant results at the front. Using results from the U.S. House website as a yardstick, I estimated the point at which I should stop digging for each topic on each included website: about forty relevant documents per topic, or (if I had not already found the maximum number of relevant documents) about the first 100 Google results. Even with this limited search strategy, I still found nearly a thousand relevant documents.

Looking at Each Document

For every document included, I asked the same small set of basic questions. First, what year was it produced? Second, what sector does its author(s) represent? Here, I put each policy actor into one of eleven categories, such as media industry, technology industry, elected government official, appointed official, scholar, librarian, or nonprofit group. Finally, and most importantly, I asked of each document, what copyright viewpoint does it adopt? Here, I put each document in one of three categories, assigning each a corresponding number from one to three: strong copyright (1); mixed, neutral, or unclear (2); or strong fair use (3). For documents in the mixed/neutral/unclear category, I also examined each paragraph to decide if it was relevant to the debate at hand and, if so, I also categorized each paragraph as SC, neutral, or SFU, using the same 1–3 scale. For each of these neutral documents, I then took the mean copyright viewpoint of each relevant paragraph; this allowed me to assign a fairly precise score for each document's leaning toward one side or the other in the debate. All documents could then be placed on what I call the "copyright viewpoint scale," which ranges from 1 to 3, with 1 representing the SC position, 3 representing the SFU position, and neutral/mixed documents representing a range of positions between 1 and 3. With all these data in hand, I was able to have real precision in measuring which side of each DRM debate was better represented. Not only could I answer this question in general, but specifically for each medium (hearings, newspapers, and online), as well as over time.

How These Different Methods Work Together

This study presents an unusual combination of methods; to my knowledge, this combination is unprecedented. In fact, one could break the study in two, presenting only the detailed case study or only the quantitative findings, and have two separate studies. In fact, I have published two journal articles along these lines, one a quantitative study in a social science journal, and the other a political history in a law review.[46] In combination, though, the two parts show my central argument in a way that neither part alone cannot. Specifically, this study shows that, in the debate over copyright, internet advocacy has played an essential role in the rise of the SFU coalition and the shift in the politics of copyright. The quantitative analysis shows the degree to which online advocacy differs from the offline debate – how only the SFU coalition is actually making a sincere effort to reach out to the broader public on this issue. It also shows how very different the politics of DRM became in just a short period, especially as reflected in the congressional debate, with profound changes in both the balance of the debate and the makeup of the witness lists. Yet these changes do not themselves show changes in policy outcomes; for that, the detailed political history is necessary. Here, the study shows a change in policy outcomes as dramatic as the change in the debate – a change from formerly easy passage of statutes increasing copyright's reach into the regulation of digital technologies in the 1990s, to a far more difficult road to passage for such laws by the early 2000s. The history even shows an SFU coalition that has gone from virtual nonexistence to one with the capacity to make aggressive legislative moves, even if those moves were also stalled. The quantitative analysis demonstrates that the tenor of the debate and the roster of participants changed

---

[46] Herman, "Taking the Copyfight Online;" Herman, "Political History of DRM."

substantially, including a major push toward online communication by the SFU coalition; the political history shows that these differences preceded major changes in the types of policy outcomes.

As designed, this study was not originally going to be able to prove, definitively, that the internet had changed outcomes in the copyright debate. Such definitive proof would be unreasonable to expect when talking about something as complex as our political system. The correlation, though, was already undeniable by 2006, and it strongly suggested causality. Why would SFU advocates invest so heavily in online communication unless it made a substantial difference? Further, if not for the SFU coalition's rise, how could the policy outcomes not have been different? The view that online communication really had made a difference even lined up with the views of several on-the-ground participants, as expressed in off-the-record conversations with several advocates and policymakers.[47] Although not definitive in proving causality, all this evidence at least strongly suggested that online communication has shaped the debate in myriad ways, even if it obviously does not change all of the rules.

Then, in late 2011 and early 2012, the response to SOPA and PIPA unleashed a series of events that were far more than definitive – and exciting – than anyone expected. In this case at least, everyone agrees that strong fair use advocates leveraged the internet to kill a bill that was otherwise headed toward near-certain passage. Again, the mainstream reporting on these events lacked the historical and organizational understanding that could lead to a genuine grasp on what really happened. To some extent, this is understandable; even the people who were fighting on the front lines to cause this outcome were genuinely shocked by their success, so it should hardly be surprising that reporters and commentators were not ready for what happened. Yet as the SOPA strike transitions from news to history, more needs to be known about the decades leading up to it. It would not be too much of a stretch to say that this study and the SOPA strike complete each other; this study gives the needed context to reach a fuller understanding of the strike, and the strike underlines

---

[47] I interviewed too few of each to be able to use quotations or specific details from these conversations in this study's results without threatening promises of anonymity. I am quite grateful to participants for their time, however, as they provided me with invaluable insights into online advocacy generally and communication policy advocacy specifically. The time spent with them definitely contributed to how I reported my findings.

and extends this study's findings from the pre-strike era. The copyright debate was already a great illustration of the power of internet-fueled mobilization – and that was true even before SOPA's opponents caught lightning in a bottle.

HOW THIS BOOK IS ORGANIZED – AND SUPPLEMENTED

The rest of the book is divided into three parts. Part I is a political history of digital copyright through 2006. This covers the two DRM regulations that became law in the 1990s, the 1992 AHRA (Chapter 2) and the 1998 DMCA (Chapter 3). The next four years, 1999–2002, were not marked by any passed or nearly passed DRM proposals, but they did see several major developments in copyright and digital technology; I thus discuss these in Chapter 4. Then, in Chapter 5, I discuss the political histories of the two major DRM proposals that were debated from 2003 to 2006, the first being the SFU coalition's proposals to limit the reach of the DMCA, and the second being the various broadcast flag proposals.

Part II uses the quantitative results to examine the political communication around the four key DRM debates. In Chapters 6 and 7, respectively, I look at how these debates were represented in Congress and in the newspapers. Chapter 8 explores the debates over DMCA reform and the broadcast flags as these debates happened online. Here, I explore which sites were substantial participants, which among these got the most links from other participants, how much each site contributed to the debate, and how strongly each site lined up in the continuum from strong copyright to strong fair use. Chapter 9 compares these three media for the two most recent debates, showing the very high degree to which copyright advocacy online differs from the debates' representations in Congress and national newspapers.

Finally, in Part III, I look at the changes in the copyright debate since 2006, as well as assessing this study's broader significance. In Chapter 10, I discuss the growing collective realization that DRM has failed to prevent widespread infringement – a realization that is nonetheless not reflected in policy advocacy, as reflected by the waning interest in DMCA reform and SC advocates' push to export DMCA-like DRM restrictions. Chapter 11 explores the various proposals to further limit online infringement that have been discussed since 2010. These include the Combatting Online Infringements and Counterfeits Act (COICA) and ongoing Administration actions seizing foreign websites that have been accused of infringement. This chapter is also where I discuss SOPA and PIPA, as well as the remarkable response and substantial political fallout. Finally, in Chapter 12, I step back and say a few words about what this study suggests for the future of copyright, political communication, and the study of each.

Part I

A Political History of Digital Copyright Through 2006

2

The Audio Home Recording Act, 1987–1992

In the 1980s, consumers had limited ability to commit copyright infringement. Yes, they could use their videocassette recorders (VCRs) to record movies from broadcast television – or even from the rented videotape in one VCR through to a blank tape in a second VCR – in lieu of buying copies. They could record songs from the radio and even make whole copies of cassette albums using dual-cassette decks. They could make infringing photocopies of printed works, although, except for limited types of works such as sheet music, the cost of buying a licensed copy was often cheaper and remains so to this day. VHS and audio cassettes also imposed a real cost on would-be copiers, albeit a substantially lower cost than that of a licensed copy. All of these methods also represented real trade-offs in quality. Even the first-generation photocopy or magnetic cassette copy is notably inferior to the original, and the second generation (a copy of a copy) and each subsequent generation is exponentially worse. Furthermore, making such copies takes time, making it comparatively more attractive to buy originals. Thus, although many people had at least a few copies that were arguably or even clearly infringing, and although a few people had many such copies, there was still a unique demand for the quality and convenience of original copies.

In this analog world, companies selling copyrighted works were fairly secure. Although a few people were too cheap or too poor to pay for the quality and convenience of authorized copies, most people consumed authorized copies most of the time. Video rental stores, record stores, and bookstores were the profitable retail face of the profitable analog media economy. The record industry in particular used its ridiculous profitability to fuel rampant excess.[1]

Into this analog world, Sony sought to introduce the digital audio tape (DAT) machine, a device to enable digital audio recording for consumers. For the music industry, this was an unwelcome development, although, in just a few years, the internet would make all stand-alone media recording devices seem like media industry allies. Yet even the modest threat posed by higher quality digital recording was enough to initiate the first step in the transition from a copyright system that regulates behavior to one that regulates technology.

DIGITAL AUDIO TAPE AND SERIAL COPYING

In the early 1980s, electronics manufacturers began developing devices to record and play DAT. By 1987, Sony had begun mass production and hoped to have DAT decks on U.S. store shelves. DAT promised consumers the ability to make their own recordings with the kind of perfect audio fidelity that was then only available via compact disc (CD). At the time, CD was a read-only medium, so DAT's promise of noiseless personal recordings was music to the ears of audiophiles. Yet not everybody was excited by the prospect of consumers having the capacity to make perfect digital copies – let alone copies of copies.

Even then, in the analog world, the music industry was already groaning that "Home taping is killing music."[2] This motto was so obviously false that it was never taken very seriously, but in DAT, they found an even more dire threat. As the *New York Times* observed:

> [T]he president of the Recording Industry Association of America, Stanley Gortikov,.... characterized the Japanese-dominated audio hardware industry as an "assassin" bent on destruction of the largely American recording

---

[1] I was fortunate enough to have one such executive in one of my courses recently. She had risen to the level of vice president at one of the major labels before the music industry's decline led to her being laid off. The irony of having a former music industry executive in the front row of my media studies course was particularly poignant during my lecture about copyright. In private conversations, she has told some funny stories, confirming the well-established record of lavish excess in the music industry of that era, including free alcohol for everybody, including the interns; nearly unlimited expenditures on travel and accommodations; and generous pay for a deep roster of executives. In this light, some of the recent changes in the music industry represent an unwelcome shift toward conditions in which most sectors already live. Although the layoffs are a real loss, we might not shed too many tears about the end of an era of shameless indulgence.

[2] Jim Sullivan, "Rock the Boat, Billy Bragg," *Boston Globe*, October 28, 1988, 51.

industry. "We are already losing billions to home taping," Mr. Gortikov said recently in a telephone interview. "Imagine what it will be like if the tape copy is equal to the original."[3]

Here, the concern was about *lossless serial copying* – that is, copies of copies with no degradation over successive generations. If some consumers were already willing to settle for lower quality analog copies of albums, then perfect copies would only exacerbate the issue. In principle, a few original copies could lead to thousands of illicit copies – a real boon to Sony, but a problem for the music industry.

LEGAL THREATS AND A LEGISLATIVE COMPROMISE

DAT decks were expected to arrive on U.S. store shelves by 1987,[4] but the recording industry used lobbying, threatened and actual litigation against Sony, and market pressure to stop the manufacturer from importing DAT machines.[5] As I'll discuss shortly, any court case against Sony over DAT would have a very shaky legal basis, but the threat of lawsuits alone was enough to stop Sony in its tracks; even if it had won the court case, the attorney fees and opportunity costs due to delayed entry into the U.S. market would add up quickly. In addition, the recording industry had political and market advantages over Sony. The labels had much greater clout in Congress,[6] especially since most manufacturers were based in Japan, so even a court decision favoring Sony would have been vulnerable to being overturned by later legislation. Also, record labels could and did refuse to release music in DAT format, thus greatly diminishing the potential demand for the machines.[7]

Starting in 1987, the recording industry supported legislation to require that DAT recorders sold or imported into the United States include copy control technologies.[8] CBS Records developed a system using very minor changes to the audible sound of a recording, albeit in a narrow band at the high end of the audible frequency. Record labels would be able to make these changes for their digital recordings as a form of copy

[3] Will Crutchfield, "Next Home Stereo Advance: Digital Tape Cassettes in 1987," *New York Times*, October 24, 1986, A1.
[4] Ibid.
[5] Menell and Nimmer, "Legal Realism in Action," 19–20.
[6] Litman, *Digital Copyright*.
[7] Andrew Pollack, "Digital Tape Machines Expected by July," *New York Times*, January 8, 1990, D1.
[8] Lee, "Audio Broadcast Flag System."

protection, knowing that copy control–equipped DAT decks would not make reproductions of these protected works. The change likely would have been inaudible to most listeners – but it might have been audible for the very audiophiles who were DAT's primary target market.[9] Proposals to mandate this technology met substantial electronics industry resistance,[10] and the lack of interindustry consensus around a workable technology kept legislation from moving forward. Tensions between the recording industry and electronics manufacturers eased when Sony purchased CBS Records in January of 1988.[11] Still, the legal threats kept DAT decks out of U.S. stores.

In 1989, the industries came to terms around a new, inaudible technology, apparently clearing the legal cloud around DAT.[12] The breakthrough copy control technology, the *serial copy management system* (SCMS), does not alter the audible sound of recordings; rather, it adds an inaudible, one-bit signal that indicates whether the tape is an original or a copy. Using SCMS-equipped recorders, consumers can make a perfect digital copy of an original recording but cannot make copies of copies. Allowing only first-generation copies represented a compromise between the industries; in return for this limitation, record labels agreed not to sue DAT manufacturers or users over home recording.[13]

Both industries sought legislation codifying this deal.[14] However, record companies were not the only music industry group with a legal threat in store; songwriters and music publishers were not satisfied by the proposed accord and used their own legal threat against DAT:

> The National Music Publishers Association [NMPA], a New York group representing music copyright holders...thinks [SCMS] does not restrict copying enough and can be circumvented easily. The organization favors charging buyers of tape machines and blank tapes a royalty fee that would go to compensate the songwriters and music publishers.[15]

---

[9] Andrew Pollack, "Move to End Digital Tape Dispute," *New York Times*, January 16, 1988, A35.

[10] *Digital Audio Tape Recorders: Hearing on H.R. 1384 Before the Subcommittee on Commerce, Consumer Protection, and Competitiveness*, 100th Cong. (1987); *Digital Audio Tape Recorder Act of 1987: Hearing on S. 506 Before the Committee on Commerce, Science, and Transportation*, 100th Cong. (1987).

[11] "CBS Records' Dispute Seen," *New York Times*, February 23, 1988, D19.

[12] Andrew Pollack, "Accord Clears the Way for Digital Tape Recorders," *New York Times*, July 26, 1989, A1.

[13] Ibid.

[14] Digital Audio Tape Recorder Act of 1990, H.R. 4096/S. 2358, 101st Cong. (1990).

[15] Andrew Pollack, "Suit Seeks to Bar Sale of New Audio Players," *New York Times*, July 11, 1990, D5.

The NMPA funded a lawsuit, *Cahn v. Sony Corp.*, with songwriter Sammy Cahn as the lead plaintiff.[16] The suit accused Sony of contributory infringement.[17] The publishers pursued the action even though their case faced long odds. In *Sony v. Universal*, the Supreme Court had already ruled that "copyright law did not impose such secondary liability where the device in question was capable of substantial noninfringing uses."[18] Despite the weakness of the music publishers' case in the *Cahn* suit, Sony decided against another extended legal fight and "settled about a year into the litigation,"[19] in June of 1991.[20]

In addition to implementing SCMS, the manufacturers agreed to pay a copyright royalty on DAT decks and blank tapes. Furthermore, they agreed to support new legislation that would require SCMS and the collection of royalties for all digital audio recording devices.[21] With all three industries on board, the Audio Home Recording Act (AHRA) sailed into law in 1992. In return for the electronic industries' support, the music industry agreed to statutory language that, first, gives consumers the explicit legal right to make noncommercial recordings for personal enjoyment; and, second, gives manufacturers the legal right to help them do so.[22]

THE AUDIO HOME RECORDING ACT'S EFFECTS AND POLITICAL SIGNIFICANCE

The AHRA was outdated quickly after it became law. To avoid the imposition of royalties on their products – which, in 1992, were rarely used to produce or copy audio recordings – computer companies had helped to make sure that the act did not regulate general purpose computers, computer software, or blank computer media, such as floppy disks or hard disk drives.[23] As today's consumer well knows, this demarcation between personal media equipment and computing equipment did not hold for long. By the mid 1990s, computer CD burners allowed music fans to engage in unlimited serial copying without paying royalties, and the personal computer (PC) as home entertainment center was already

---

[16] *Cahn v. Sony.*
[17] Menell and Nimmer, "Legal Realism in Action," 19–20.
[18] Reese, "Temporal Dynamics."
[19] Menell and Nimmer, "Legal Realism in Action," 20.
[20] Lee, "The Audio Broadcast Flag System," 452.
[21] Eben Shapiro, "Accord on Digital Taping Now Faces Congress Debate," *New York Times*, July 12, 1991, D1.
[22] 17 U.S.C. § 1008.   [23] 17 U.S.C. § 1001.

becoming a reality.[24] The courts also found that the act does not regulate MP3 players,[25] a ruling that helped keep costs low for the iPod and all its progeny.

In 1992, policymakers and interested industries envisioned a future for digital music that looked like a higher fidelity version of what was then the present – one in which media consumption was tethered to stand-alone media players playing special purpose media. What happened instead was nothing less than a home entertainment revolution founded on computer-based copying and consumption, all of which falls outside the act's regulatory bounds. It began with computer-based, royalty-free burning of CDs for playback on home and car CD players. Then the invention and explosive adoption of peer-to-peer systems, such as Napster, put the PC squarely in the center of music consumption.[26] By persuading the record labels to sign on to the iTunes music store in 2002,[27] Apple provided the first commercially successful means of collecting on the internet distribution of music, but there was no putting the internet genie back into the bottle – and certainly no going back to the era of the stand-alone music player.[28]

Because policymakers and the electronics and music industries understandably did not foresee this revolution in how music would be acquired, distributed, and consumed, the AHRA was drafted in such a way that it quickly became irrelevant. DAT decks and other regulated technologies, such as the Sony MiniDisc, never caught on with consumers; consumers were generally quite happy with the lower-fidelity recordings of analog cassette decks. To the extent that they demanded digital quality, they greatly preferred unregulated computer-based CD burners to both DAT decks and AHRA-compliant stand-alone CD burners.[29] Since AHRA-regulated technologies never achieved widespread adoption, the legislative history of the act has received light treatment by legal scholars, and commentators who do discuss it have dismissed it as a minor step on the route to more substantial digital rights management (DRM) regulation.[30]

---

[24] Dan Stets, "Pump up the PC," *Philadelphia Inquirer*, April 11, 1996, F1.

[25] *Recording Industry Association of America v. Diamond.*

[26] Alderman, *Sonic Boom.*

[27] Goldsmith and Wu, *Who Controls the Internet?*, 117–9.

[28] In our large-lecture Introduction to Media Studies, I often have occasion to ask my undergraduate students how many of them even still use CD players at home. In a class of 150, perhaps five will raise their hands.

[29] Kolff, "MP3."

[30] For instance, see Van Houweling, "Communications' Copyright Policy," 106, n51; Lee, "Audio Broadcast Flag System," 411, n197. Had AHRA-regulated technologies become widely adopted, the act would have been more significant. It is the more recent

The AHRA is historically significant as the first DRM regulation of any kind, as well as being the first copyright law mandating the adoption of a specific technology. On both counts, the AHRA thus represents the first step in copyright's transition into a vehicle for regulating devices. After the AHRA, it became illegal to make and sell stand-alone digital audio recording devices with unrestricted functionality. The law effected this outcome even though unrestricted devices would have had the same kinds of substantial noninfringing uses as the video recorder – the same noninfringing uses that led to the Supreme Court's technology-shielding *Sony* ruling.[31]

The passage of the AHRA also shows how DRM policy debates through the end of the twentieth century continued to follow the industry-led legislation process that Jessica Litman identifies in copyright generally.[32] As in other instances, Congress urged the affected industries to reach a generally acceptable compromise and, once one was reached, passed it as law. The motivation for record companies and music publishers was clear enough; the former wanted to reduce the number of illicit digital copies competing with their official recordings, and the latter wanted another source of licensing revenues. Technology companies supported the bill – not on principle, but because they wanted to design and sell their products without being sued. Even though Sony and others disliked the need for protective legislation, they grudgingly accepted it as better than unending litigation. By the early 1990s, the electronics industry was practically begging for the AHRA's passage so they could finally import DAT decks – a technology that had already been available abroad for years by that point.[33]

Voices of resistance were raised during the legislative process. Several opponents voiced their opposition, and some of their reasons for opposing the bill were insightful or even prescient.[34] Well-reasoned though

changes in the music industry, rather than the text of the act itself, that made it relatively unimportant.

[31] *Sony Corp. of America v. Universal*, 442.

[32] Litman, *Digital Copyright*, 23. "About one hundred years ago, Congress got into the habit of revising copyright law by encouraging representatives of the industries affected by copyright to hash out among themselves what changes needed to be made and then present Congress with the text of the appropriate legislation."

[33] Pollack, "Suit Seeks to Bar Sale." As of July, 1989, DAT decks had "been available in Japan, and to a limited extent in Europe, for about two years."

[34] For instance, in one hearing, Philip Greenspun, President of Isosonics Corp., argued that neither DAT nor the AHRA would substantially change the amount of infringement and that consumers would generally not adopt DAT. *Digital Audio Tape Recorder Act of 1990: Hearing on S. 2358 Before the Subcommittee on Communications*, 101st Cong. 169 (1990).

they were, however, these voices of opposition were not part of any substantially mobilized resistance and thus went unheeded. For instance, consumer groups expressed their doubts but participated lightly – and rather than opposing the bill outright, they described it as a regrettable necessity in the face of the music industry's legal threats. The National Consumers League appeared at one hearing and backed the bill on these terms.[35] Consumers Union representatives appeared in two *Washington Post* articles, describing the royalty as unfair but assessing the bill as the only means to get DAT into the market.[36] Scholarly opposition was more genuinely against the bill as drafted, but their participation was also light; law professor Jessica Litman voiced her opposition to the bill,[37] as did Philip Greenspun, then a research assistant at MIT – although he was also serving as president of a small technology company.[38] With all the major affected industries signing on and little systemic resistance, the bill passed with relative ease. Copyright holders would not enjoy such easy passage in future DRM policy debates.

Finally, the debate also foreshadowed the battle lines that would be hardened in later debates. The AHRA is the first effort to use copyright law to shape product design, growing from supporters' belief that if technology can cause them problems in the form of easier copying, other technology – backed by law – can also solve that same problem. In contrast, opponents argued that DRM and a law against its circumvention would inconvenience customers, drive up prices, and prevent noninfringing uses, all while failing to prevent infringement to any significant degree. These battle lines grew more entrenched during the debate leading up to and following the passage of the Digital Millennium Copyright Act (DMCA).

[35] *Audio Home Recording Act: Hearing on S. 1623 Before the Subcommittee on Patents, Copyrights, and Trademarks,* 102nd Cong. 74 (1991) (statement of Linda F. Golodner, Executive Director, National Consumers League).

[36] Stephen Levine, "The Digital Duel Could Be Ending: Manufacturers, Music Industry Reach Pact," *Washington Post,* July 11, 1991, B8; John Burgess, "Bill Imparts the Sound of Music: Congress Settles Long-Standing Dispute Over Digital Recording," *Washington Post,* October 9, 1992, F1.

[37] *Audio Home Recording Act: Hearing on H.R. 3204 Before the Subcommittee on Intellectual Property and Judicial Administration,* 102nd Cong. (1992).

[38] *Digital Audio Tape Recorder Act of 1990: Hearing on S. 2358 Before the Subcommittee on Communications,* 101st Cong. 169 (1990) (statement of Philip Greenspun, President of Isosonics Corp.).

3

The Digital Millennium Copyright Act

The Digital Millennium Copyright Act (DMCA) is the most sweeping revision to copyright law since 1976, and it "arguably represents the most dramatic change in the history of U.S. copyright law."[1] The act was an effort "to bring U.S. copyright law 'squarely into the digital age,' ... [and] the primary battleground in which the [Act] achieved this goal is its first title."[2] Title I of the DMCA was billed as an implementation of two World Intellectual Property Organization treaties,[3] which the United States signed in 1996. These provisions add the force of law to digital rights management (DRM) systems designed by copyright holders to prevent unauthorized use of copyrighted works. Users cannot circumvent many kinds of DRM, even if their intention is otherwise noninfringing. The law also bans almost all acts of developing, marketing, or offering technologies or services that circumvent DRM systems.

Although not specific to DRM regulation, another very significant part of the DMCA is embodied in Title II, which limits the liability that online service providers face for online infringement. Although this book is primarily about the regulation of DRM, potential liability for service providers is also an important, related area of law. This is true not only for what most people would identify as internet service providers (ISPs) – those companies that sell connections to the internet, such as the local phone and cable companies that sell broadband service – but also other members of the internet ecosystem that transmit, host, store, serve, and help users find content. Title II of the DMCA is still the statute that most

---

[1] Gillespie, *Wired Shut*, 177.   [2] Nimmer, "Riff on Fair Use," 681–2.
[3] World Intellectual Property Organization Copyright Treaty (WCT), Arts. 11–12; World Intellectual Property Organization Performances and Phonograms Treaty (WPPT), Arts. 18–19.

directly governs service provider liability, and it continues to be extremely relevant to this day. Especially because it was bundled with the anticircumvention provisions, the passage of Title II is a crucial part of this story. Particularly in combination, the DMCA's two big changes – the anticircumvention provisions embodied in Title I and the limitations on ISP liability in Title II – add up to the most important digital copyright statute to date in the United States.[4]

PREPARING FOR THE LOOMING INTERNET AGE

The story of the DMCA begins with strong copyright (SC) advocates seeking to prepare for the new era of internet-delivered content. Beginning in 1994, the World Wide Web exploded in popularity,[5] drawing tens of millions online and making it apparent that most households would be online in the near future. This had copyright holders and their allies searching for a way to ensure their viability in a future marked by internet distribution. For instance, Bruce Lehman, then-head of the Patent and Trademark Office, was the prime force behind the anticircumvention provisions, and, in his testimony at a 1995 hearing, he correctly predicted that the internet would become an essential medium for the transmission of media content.[6] Throughout the several congressional hearings on the bill, other SC advocates also predicted a future marked by online distribution.

Bracing for the Worst

Of course, SC advocates did not merely predict an online future; they always coupled that prediction with the warning that much of the content online could be infringing unless Congress passed new laws for the

---

[4] The DMCA actually contained three more titles. Each represents a relatively minor change – especially in comparison to Titles I and II – and covers subjects not of direct relevance here.

[5] Kelty, *Two Bits*, 223.

[6] *NII Copyright Protection Act of 1995: Joint Hearing before the House and Senate Subcommittees on Courts and Intellectual Property*, 104th Cong. 30 (1995) (statement of Bruce A. Lehman, Asst. Sec. of Commerce and Commissioner of Patents and Trademarks, Patent and Trademark Office). For instance, he argues that the Internet, going forward, "will now offer an opportunity, a new marketplace, for [both traditional media producers] and new kinds of commercial content providers. Copyright law has always been at the core of these traditional industries.... And so it will be at the core of their rights when they move into this new electronic marketplace." Ibid., 32.

digital age. Testifying on behalf of a multi-industry SC coalition in a 1998 hearing, Steven J. Metalitz predicted:

> The digital revolution and proliferation of the Internet and other networks give the copyright industries new ways of reaching new customers and new markets. But these very same technologies magnify the threat of piracy.... In this environment, pirates can make limitless perfect copies, disseminate them around the world at the touch of a button, and carry out their activities with less fear of detection and capture than ever before.[7]

In yet another hearing, former Motion Picture Association of America (MPAA) chief Jack Valenti warned, "Pirates have become more sophisticated. They are armed with new technology and hackers and others are going to invade the [internet]."[8] This was all part of constructing what James Boyle describes as the "Internet Threat."[9] The incumbent media industry players correctly "see the Internet as a potential threat to their role as intermediaries between artists and creators on the one hand and the public on the other."[10] The copyright industry could not go to Congress with this argument, however – accepting that, without legislative intervention, much of the content industry would be made obsolete by a superior system of distribution. Instead, they framed a potentially unregulated internet as "a terrible menace to the American cultural industries,"[11] as well as a tool enabling widespread and profoundly immoral theft.[12] In this rhetorical construction, the internet is an existential threat not only to marginal profits for copyright industries, but to their very existence – and even to creativity itself. As copying gets cheaper, copyright must get stronger. "As copying costs approach zero, intellectual property rights must approach perfect control."[13]

Media companies also used congressional ignorance about the internet to make another threat: that unless Congress made the internet safe for content, via stronger copyright protection, copyright holders would not put their works online, thus depriving the new medium of attractive content. Policymakers generally had little online experience, leaving

---

[7] *Intellectual Property Rights: The Music and Film Industry: Hearing before the Subcommittee on International Economic Policy and Trade*, 105th Cong. 25, 26 (1998) (statement of Steven J. Metalitz, VP and Gen. Counsel, Int'l Intellectual Property Alliance).

[8] *NII Copyright Protection Act of 1995 (Part 2): Hearings before the House Subcommittee on Courts and Intellectual Property*, 104th Cong. 21, 22 (1996) (statement of Jack Valenti, Pres. and CEO, MPAA).

[9] Boyle, *Public Domain*, 54–82.

[10] Ibid., 56.   [11] Ibid., 57.

[12] Herman, "Breaking and Entering."   [13] Boyle, *Public Domain*, 61.

them open to the myth that the internet needed content – even at a time when the content online was growing exponentially without major media participation.[14] Thus, the congressional record is also filled with examples of advocates and policymakers presenting a false dichotomy. If policymakers passed the DMCA, SC advocates argued, the internet would be filled with a cornucopia of legitimate content; if they did not pass the act, however, the media industry would refuse to put their content online, yet see infringing copies of that same content all over the internet.[15]

Proposing Policy Solutions

Copyright holders correctly identified the internet as a substantial technological challenge that cannot be addressed through Audio Home Recording Act (AHRA)-style legislation, so they sought to tame it via other means. In the 1990s, the policy actor who was most directly responsible for thinking through how to change the law to tame the internet was Bruce Lehman. Lehman was Patent Commissioner from 1993 to 1998, and he also headed the White House Information Infrastructure Task Force, which released a White Paper[16] that contained several radical proposed changes to copyright. If proposed today, many of these would be incredibly controversial. James Boyle explains some of the more noteworthy:

---

[14] Litman, *Digital Copyright*, 93–4.

[15] This is something of an oversimplification, although it is one that gives content industry lobbyists credit for more consistency than they actually presented. James Boyle recounts:

> Lawmakers were assured by lobbyists that this was business as usual, that no dramatic changes were being made by the Green or White papers; or that the technology presented a terrible menace to the American cultural industries, but that prompt and statesmanlike action would save the day; or that layers of new property rights, new private enforcers of those rights, and technological control and surveillance measures were all needed in order to benefit consumers, who would now be able to "purchase culture by the sip rather than by the glass" in a pervasively monitored digital environment.
>
> In practice, somewhat confusingly, these three arguments would often be combined. Legislators' statements seemed to suggest that this was a routine Armageddon in which firm, decisive statesmanship was needed to preserve the digital status quo in a profoundly transformative and proconsumer way. Reading the congressional debates was likely to give one conceptual whiplash.

Boyle, *Public Domain*, 57.

[16] Information Infrastructure Task Force, "Intellectual Property and the National Information Infrastructure: The Report of the Working Group on Intellectual Property Rights," Washington, DC, September 1995.

Internet service providers were said to be "strictly liable" for copyright violations committed by their subscribers ... Loading a document into your browser's transient cache memory while reading it was said to be making a "copy" ... The attitude toward fair use was particularly revealing. At one point in the White Paper it was hinted that fair use might be a relic of the inconveniences of the analog age, to be discarded now that we could have automated fractional payments for even the most insignificant use.[17]

None of these became enshrined in statute, but their inclusion is a clear sign of the strongly pro-SC leanings of Lehman and the committee. Lehman's White Paper also encouraged copyright holders to deploy DRM systems. Because DRM can be circumvented, the White Paper also called for laws that would prohibit the circumvention of DRM and ban the tools of circumvention.

The White Paper was released before there was a well-organized and identifiable strong fair use (SFU) coalition, but the report caused "dismay among libraries, composers, writers, online service providers, ... and the makers of consumer electronic devices and computer hardware."[18] Several law professors also opposed the White Paper proposals. Immediately following its release, American University law professor Peter Jaszi "held informal consultations with like-thinking law professors and representatives of library organizations to see whether there was any possibility of mounting an effective opposition to the White Paper's proposals."[19] Jaszi recruited other White Paper opponents, including "library organizations, online service providers, telephone companies, computer hardware and software manufacturers, consumer electronics companies, and civil rights and consumer protection organizations."[20] This group of interests agreed to work together, calling themselves the Digital Future Coalition (DFC). The DFC succeeded in mobilizing substantial – and, from the standpoint of Lehman and the content industries, unexpected – opposition to Lehman's suggested changes.

The proposed legislation contained a categorical ban on the importation, development, and distribution of any tool to circumvent DRM.[21] The bill also banned the removal or alteration of copyright management information – data that identify the copyright holder and related

---

[17] Boyle, *Public Domain*, 55.   [18] Litman, *Digital Copyright*, 93.
[19] Ibid., 123.   [20] Ibid.
[21] NII Copyright Protection Act of 1995, § 1201 (1995). (The companion House bill – same title, H.R. 2441 – was nearly identical, and the following citations would also apply to that bill.)

information.[22] The legislation also contained provisions stipulating civil penalties, giving a victorious plaintiff the choice of actual damages or statutory damages of up to $2,500 per violation of the ban on trafficking in tools that circumvent DRM (the ban contained in section 1201) or up to $25,000 per violation of the section 1202 ban on removal or alteration of copyright management information.[23] Finally, the bill stipulated criminal penalties of up to $500,000 or five years in prison for anybody convicted of violating "section 1202 with intent to defraud."[24]

All DFC members saw this bill as a bad policy idea that would have a net negative effect on society, and many also feared it as a looming legal liability that could threaten them directly, so they mobilized and prevented the bill's easy passage. This development surprised Lehman, who was so confident of domestic passage that he had already begun pushing for an international treaty with similar provisions via the appropriate United Nations agency, the World Intellectual Property Organization (WIPO). Yet Lehman used the international momentum to his advantage.[25] Supporters were able to secure the passage of two related treaties through WIPO, the WIPO Copyright Treaty (WCT) and very similar WIPO Performances and Phonograms Treaty (WPPT),[26] even as the domestic legislation stalled. United States delegates proposed treaty language that looked much like the proposed domestic legislation: ban circumvention, and ban the tools that make circumvention possible. Much of the international community balked – like Jaszi and the DFC, they saw a lot to oppose – so proponents compromised with skeptics, weakening the treaties' language. The treaties require only that countries discourage the act of circumvention, and they do not require a ban on circumvention tools or services. On this count, the treaties are much closer to the traditional contours of copyright, which had regulated copying behavior but not copying technologies.[27]

In a second important compromise with critics, the treaties impose a rather low standard for implementing legislation. A signatory must only "provide adequate legal protection and effective legal remedies" against circumvention of DRM and removal of copyright management information.[28] United States law arguably met this standard before the DMCA's passage. It was already illegal to circumvent DRM to conduct

---

[22] Ibid., § 1202.
[23] Ibid., § 1203.
[24] Ibid., § 1204.
[25] Litman, *Digital Copyright*, 129.
[26] WCT, *supra* note 3, Arts. 11–12; WPPT, *supra* note 3, Arts. 18–19.
[27] Menell and Nimmer, "Legal Realism in Action."
[28] WCT, Arts. 11–12; WPPT, Arts. 18–19.

copyright infringement, and manufacturers of "black box" devices that only served to circumvent DRM had already been subjected to legal liability for facilitating infringement.[29] The "Clinton Administration initially considered whether the WIPO Copyright Treaty might even be sent to the Senate for ratification 'clean' of implementing legislation."[30]

Rather than merely supporting simple treaty ratification, SC advocates – including congressional allies – made a more sophisticated use of the treaties. They engaged in "policy laundering," or the use of international law-making bodies to advance one's domestic agenda.[31] As Oscar Gandy and I argue elsewhere:

> Congress used the [WIPO Copyright] Treaty as an excuse to implement a much more sweeping ban on circumvention. In short, Lehman and the bill's congressional supporters used WIPO to launder their own interests, running their political capital through the bank of international credibility and treating the final bill as something required by international law.[32]

Despite the SC coalition's disappointment with the relative weakness of the final treaties, it took advantage of the treaties' relative vagueness, urging passage of much stronger legislation in the name of compliance with treaty obligations. In congressional hearings in 1997 and 1998, at least ten witnesses made this argument.[33] Several even praised the stronger legislation for its likely effect of getting legislation passed in other countries that would similarly exceed the minimum threshold of WIPO treaty compliance. For instance, Representative Bart Gordon argued, "once we pass something here, it has to go to the international community.... They are really waiting for us to see what we are going to do. So whatever we do is the ceiling, not the floor."[34] Thus, although the patina of compliance with the WIPO treaties gave the bill some extra credibility, even supporters agreed that the bill exceeded what was required.

CRAFTING THE ANTICIRCUMVENTION PROVISIONS

The final legislation is built around the kind of strong regulation Lehman sought. Section 1201 implements three different bans. The first ban (or the

---

[29] Litman, *Digital Copyright*, 131.
[30] Samuelson, "Intellectual Property," 13.
[31] Herman and Gandy, "Catch 1201," 130–5; Hosein, "The Sources of Laws," 189.
[32] Herman and Gandy, "Catch 1201," 131.
[33] Ibid., 133.
[34] *The WIPO Copyright Treaties Implementation Act: Hearing on H.R. 2281 Before the Subcommittee on Telecomm., Trade, and Consumer Protection*, 105th Cong. 7, 8 (1998) (statement of Hon. Bart Gordon, Member, House Comm. on Commerce).

"basic ban") prohibits circumventing DRM to gain unauthorized access to copyrighted works. It reads, "No person shall circumvent a technological measure that effectively controls access to a work protected under this title."[35] For example, if a computer program requires a unique serial number during installation, this makes it illegal for a technically sophisticated user to defeat or hack this requirement and install the software without such a serial number. Although doing so for the purpose of infringing copyright was already illegal, this clause bans it for nearly any reason – even if one has misplaced the serial number for a legally purchased software package and intends to install it on just one computer. The statute itself makes few allowances for even the most benign of uses, such as efforts to preserve the data on a decaying disk.

The second ban prohibits manufacturing, importing, and trafficking in tools that would help circumvent access-controlling DRM.[36] A technology is covered by this ban if it is developed, marketed, or primarily used for such circumvention. This ban (the "access trafficking ban") prohibits computer repair services from assisting a librarian in the preservation of software stored on decaying media, and it prohibits librarians from developing a technology to facilitate circumvention.

Some DRM systems do not prevent unauthorized access but instead prevent certain uses of copyrighted works, especially unauthorized copying. The third ban (the "additional violations ban") prohibits trafficking in tools to facilitate the circumvention of DRM if that DRM protects any copyright holder's right.[37] For example, the music industry had briefly experimented with DRM-restricted compact discs (CDs). These discs are not easily copied by computers, but the DRM systems do not prevent access; CD players require no access key or code to play them and thus computers generally play them without problems. This provision would ban a technology designed or marketed to circumvent this DRM system – for instance, a tool that would allow a consumer to convert the audio files from a CD into MP3 format on her hard drive. The proposed bills and final legislation all left untouched the right to circumvent use-controlling DRM such as this. Thus, a determined end user would be well within her rights to circumvent the DRM on a music CD, but it would be illegal for her to develop, sell, or market a service or software program that did so.

---

[35] 17 U.S.C. § 1201(a)(1)(A).
[36] 17 U.S.C. § 1201(a)(2).
[37] 17 U.S.C. § 1201(b).

The 105th Congress added a number of amendments to the bill. In the House bill as introduced,[38] a very brief section 1201 lays out the three bans with no explicit exceptions. It contains the following caveat, which is also included in the final legislation: "Nothing in this section shall affect rights, remedies, limitations, or defenses to copyright infringement, including fair use, under this title."[39] Although this may seem like a large caveat, the DMCA does not change the definition of infringement; it simply adds an additional set of prohibitions. Thus, most of the limitations, exclusions, and affirmative defenses built into copyright law do not limit the DMCA's reach. Most importantly, fair use is not a defense against charges of circumvention or trafficking in circumvention devices. The language in the 1997 bill also applies criminal penalties of up to $1 million in fines and up to ten years in prison for violating section 1201 or 1202 "willfully and for purposes of commercial advantage or private financial gain."[40] These penalties remained in the final legislation as enacted.[41]

Facing mobilized opposition, the bill's supporters made several narrow concessions, each creating a limited reprieve from one or more of the three bans. These caveats are clear attempts to address the concerns of a specific sector without much reduction in the bill's reach. Librarians opposed the bill and got a very limited exception; they may circumvent DRM "to make a good faith determination of whether to acquire a copy of that work,"[42] but not to preserve works they have already purchased.[43] Software designers and information technology researchers spoke in

---

[38] Digital Millennium Copyright Act, H.R. 2281, 105th Cong. (1997). ["DMCA, H.R. 2281."]

[39] Ibid., § 1201(d), encoded at 17 U.S.C. § 1201(c).

[40] DMCA H.R. 2281, § 1204.   [41] 17 U.S.C. § 1204.

[42] 17 U.S.C. § 1201(d)(1).

[43] This exemption is not very useful in practice, to say the least. Librarians who want to make informed decisions about DRM-encrypted media such as DVDs can borrow them from other libraries, and they will only buy them if they have the appropriate technology to view them without circumvention. This exemption could apply to a librarian who wants to decide whether to purchase a networked resource, such as a specialized database, but, for it to be necessary, a librarian would need to approach a database vendor, ask for a trial subscription to a database to which the library is considering subscribing, and be rebuffed. It is highly unlikely that any company that sells their products to libraries would act so directly against their own best interests. Even in such an outlandishly unlikely scenario, a determined librarian would still likely be very uncomfortable with the legal footing for accessing such a resource, not only in light of § 1201, but also due to other federal and state laws against the unauthorized access of computing resources. For instance, in the estimation of this nonlawyer, 18 U.S.C. §§ 1029–30 would seem not to apply, but the lack of such clear applicability would be small comfort. Although the DMCA is poorly thought out on many counts – including, importantly, in its assumption of a neat cleavage between access-controlling

opposition and got some more substantial breathing room to do their jobs,[44] although not enough to prevent some major professional headaches for some bona fide researchers doing legitimate work, as discussed later. The Electronic Privacy Information Center testified in opposition, so it won the right to circumvent DRM to protect one's personal information.[45] Each opposition group got a concession in rough proportion to its political capital. For the bill's backers, this was vastly preferable to permitting a general purpose exemption for otherwise noninfringing uses – let alone an exception for technologies that are capable of substantial noninfringing uses.

The basic ban is also subject to additional, temporary exemptions. Every three years, under the supervision of the Librarian of Congress, the U.S. Copyright Office holds hearings to consider proposed exemptions from the ban on circumventing access-controlling DRM systems.[46] The procedure moves questions of fair use away from relatively fair use–friendly federal courts and into the hands of the Register of Copyrights, a clear member of the SC coalition – a shift of venue that substantially favors the SC coalition.[47] Although several exemptions have been granted in each rulemaking, the statute and the Register's interpretation of the rules for determining exemptions are heavily stacked against proposed exemptions.[48] Changes introduced in the 2006 rulemaking make it somewhat less objectionable in terms of both procedure and outcome, although the whole procedure remains deeply flawed.[49]

Ironically, the bill's opponents might have been better off had they allowed the original bill to pass without the explicit exemptions that were later added. As Jessica Litman explains:

> The original Lehman bill granted copyright owners sweeping new rights, but its silence on available exceptions invited the courts to apply copyright's traditional limitations [such as fair use]. The DMCA also grants copyright owners sweeping new rights. Its laundry list of narrow exceptions, however, discourages the inference that the classic general exceptions and privileges apply.[50]

---

and use-controlling DRM – this exemption borders on the silly. I doubt it has ever been used.

[44] 17 U.S.C. §§ 1201(f), 1201(g)(2).   [45] 17 U.S.C. §1201(g).

[46] 17 U.S.C. § 1201(a)(1).

[47] Herman and Gandy, "Catch 1201," 143–4.

[48] Ibid., 187–90.

[49] Bill D. Herman, "Copyright Office grants 6 exemptions for circumventing TPMs," *Shouting Loudly*, November 22, 2006, http://www.shoutingloudly.com/2006/11/22/copyright-office-grants-6-exemptions-for-circumventing-tpms.

[50] Litman, *Digital Copyright*, 145.

This inapplicability of general exceptions became the cause for much political wrangling later, as discussed in later chapters.

In the debate over what became Title I of the DMCA, the SC coalition argued that the legal backing behind encryption would turn the internet into a safe place for the transmission of digital content. Among the many predicting its success, Robert W. Holleyman, II, head of the Business Software Alliance (BSA), described section 1201 as "the model,...the gold standard that we need to take to show the world how they protect intellectual property against piracy."[51] Allan R. Adler, Vice President for Legal and Government Affairs, supported the domestic implementation enthusiastically, predicting that the WIPO treaties would "benefit the U.S. economy by ensuring effective protection for U.S. copyrighted works in the digital environment."[52] These SC advocates and many more predicted that Title I would greatly reduce online infringement.

A DEAL TO LIMIT SERVICE PROVIDER EXPOSURE

In return for the anticircumvention provisions, the SC coalition also accepted the proposal limiting online service provider liability. This limitation, which became Title II of the DMCA, was written in a way that was palatable to the SC coalition. Even on its own, Title II represents a compromise between online service providers and copyright holders.[53] This is fairly clear from both the statute's content and the critiques that, in retrospect, should have been both obvious and disconcerting.

The Shape of Title II: A Notice-and-Takedown Process

In general, the act provides that service providers are not liable for the infringements committed by their users as long as the service provider

---

[51] *The WIPO Copyright Treaties Implementation Act: Hearing before the Subcommittee on Telecommunications, Trade, and Consumer Protection of the House Committee on Commerce,* 105th Cong. 36, 37 (1998) (statement of Robert W. Holleyman, II, President and CEO, Business Software Alliance).

[52] *H.R. 2281, WIPO Copyright Treaties Implementation Act; and H.R. 2180, Online Copyright Liability Limitation Act: Hearing before the Subcommittee on Courts and Intellectual Property of the House Committee on the Judiciary,* 105th Cong. 205, 207 (1997) (statement of Allan Adler, Vice Pres. for Legal and Governmental Affairs, Assn. of Amer. Publishers).

[53] Miller, "Fair Use." Miller observes: "Section 512(c) of the DMCA is the end product of a compromise between OSPs [Online Service Providers] and copyright holders. It absolves OSPs from liability when they comply with demands from copyright holders to remove potentially infringing material." Ibid., 1702.

meets certain conditions.[54] These include not knowing that the material in question was infringing, promptly complying with requests to take down infringing materials, and publicly identifying the service provider's contact information by which such takedown requests can be made.[55] For instance, if I post a five-minute clip of a Warner Brothers movie on YouTube, the studio can simply contact YouTube requesting that it be taken down; the service provides a web form for doing so, but copyright holders may also contact them via e-mail, fax, or post. As long as YouTube promptly complies with this request, it has no legal exposure for having helped me commit infringement. In this way, the bill addresses concerns by both service providers and copyright holders. Service providers have a mechanism for escaping legal liability; for services that host user-generated content, this is extremely reassuring. Likewise, this ability to escape liability provides very strong incentives to take content down, which is decidedly to the benefit of copyright holders.

This compromise was generally acceptable to the SC coalition. For instance, in her written testimony, then-head of the Recording Industry Association of America (RIAA) Hilary B. Rosen said, "This section represents an historic achievement in establishing new rules of the Internet road, balancing the legitimate needs and concerns of copyright owners with those of Internet service providers."[56] Likewise, Holleyman expressed support for the pairing of Title I and Title II in the DMCA, saying the combination "allows us to have an appropriate balance that we need to move ahead in a technological era."[57] The SC coalition also included holdouts such as then-MPAA head Jack Valenti, who argued that the mechanism for granting immunity to service providers was unnecessary; he argued that the then-current case law worked "very well" by giving "judges discretion to deal on a case by case basis."[58] Much more

---

[54] 17 U.S.C. §512. See also, Senate Committee on the Judiciary, *The Digital Millennium Copyright Act of 1998*, S. Rep. No. 105–190 (1998), http://www.hrrc.org/File/S._Rept._105-190.pdf.

[55] E.g., 17 U.S.C. §512(c) (covering "Information Residing on Systems or Networks at Direction of Users").

[56] *The WIPO Copyright Treaties Implementation Act: Hearing before the Subcommittee on Telecommunications, Trade, and Consumer Protection of the House Committee on Commerce*, 105th Cong. 45 (1998) (statement of Hilary B. Rosen, Pres. and CEO, RIAA).

[57] Ibid., 36 (statement of Robert W. Holleyman, II, Pres. & CEO, Bus. Software Alliance).

[58] *H.R. 2281, WIPO Copyright Treaties Implementation Act; and H.R. 2180, Online Copyright Liability Limitation Act: Hearing before the Subcommittee on Courts and Intellectual Property of the House Committee on the Judiciary*, 105th Cong. 78 (1997) (statement of Jack Valenti, Pres. & CEO, MPAA).

important, however, was the SC coalition's concerns that the internet industry's desires for an immunity provision not stand in the way of the passage of the anticircumvention provisions. Valenti voiced this concern most clearly, insisting that the DRM mandates not be held "hostage" to the service providers' interests and that Congress act quickly so as to create a sense of momentum toward international ratification of the WIPO treaties.[59]

Whether embraced enthusiastically or accepted as a condition for the passage of the anticircumvention provisions, the SC coalition as a whole enthusiastically accepted what became Title II of the DMCA. Members of the SC coalition viewed the whole bill as being very much an advancement of their interests and a fair deal. With this kind of limitation enshrined in statute, the burgeoning internet industries were also justified in supporting the whole legislative package. Especially with the SC coalition's vocal support for the final bill, service providers were also justified in walking away from the DMCA debate with the reassurance of having reached a deal with the content industries.

The Concerns with Title II: Largely Foreseeable, At Least in Hindsight

Even when the most closely affected industries like a bill, that does not mean it is a good deal for everybody. The kind of horse-trading between industries that went into the DMCA is not exactly the most democratic way to make law – and, as Jessica Litman argues persuasively, this kind of process has helped lead copyright away from the public's interest for decades.[60] From internet users' perspective, there is much to criticize in Title II. In particular, several scholars have argued that the statute leads to a suppression of free expression online.[61] The law provides strong incentives for taking content down and weak incentives for leaving it up or restoring it after an initial takedown, as well as making it unlikely that sloppy or even bogus copyright claims will be punished. When confronted with a takedown request, a service provider can escape all cause of action by complying quickly. In contrast, refusal to comply leaves the provider exposed to substantial legal liability for contributory liability, especially since the provider will have received notice of the allegation of infringement.[62] Should a provider be found liable for willful infringement, the provider could be subject to massive statutory damages – up

---

[59] See ibid. [60] Litman, *Digital Copyright*.

[61] Seltzer, "Free Speech Unmoored;" Miller, "Fair Use;" Koss, "Protecting Free Speech."

to $150,000 per work – as well as plaintiff's costs and attorney's fees.[63] Thus, the incentive to comply with any takedown request is incredibly strong.

The act does provide a mechanism for an affected user to issue counter-notice to the service provider. A subscriber to an online service whose content is removed may ask that it be reposted by submitting to the service provider a "statement under penalty of perjury that the subscriber has a good faith belief that the material was removed or disabled as a result of mistake or misidentification of the material to be removed or disabled."[64] If a subscriber does file such a counter-notice, the service provider can repost the material in question, although they must do so "not less than 10, nor more than 14, business days following receipt of the counter notice, unless [the copyright holder] has filed an action seeking a court order to restrain the subscriber from engaging in infringing activity relating to the material on the service provider's system or network."[65] By following this procedure, a service provider is legally protected against claims by both copyright holders and subscribers who have their content removed.

For those who would prefer a system that errs on the side of free expression, the incentives and procedures set up by this statute are obviously disconcerting. The ten-day window is one cause for concern. For many communicators, especially online, ten days can be a very long time. Wendy Seltzer recounts the case of the McCain-Palin campaign having several of their videos taken down for ten days during the last month leading up to the 2008 presidential election.[66] The service kept the videos offline for the full ten-day window even though they were "a clear case of non-infringing fair use – speech protected by the First Amendment..."[67] If the statute can have a chilling effect on a presidential campaign, it takes little to imagine the staggering obstacles a takedown notice can be for an ordinary individual. Surely, a vast majority of those who have their content taken down do not even know about the counter-notice provisions, and, even among those who do, few understand copyright well enough to be confident in filing a counter-notice. Further, if a potential penalty of $150,000 per work and a plaintiff's legal fees are large enough to shape Google's strategies, these amounts are crippling for ordinary individuals, small businesses, and not-for-profit institutions, such as colleges. A

---

[62] Seltzer, "Free Speech Unmoored," 208–9.
[63] 17 U.S.C. §§ 504–505.
[64] 17 U.S.C. § 512(g)(3).
[65] 17 U.S.C. § 512(g)(2)(C).
[66] Seltzer, "Free Speech Unmoored," 171–5.
[67] Ibid., 173.

section 512 counter-notice is essentially a dare to the copyright holder: "Go ahead, sue me." Very few people are in a position to make such a dare, and even those who do file counter-notices still may never have their content restored.[68]

Takedown notices have been issued in genuine bad faith as well, and they are increasingly being made in automated ways that lead to incredible sloppiness. The statute does provide for damages to be assessed against anyone who "knowingly materially misrepresents" whether an infringement has taken place in a takedown request (or counter-notice).[69] Rulings of bad faith under section 512(f) are vanishingly rare, but in one, *Online Policy Group v. Diebold*,[70] the court was prepared to award damages for bad faith DMCA takedown requests. This case featured some of the most brazen bad faith copyright claims imaginable, inviting what became a strategic lawsuit pursued by the Electronic Frontier Foundation (EFF) and the Center for Internet and Society Cyberlaw Clinic at Stanford Law School.[71] The sizable amount of the out-of-court settlement reached before final judgement, $125,000,[72] serves as at least some deterrence to filing bad faith takedown requests, but the impact of that deterrence has been minimal. One study of hundreds of takedown requests found results that show widespread misuse, ranging from notices for noncopyrightable material to obvious fair uses to competitors using the process strategically.[73] Some people have used the takedown process

[68] Those who file a counter-notice have little if any recourse against service providers. The act's immunity clause is only a supplement to the protections given to providers by their end user license agreements. The latter generally give users little if any potential for relief for any reason, and service providers act accordingly – including, in this case, often ignoring counter-notice claims and not re-posting the content in question. One could argue about whether this strikes the right balance in copyright, but it surely cuts at least some legitimate speech out of the public sphere.

[69] 17 U.S.C. § 512(f).

[70] *Online Policy Group v. Diebold*. Diebold, makers of electronic voting machines, was the subject of criticism that their machines failed to correctly tabulate vote totals. There was an online leak of thousands of internal company e-mails, many featuring employees openly acknowledging the flaws in the company's voting machines, and the company issued dozens of DMCA takedown notices in an effort to suppress the circulation of these memos. The works in question had no protectable commercial value as copyrighted material, and the people circulating them online – including then-Swarthmore undergraduates Nelson Chu Pavlosky and Luke Thomas Smith – were doing so as part of a political discussion about the concerns with the company's technology, rather than for commercial gain.

[71] Electronic Frontier Foundation, "*Online Policy Group v. Diebold*," https://www.eff.org/cases/online-policy-group-v-diebold.

[72] Ibid.

[73] Urban and Quilter, "Efficient Process or Chilling Effects."

to silence the speech of Facebook groups with whom they disagree – even doing so with fake contact information, as well as coordinating and bragging about their behavior on other websites.[74] Finally, the number of automatic computer-produced takedowns is so large, and the incentives against sending out mistaken takedowns so weak, that thousands of computer-generated takedowns have been sent even in cases of gross error, such as media companies demanding the takedown of works to which they do not own the copyright.[75]

Although the specifics of these stories were not foreseeable, it certainly was clear that the law set up incredibly strong incentives for the takedown of material in response to any claim of infringement – powerful incentives decidedly not counterbalanced by weak to nonexistent reasons to ignore even the flimsiest takedown request. It would have taken little forethought to see that this would lead to at least some legitimate speech being suppressed online. Yet, at the time, there was little outcry. The SFU coalition was still being built, and the push behind the organization of the Digital Future Coalition was based on concern with the anticircumvention provisions rather than the service provider liability provisions. Understandably, service providers and other computer industry voices were worried about sheltering their industry from legal liability. This included both established telecommunications companies, hardware and software firms, and a few internet companies such as AOL and Netscape (Google was still based in a garage). All the push was to find a system for rapid enforcement that would shelter members of the internet ecosystem from potentially massive legal liability. The DMCA was not crafted as an effort to maximize the public's interest or the free circulation of ideas online, but as a deal between copyright holders and service providers. Even Title II, which was the part that service providers requested, was crafted as a compromise that was generally accepted by copyright holders. Unfortunately for both service providers and the public, however, even this deal was not enough to satisfy the SC coalition – a point I explore in Chapter 11.

---

[74] Violet Blue, "Neowin's Facebook Page Downed by Bogus Complaints – Again [UPDATED]," *ZDNet* (April 28, 2011), http://www.zdnet.com/blog/violetblue/ neowins-facebook-page-downed-by-bogus-complaints-again-updated/3317.

[75] Mike Masnick, "EFF Argues That Automated Bogus DMCA Takedowns Violate The Law And Are Subject To Sanctions," *Techdirt* (March 8, 2012), http:// www.techdirt.com/articles/20120308/03505018034/eff-argues-that-automated-bogus -dmca-takedowns-violate-law-are-subject-to-sanctions.shtml.

DIGITAL MILLENNIUM COPYRIGHT ACT AS POLITICAL MILESTONE

Compared with the AHRA, the passage of the anticircumvention provisions of the DMCA represented a much more significant shift in copyright law as a vehicle for the regulation of technology. The AHRA regulates only one small class of technologies – stand-alone digital audio recording devices. In contrast, the DMCA regulates a potentially infinite number of devices, including computers. Every copyrighted work that can be digitized can be wrapped in encryption or flagged by copyright management information. Those who design and manipulate technologies to handle such copyrighted works are on thin legal ice. As scholars such as Kembrew McLeod note, this discourages even legitimate academic encryption research, despite the statutory exception protecting it.[76] Unauthorized but legal uses of DRM-protected works are also discouraged, both via the ban on circumvention and the ban on tools of circumvention.[77] This regulation of technology is a substantial departure from the behavior-regulating tradition of copyright; the anticircumvention provisions share "neither the logic nor the strategy of copyright."[78]

Like the debate around the AHRA, the process leading up to the DMCA also says a great deal about the politics of copyright – although whereas the AHRA debate was more of an extension of the previous politics of copyright, the run-up to the DMCA sowed the seeds of a major change. Before Lehman began advancing his ideas, there was still no cohort of policy actors that advanced an agenda directly opposed to that of the SC coalition. Lehman's proposal, however, scared opponents into coordinated action. Starting with Peter Jaszi and other like-minded law professors, opponents began recruiting others to the cause, in hope of stopping or amending the proposal before it could become law. Importantly, they successfully recruited additional voices of resistance that policymakers could not ignore – that is, not just law professors and librarians, but industry voices. Weighing in to voice concerns about the bill were computer and electronics industry trade groups such as the Home Recording Rights Coalition, Consumer Electronics Manufacturers Association, and the Computer and Communications Industry Association. Another notable voice of opposition was the Institute of Electrical and Electronics Engineers (IEEE), which functions like an academic body

[76] McLeod, *Owning Culture*, 261–2.
[77] Herman and Gandy, "Catch 1201," 132.   [78] Gillespie, *Wired Shut*, 177.

and has many academic members but is also substantially populated by and representative of industry professionals. As copyright increasingly became a potential threat to new technologies, the people seeking to develop and sell new computer technologies began to see what the consumer electronics industry had already seen after the introduction of the videocassette recorder (VCR) – their need to mobilize to protect their interests as makers of copying technologies. They did not mobilize as core members of what would become the SFU coalition, but more as what might be called "persuadable technology actors," or industry voices that could produce more vocal opposition to the expansion of copyright in the years to come.

The difference in the dynamics between the AHRA and the DMCA processes was subtle, but palpable. The AHRA opposition was not coordinated to even the same degree as the DFC, which itself was a hastily organized coalition rather than a well-coordinated strategic machine. This kind of principled opposition from civil society actors and scholars, organized and coordinated even to this modest degree, was new in the copyright debate. Furthermore, the AHRA process required substantial input from just one technology industry: the consumer electronics manufacturers who strongly supported the bill as a legislative permission slip to finally begin selling DAT decks.[79] In contrast, the DMCA process brought several into the copyright debate. Each of these sectors needed to be accommodated and, more or less, each was. Congress was not used to legislating copyright law in the face of such a melange of conflicting, technologically complicated requests and even substantial skepticism. The unexpected outburst of opposition and calls for specific exceptions slowed down what Lehman had expected to be an easy process.

Another important development was the addition of Representative Rick Boucher to the voices of opposition. Over the course of nearly three decades in service, Boucher earned a reputation as one of the most technologically literate members of Congress and an informed, thoughtful voice in technology policy discussions.[80] In expressing his own views in congressional hearings, he eloquently advanced the arguments of the bill's opponents. For instance, he argued that the bill would erode the *Sony* decision and that this would prevent legitimate technologies from coming

---

[79] I am excluding the computer industry, which sought only to ensure that the bill did not regulate them (e.g., by charging the blank media and device royalties on their technology).

[80] Tony Romm, Tech Community Laments Rick Boucher Loss, *Politico*, November 2, 2010, at http://www.politico.com/news/stories/1110/44589.html.

to market.[81] He also proposed legislation with an alternate version of section 1201.[82] It read, in part:

> No person, for the purpose of facilitating or engaging in an act of infringement, shall engage in conduct so as knowingly to remove, deactivate or otherwise circumvent the application or operation of any effective technological measure used by a copyright owner to preclude or limit reproduction of a work or a portion thereof. As used in this subsection, the term "conduct" does not include manufacturing, importing or distributing a device or a computer program.[83]

If passed in this form, the DMCA would have tethered violations to the question of infringement; if a user's purpose was not infringing, circumvention would have been entirely legal. Thus, exemptions and affirmative defenses such as fair use would have limited the reach of the DMCA. In this bill, the basic ban is the only ban – there are no bans on developing or selling products or services that circumvent DRM, whether access-controlling or use-controlling. Instead, the language specifically exempts manufacturers and vendors of such devices and services. This would have left the *Sony*[84] standard as the rule governing liability for creating or marketing circumvention technologies; manufacturers of circumvention devices that are "capable of substantial noninfringing uses"[85] would not be liable for their products' infringing uses. Instead, under the law that passed, even technologies that are exclusively capable of noninfringing uses are still illegal if they circumvent DRM.

Obviously, members of Congress make for powerful political allies, and the DMCA debate saw Boucher's full-throttle entry into what was blooming as the SFU coalition. Just one other member of Congress, Scott Klug, the former Representative from Wisconsin, voiced substantial concern about the DMCA during the debate over the bill.[86] Since Klug kept his initial campaign promise only to stay in the House for eight years, ending his tenure in early 1999, he would not have the chance to have the same kind of substantial influence that Boucher exercised in future debates on copyright. Yet he would not be the last member of Congress to

---

[81] *NII Copyright Protection Act of 1995 (Pt. 2): Hearings Before the Subcommittee on Courts and Intellectual Property*, 104th Cong. 16 (1996) (statement of Hon. Rep. Rick Boucher).

[82] H.R. 3048, Digital Era Copyright Enhancement Act, 105th Cong., §8 (1997), http://thomas.loc.gov/cgi-bin/query/z?c105:H.R.3048:.

[83] Ibid., §1201(a).

[84] *Sony v. Universal*, 464 U.S. 417 (1984).   [85] Ibid., 442.

[86] Herman and Gandy, "Catch 1201," 146–7.

join Boucher in the call for greater fair use. Quite the contrary, Boucher would only find a growing number of allies on this count in the years to come. Combined with the beginnings of a permanent civil society voice for fair use, Boucher could be considered a founding member of what would become the SFU coalition. Having even one coalition member in Congress undoubtedly gave those outside Congress considerably greater legitimacy and momentum. Even though they were just forming into a coalition as the bill passed, their resistance was unexpected, and it forced changes in both the SC coalition's strategy and the bill's final language.

On at least one count, however, the passage of one part of the DMCA sought by the copyright industries happened with even less resistance than came during the process leading up to the AHRA. The DMCA contains a little-noticed, AHRA-like affirmative requirement that all VCRs marketed and sold in the United States implement a specific anticopying technology.[87] The technology, developed by DRM vendor Macrovision, looks for a "do not copy" signal that movie studios can build into prerecorded videos; if the signal is present, the VCR will not make a useful copy of the original. This DRM system is more stringent than the serial copy management system (SCMS) system required by the AHRA; the SCMS allows copies of originals, just not copies of copies, whereas the Macrovision system does not even allow copies of originals. Yet, although the AHRA requirement was subject to hearings and a public debate, the DMCA's VCR requirement was subject to little if any public scrutiny. Nothing like the relevant section appeared in either of the versions that passed the House and the Senate; rather, it was "added during conference committee markup."[88] Thus, this AHRA-like mandate, of obvious benefit to Macrovision and the movie industry, was passed in a manner that suggests an evasion of public input – hardly an example of good, transparent government.

The most significant part of the anticircumvention provisions, however, was and remains the three bans on circumvention and trafficking in circumvention devices. The law's passage was a wake-up call to those in the formerly cozy confines of the copyright debate. It saw the birth of the SFU coalition and its capacity to slow and even modify copyright industry–backed legislation. The SFU coalition was not yet powerful enough to stop the DMCA from passage, but catching Lehman off-guard

---

[87] 17 U.S.C. § 1201(k).
[88] Herman and Gandy, "Catch 1201," 148, n. 146.

and forcing changes to the bill was a promising beginning for the group. By 2003, opposition to the DMCA became one of the main issues driving the rapid growth of the SFU coalition. In the four years between the bill's passage and the first credible efforts to reform it, however, other major events fundamentally reshaped the landscape of the copyright debate.

4

A Digital Rights Management Interlude:
1999–2002

In the four years between the passage of the Digital Millennium Copyright Act (DMCA) and the next major legislative fights over credibly advanced digital rights management (DRM) proposals, several notable events happened that reshaped the playing field. The most visible events happened in technology and the courts, but some less widely discussed developments from that period have had comparable or even greater long-term political significance. Several of these developments would warrant discussion on their own, but since they all happened in a very short time, they add up to a very turbulent period. All told, the turn of the century was nothing less than a time of watershed changes in copyright advocacy.

THE PEER-TO-PEER EXPLOSION

Most visibly, 1999 marked the year in which Napster first gave millions of users the ability to acquire nearly all of the world's recorded music for free. This represented a tectonic shift in the media industry; suddenly, the music industry wished that its biggest threat were from illicit cassette recordings (digital or otherwise) rather than the internet. Most readers will likely know at least the basics of the story, and of course, there are more thorough examinations of the birth and early growth of Napster,[1] the record industry's reaction,[2] and the current state of the music industry in light of peer-to-peer (P2P) trading.[3]

Even during hearings leading up to the DMCA, the media industries were already expressing fears about the internet. If the untamed web of 1998 was scary, however, the explosive adoption of P2P software was

[1] Alderman, *Sonic Boom.*   [2] Knopper, *Appetite for Self-Destruction.*
[3] Madden, "The State of Music Online."

mortifying. The record industry responded with a multipronged legal strategy. First, along with the motion picture industry, they sued the companies behind P2P technologies. They started by suing Napster, winning a finding that the company was liable for their users' widespread infringement.[4] After the 2001 *Napster* decision led to the service's shuttering, several newer companies sprung up to fill Napster's shoes; the recording and movie industries responded by suing these companies as well, resulting in the 2005 *MGM v. Grokster* decision by the Supreme Court. This decision substantially reduced the value of the *Sony* safe harbor, placing technology innovators in a much more precarious legal position.[5] Yet this strategy did not prevent the further development and adoption of still further P2P programs.[6] "In short, suing the technology hasn't worked,"[7] as P2P software is still readily available and widely used for infringement.

The other part of the Recording Industry Association of America (RIAA)'s legal strategy was suing thousands of users – approximately 35,000, from 2003 to 2008.[8] It was a public relations debacle, highlighted by lawsuits against "several single mothers, a dead person and a 13-year-old girl."[9] Although the RIAA certainly embarked on this campaign with some reluctance and with a readiness to be subjected to some degree of public scorn, the suits did not even achieve the intended effect of discouraging P2P use.[10] The message that illicit P2P trading is illegal did get through to users, but peer pressure provided a far more powerful force in favor of continued use.[11] Beginning in 2008, the RIAA thus stopped pursuing new cases, although it continued with cases that had already begun.[12]

Even though the RIAA has stopped suing users and even scaled back their scorched-earth litigation against technological innovators, the group

---

[4] *A&M Records v. Napster*.

[5] Menell and Nimmer, "Legal Realism in Action."

[6] The most significant contemporary P2P application is BitTorrent, which is used for widespread infringement but also has been adopted for legitimate purposes, such as distributing open source software.

[7] Electronic Frontier Foundation (EFF), "RIAA v. the People," 2.

[8] Sarah McBride and Ethan Smith, "Music Industry to Abandon Mass Suits," *Wall Street Journal*, December 19, 2008, http://online.wsj.com/article/SB122966038836021137.html.

[9] Ibid.   [10] EFF, "RIAA v. the People," 9.

[11] Oksanen and Välimäki, "Theory of Deterrence," 693.

[12] Sarah McBride and Ethan Smith, "Music Industry to Abandon Mass Suits," *Wall Street Journal*, December 19, 2008, http://online.wsj.com/article/SB122966038836021137.html.

may never recover from the public relations damage. After their response to Napster, the trade group that had formerly had relatively little public visibility was suddenly the object of hatred by young people and technology enthusiasts across the country. Although few of these people were being tapped for direct political action, their opposition to the RIAA's political agenda was suddenly boundless and effusive.[13] Even among the very substantial subset who do not trade illicit files, there has been little public support for the industry in their war against downloaders. This ethos of visceral resentment toward the RIAA and the Motion Picture Association of America (MPAA) has also been reflected on and fueled by virtually every major technology website – from *Wired* to technology-themed blogs and user-generated content sites. On the rare occasions when high-profile sites do host a guest commentary from a strong copyright (SC) ally, the stream of outraged user comments let the editors know that this viewpoint is not appreciated.[14] Although the DMCA had passed in relative obscurity, the RIAA's actions quickly pushed copyright to the front page – while drawing millions to view the content industry as the enemy in a war between new technologies and copyright holders.

SENATOR HOLLINGS' PROPOSAL

Not content with the DMCA, the content industries and their allies in Congress soon advanced additional legislative proposals intended to limit internet users' ability to continue engaging in infringement. The most significant of these legislative proposals, if enacted, would have represented a change in copyright exceeding the significance of the DMCA. That proposal, S. 2048, the Consumer Broadband and Digital Television

[13] On literally every major site that I can name that draws the young or technologically savvy, open contempt for content industry lobbyists has been the norm since these lawsuits began. The drumbeat is the loudest on technology sites, such as Slashdot.org, Wired.com, Techdirt.com, and Gizmodo.com, where the legal environment for technology is discussed with the highest relative frequency. On other sites that are popular with young audiences – such as YouTube and social networking sites such as MySpace (dominant during the heart of the RIAA's legal campaign) and Facebook – the subject comes up with much less proportional frequency, but when it does, users are more openly hostile to the RIAA than sympathetic to its goals.

[14] For instance, in 2005, *CNet* published an anti-DMCA–reform piece by Patrick Ross, then-VP of the now-defunct SC-aligned Progress and Freedom Foundation. Patrick Ross, "Perspective: Here's a Surefire Way to Stifle Innovation," *CNet News*, October 6, 2005, http://news.cnet.com/2010_1025_3-5889596.html. The article drew 124 comments, virtually all of them scathing critiques – including one by this author.

Promotion Act, "would have prohibited the manufacture, sale, import, or provision of any 'interactive digital media device' that didn't incorporate certain security technologies."[15] From computers to iPods to a good portion of today's advanced home audio/video equipment, the bill would have required government-specified copy protection to be built into each device.

Sponsored by Senator Fritz Hollings, S. 2048 created a firestorm. "Several consumer groups and electronics companies aligned themselves against" the bill.[16] A *Salon* headline warned, "U.S. Prepares to Invade Your Hard Drive," and noted that Hollings' sponsorship of the bill had moved him into the "axis of evil for technology."[17] Faced with this coordinated – and now predictable – resistance, the bill was unlikely ever to become law. As if this were not enough of an obstacle, the Hollings bill also ran into a problem of committee jurisdiction; by introducing this bill from the Senate Commerce Committee, Hollings stepped squarely on the Judiciary Committee's traditional domain of copyright legislation. This breach of jurisdiction upset Judiciary member Patrick Leahy, who is normally a reliable supporter of copyright industry requests but who, in this case, actually threatened a filibuster.[18]

If the music and movie industries had wanted to give something like the Hollings bill a real shot at passage, they would have engaged the electronics and computer industries in the kind of negotiations that led to the passage of the Audio Home Recording Act (AHRA). They also would have chosen the "right" committee to introduce the bill. Instead, Disney's then-CEO Michael Eisner, reportedly the industry voice who led to Hollings' sponsorship of the bill,[19] jumped several steps ahead in the process and moved forward with a sponsor who further reduced the odds of passage. There are a range of theories about why Eisner and Hollings teamed up on this effort, all the more so because the Hollings bill would have gone further than even other media companies and allied congresspersons supported,[20] meaning that the strategies they did choose sealed the bill's fate.

---

[15] Gillespie, *Wired Shut*, 196.

[16] Brad King, "Howling Mad Over Hollings' Bill," *Wired*, March 3, 2002, http://www.wired.com/gadgets/portablemusic/news/2002/03/51337?currentPage=all.

[17] Paul Boutin, "U.S. Prepares to Invade Your Hard Drive," *Salon*, March 29, 2002, http://www.salon.com/2002/03/29/hollings_bill/.

[18] Jeffrey H. Birnbaum, "The Hollings Bill: Doomed But Effective," *CNN*, May 27, 2002, http://money.cnn.com/magazines/fortune/fortune_archive/2002/05/27/323686/index.htm.

[19] Ibid.   [20] Ibid.

Rather than a sincere effort to change the law, the Hollings bill was far more likely intended as a rhetorical move – an addition to the conversation or an implicit threat to the technology sector, depending on one's perspective. It was reported as an effort to spur "Hollywood and Silicon Valley to redouble their efforts to find a technological fix to the problem of digital duplication.... In other words, think of Washington as a legislative cattle prod."[21] One could debate whether this prod was effective or counterproductive, although there is no clear link to any industry outcomes. The next April, Apple finally offered consumers a legitimate way to purchase most big-label music – contained within Apple's proprietary DRM scheme, FairPlay – with the iTunes Music Store. Many other stores soon cropped up selling their own packages of DRM-wrapped media. Yet it is not at all clear that the Hollings bill helped foster any of these outcomes. Instead, it took Apple – and, to a large degree, Steve Jobs personally – to persuade a reluctant recording industry to embrace internet distribution.[22] Once the money started rolling in from that agreement, deals with other companies became far more conceivable.

The Hollings bill did at least serve as a loud and clear threat to the technology industry: make DRM systems that satisfy the content companies, or Congress might design and mandate one for you. It also sent a strong message to technology companies that they needed to pay more attention to the debate over copyright in Washington, D.C. This is especially significant because the technology sector is not united on copyright issues. Some are principled, permanent members of the strong fair use (SFU) coalition; these include nonprofits that support free (as in freedom) software[23] and other copyrightable content, such as the Free Software Foundation (founded in 1985), the Mozilla project (created in 1998), and the Wikimedia Foundation (founded in 2003). In contrast, the proprietary/closed source software industry (in particular, Microsoft and Adobe) and vendors of DRM technologies (e.g., Macrovision) are generally members of the SC coalition. The rest of the technology sector generally leans toward

---

[21] Ibid.

[22] Ben Sisario, "He Pushed a Reluctant Industry Toward Digital Music," *New York Times Media Decoder Blog*, October 5, 2011, http://mediadecoder.blogs.nytimes.com/2011/10/05/he-pushed-a-reluctant-industry-toward-digital-music/.

[23] Here I use the term "free software," which is the term of choice for those who view this as a political and human rights issue. In the index and many places throughout the book, though, I use the hedged term "free/open source software" to add clarity for those who may be more familiar with the (depoliticized) term "open source." For more, see Richard Stallman, "Why Open Source Misses the Point of Free Software," 2010, http://www.gnu.org/philosophy/open-source-misses-the-point.html.

the SFU position but are better described as the "persuadable technology" (or PT) division or group. This division – which I do not label as a coalition since they do not necessarily act in coordination – is filled with very important potential allies for either the SC or the SFU coalition. Those in the PT group include the consumer electronics industry, makers of computer hardware, internet service providers, web content companies, and online retailers. Collectively, these represent a significantly larger share of the economy than the SC-affiliated industries,[24] allowing them a real chance to swing the debate in either direction.

The bulk of the technology industry is persuadable on issues of digital copyright regulation. If proposed copyright legislation would drastically reduce consumer rights in a way that would sharply reduce the value of their wares, they will weigh in alongside the SFU coalition. Yet, as discussed in the other chapters in Part I, in relation to the AHRA (Chapter 2), DMCA (Chapter 3), and broadcast flag (Chapter 5), they are also willing to go along with increases in copyright as long as they can shape the legislation such that it reduces their liability or does not substantially reduce their profitability. Because of their substantial economic clout, the SFU and SC coalitions each spend a great deal of effort trying to draw this PT division to support their respective sides. To the extent the Hollings bill – as well as the suits against P2P companies – pushed the PT division closer to the SFU coalition, it probably had the ironic effect of harming the SC coalition's interests. Regardless of whether its impact led to any

---

[24] In 2009, the latest year available, the entire publishing industry (including software) accounted for 1 percent of gross domestic product (GDP), and the movie and record industries made up just 0.4 percent. The SC coalition could also claim a portion of the "arts, entertainment, and recreation" sector – particularly that portion such as sports leagues that also sell their rights to media companies – that totals 0.9 percent. In contrast, the computer and electronics industry alone made up 1.5 percent, and the sales of these items are a substantial and lucrative portion of the retail (5.8 percent) and wholesale (5.5 percent) trade sectors. (For instance, the items that draw the largest crowds for Black Friday sales are almost always technology products, including televisions, computers, and video game systems.) The IT services sector ("computer systems design and related services") accounted for 1.2 percent, information processing came in at 0.5 percent, and telecommunications and broadcasting (unfortunately lumped together) accounted for 2.5 percent. Depending on estimates for the telecommunications industry (vs. broadcasting) and its impact on wholesale and retail trade, the PT division in the copyright debate could claim credit for 5 to 10 percent of the U.S. economy. In contrast, the SC sectors might weigh in at 3 to 5 percent. In other words, the PT division is roughly twice as large as all SC-affiliated industries, and as much as ten times as large as the industries at the very core of the SC coalition – the record and movie industries. Gilmore, Morgan, and Osborne, "Annual Industry Accounts."

actual business decisions, then, the bill's political significance is hard to ignore.

NONGOVERNMENTAL ORGANIZATIONS TAKE A CENTRAL ROLE

In addition to rousing the slumbering giant of the technology sector, aggressive copyright industry litigation and lobbying helped spark the permanent involvement of nonprofit groups. Leading up to the passage of the DMCA, the internet and media policy nongovernmental organizations (NGOs) had little to say by way of opposition. The Electronic Frontier Foundation (EFF), which was founded in 1990 as roughly the online equivalent of the American Civil Liberties Union (ACLU), could have joined as an opponent of the DMCA's anticircumvention provisions. Instead, in 1995, the *Washington Post* quoted then-chair Esther Dyson as supporting Lehman's proposal.[25] The Digital Future Coalition was really just an umbrella group for other actors, and it was conceived, founded, and run by people who had day jobs other than as full-time policy advocates. Although this was an important start, there were no NGOs dedicated to the public's side in the copyright debate.

In the early 2000s, however – especially in 2001 – NGOs got heavily involved, and computer science researchers became the cause célèbre that helped spur such heavy involvement. First, in 2001, a team of computer scientists at Princeton faced legal threats for their study of a DRM system then in development. The Secure Digital Music Initiative (SDMI), a coalition of recording industry and technology firms, was developing the DRM system, and the RIAA caught the researchers utterly off-guard with surprisingly stark legal threats. Lawrence Lessig tells the story:

> Using encryption, SDMI hoped to develop a standard that would allow the content owner to say "this music cannot be copied," and have a computer respect that command. The technology was to be part of a "trusted system" of control that would get content owners to trust the system of the Internet much more.
>
> When SDMI thought it was close to a standard, it set up a competition. In exchange for providing contestants with the code to an SDMI-encrypted

[25] Elizabeth Corcoran, "A Digital Duel: Whose Property Is This? Business and the 'Net Cruisers' Debate How – and Whether – Copyright Applies in Cyberspace," *Washington Post*, September 3, 1995, H1.

bit of content, contestants were to try to crack it and, if they did, report the problems to the consortium.

[Princeton Professor Ed] Felten and his team figured out the encryption system quickly. He and the team saw the weakness of this system as a type: Many encryption systems would suffer the same weakness, and Felten and his team thought it worthwhile to point this out to those who study encryption.

. . .

And though an academic paper describing the weakness in a system of encryption should . . . be perfectly legal, Felten received a letter from an RIAA lawyer that [threatened legal action].[26]

The RIAA invoked the DMCA in its threats to Felten's team. Of course, it is a rare event when scholars are threatened with legal action for attempting to share their research results at an academic conference. This drew substantial publicity – and much of it negative – for the DMCA. The researchers were able to attract substantial donations of money, pro bono legal work, and favorable publicity to support their case, all of which led the SDMI attorneys to drop the suit – although not before the ordeal wreaked professional havoc for the researchers.[27] The EFF, which had not previously been a major player in copyright politics, went to work *pro bono* on Felten's behalf, giving him and his team the kind of legal and public relations resources that led the RIAA to drop its suit.[28] Even after the immediate legal threat was withdrawn, Felten and the EFF still wanted a court precedent to create a legal umbrella over his research and work like it, so they filed a suit seeking such a ruling. Since the recording

---

[26] Lessig, *Free Culture*, 155–7. Even though the researchers won in the end, they endured tremendous professional difficulties.

[27] Ed Felten, "Happy Endings," *Freedom to Tinker*, April 28, 2006, https://freedom-to-tinker.com/blog/felten/happy-endings. Felten writes:

> Let's catalog the happy consequences of our case. One person lost his job, and another nearly did. Countless hours of pro bono lawyer time were consumed. Anonymous donors gave up large amounts of money to support our defense. I lost at least months of my professional life, and other colleagues did too. And after all this, the ending was that we were able to publish our work – something which, before the DMCA, we would have been able to do with no trouble at all.
>
> In the end, yes, we were happy – in the same way one is happy to recover from food poisoning. Which is not really an argument in favor of food poisoning.

[28] Jennifer B. Lee, "Delayed Report on Encryption Flaws to Be Presented," *New York Times*, August 15, 2001, C3.

industry had backed down, however, the New Jersey Federal District Court dismissed the case, and Felten's side declined to pursue an appeal.[29]

Also in 2001, Russian programmer Dmitry Sklyarov faced his own, more serious legal problems. During a visit to the United States, he was arrested and jailed for nearly a month, charged with criminal violations of the DMCA. Sklyarov was a Ph.D. student researching cryptography and an employee of Russian software firm Elcomsoft. He had helped create a program called the Advanced eBook Processor, which removed the restrictions in Adobe Systems' eBook software. After he gave a presentation about the software at the 2001 DEF CON hacker[30] convention in Las Vegas, Federal Bureau of Investigation (FBI) agents arrested and charged him with trafficking in a circumvention device for profit, a criminal offense under § 1204. After several weeks in jail, Sklyarov was released on the condition that he testify against his employer Elcomsoft. In 2002, the jury found the company not guilty; they believed the company's defense of not knowingly violating the law.[31] Again, the EFF worked on behalf of the defendant, and again they were able to leverage the case into substantial negative publicity against the DMCA. Although the EFF had not previously been involved in copyright litigation or advocacy to any substantial degree, the Felten and Sklyarov cases drew them immediately into the very center of the fray.

Likewise, in 2001, the Washington, D.C.-based NGO Public Knowledge was born. The group was founded largely to serve as a permanent D.C. presence to counterbalance the content industry's lobbying efforts – or, as the group puts it more positively on its site, Public Knowledge "preserves the openness of the internet and the public's access to knowledge, promotes creativity through balanced copyright, and upholds and protects the rights of consumers to use innovative technology lawfully." Public Knowledge plays an absolutely central role in the SFU coalition's Washington, D.C. presence. During congressional hearings on copyright,

---

[29] EFF, "Security Researchers Drop Scientific Censorship Case: Government, Industry Claim DMCA Not a Threat to Science," February 6, 2002, http://w2.eff.org/IP/DMCA/Felten_v_RIAA/20020206_eff_felten_pr.html.

[30] News media often portray hackers as people who use their technological skills to commit crimes. As used here, and as represented at DEF CON, a hacker is better thought of as a tinkerer. Some computer tinkerers are criminals – which is to say that they are a subset of the general population. Thankfully, the rise of geek chic seems to be helping to rehabilitate the term.

[31] Matt Richtel, "Russian Company Cleared of Illegal Software Sales," *New York Times*, December 17, 2002, http://www.nytimes.com/2002/12/18/business/technology-russian-company-cleared-of-illegal-software-sales.html.

it is often the only NGO present. By 2002, Public Knowledge President Gigi Sohn was already appearing in the national media as a voice for moderation in copyright law.[32] In the decade since, Public Knowledge in general and Sohn in particular have become the primary voice for fair use inside the Beltway, even though their centrality is not as widely appreciated as it should be. This mismatch led to Sohn being named one of technology's twenty "most underrated founders."[33]

SCHOLARS STEP INTO THE SPOTLIGHT

Finally, the period from 1999 to 2002 was the beginning of a major public outreach effort by scholars. Peter Jaszi might have put the DFC in motion, but most outside the world of copyright are (unfortunately for them) not familiar with Jaszi or with the other key scholars who were the heart of the DFC.[34] In sharp contrast, by the early 2000s, law professor Lawrence Lessig had appeared in public so often that he became known to millions as the face of a growing movement to reform copyright. He published several books aimed at non-lawyers, helping to raise a high degree of public consciousness around questions of internet design and regulation. Lessig also served as the attorney for Eric Eldred in *Eldred v. Ashcroft*, argued in 2002 and decided in 2003. Eldred asked the Supreme Court to overturn the 1998 Copyright Term Extension Act – named for the late Sonny Bono – which extended copyright terms by twenty years, even

---

[32] David Lieberman, "Reshaping Industries, Lifestyles," *USA Today*, June 25, 2002, http://www.usatoday.com/life/cyber/tech/2002/06/25/bonus-panel.htm; Amy Harmon, "Movie Studios Press Congress in Digital Copyright Dispute," *New York Times*, July 29, 2002, http://www.nytimes.com/2002/07/29/business/movie-studios-press-congress-in-digital-copyright-dispute.html?pagewanted=all&src=pm.

[33] Mez Breeze, "20 of Technology's Most Underrated Founders," *The Next Web Insider*, October 23, 2012, http://thenextweb.com/insider/2012/10/21/technologys-underrated-founders.

[34] The other law professors at the earliest meetings included Jessica Litman, Pamela Samuelson, James Boyle, Lolly Gassaway, Bob Oakley, Julie Cohen, and David Post. Litman, *Digital Copyright*, 145. These scholars were also public intellectuals – and not just by virtue of participating in founding the DFC, although that alone would qualify. For instance, in congressional hearings leading up to the DMCA, Boyle and Oakley testified against the bill. Other academics who testified include law professor Keith Aoki and Douglas Bennett, a political scientist who was then the president of Earlham College. Furthermore, more than sixty law faculty signed letters urging Congress to strip those portions of the bill that ban circumvention devices, instead calling for a conduct-based approach much more like Boucher's proposal. To my knowledge, however, none engaged in the kind of full-frontal publicity campaign that would come a few years later.

retroactively. They failed to get their desired ruling, but the case helped bring additional attention to the fair use coalition's message on copyright law. Although Lessig's role has been singular, many other scholars have also taken the SFU coalition's message to the public – not only legal scholars, but also scholars in fields such as communication and computer science. Once copyright became a hot issue – especially, as in Ed Felten's case, once it became a hot issue in some researchers' laps – these scholars were happy to help spread the agenda of copyright moderation, not only writing volumes online, but also appearing in newspapers and on radio and TV news.

CONCLUSION

The combination of all these events turned the period from 1999 to 2002 into an inflection point in the history of copyright. Before that point, copyright was perceived as a topic of little interest to the general public, but in those few short years, the subject suddenly captured the public's attention.[35] For a brief window, it seemed like the internet might destroy the media industry's business model of large, centralized distribution systems; the future of music, movies, publishing, and news media seemed to hang in the balance. Digital utopians like John Perry Barlow promised that the internet would remove the need for centralized media industries and for copyright protection in general.[36] Meanwhile, some agreed with Barlow's contention in fact, but took up a wholly different estimation of that outcome's desirability – promising doom and gloom for the future of cultural creativity.[37] In hindsight, the debate of ten years ago seems

---

[35] Vaidhyanathan, "The State of Copyright Activism."

[36] John Perry Barlow, "The Next Economy of Ideas: Will Copyright Survive the Napster Bomb? Nope, But Creativity Will," *Wired*, October, 2010, http://www.wired.com/wired/archive/8.10/download.html.

[37] See, e.g., David Higgins, "Download and Be Damned," *Sydney Morning Herald*, May 19, 2000, http://newsstore.smh.com.au/apps/viewDocument.ac?page=1&sy=smh&kw=download+and+be+damned&pb=smh&dt=selectRange&dr=entire&so=relevance&sf=headline&rc=10&rm=200&sp=nrm&clsPage=1&docID=news000519_0609_8726. ("The Internet generation is holding the rock industry to ransom with computer programs which let it steal whole CDs at the click of a mouse.") In contrast, see Sathnam Sanghera, "Battles of the Copyright Crusader: Interview Hilary Rosen," *Financial Times*, August 14, 2002, 10. Sanghera quotes then-RIAA chair Hilary Rosen: "I don't think it's the end of the business – every survey that we've ever done says that music is an incredibly important part of people's lives, consumption of music is still extremely high – we just have to monetise that more effectively and find better ways of getting piracy under control. We will return to growth."

radically overstated, but, at the time, many believed we had to choose between continued internet freedom and the continued existence of the entertainment industries. Although the same tension remains today, and although manichean rhetoric is still common, everyone knows the policy trade-off between digital freedom and industry profits is a matter of degree rather than an either-or choice. These trade-offs would be on full display in the debates over the next DRM issues to arise.

5

Digital Millennium Copyright Act Reform
and the Broadcast Flag

From 1999 to 2002, the politics around copyright had undergone serious transformation. The issue had gone from obscurity to a topic of conversation across the country. The group of actors opposed to proposed expansions of copyright had grown from an ad hoc group to a standing coalition. These changes set the stage for a substantially different set of debates from 2003 to 2006. First, the strong fair use (SFU) coalition had grown strong enough and drawn enough congressional support to make a credible push to scale back the anticircumvention provisions of the Digital Millennium Copyright Act (DMCA). Second, the SFU coalition was able to stop the adoption of a new digital rights management (DRM) scheme, called the "broadcast flag," which was proposed as a means to protect copyrighted works in the transition to digital broadcasting.

PROPOSALS TO REFORM THE DIGITAL MILLENNIUM COPYRIGHT ACT

As discussed in the previous chapter, the turn of the century was a time of dawning realization among the technology sector that the anticircumvention provisions of the DMCA could be a headache for those engaged in formerly unobjectionable activities like encryption research. Especially in light of the cases of Ed Felten and Dmitry Sklyarov, the budding SFU coalition quickly came to see the DMCA as an extremely objectionable law in need of reform. The stories of programmers who had been harassed and even jailed quickly galvanized academics, programmers, and inventors, adding thousands to the ranks of the newly or potentially mobilized. Although the Felten and Sklyarov cases were just part of the DMCA reform movement's motivation – and efforts to reform the DMCA were just part of the intellectual property reform movement – these two stories served as a mobilizing wake-up call for untold thousands of new entrants into the copyright debate. Pushed by these horror stories and emboldened by congressional allies, SFU advocates began making a serious push for reform.

Reform Proposals

DMCA reform became a serious possibility once it attracted congressional allies. The most significant of these was Representative Rick Boucher, Democrat from Virginia. In the 108th and 109th Congresses, he introduced bills to curtail the reach of the DMCA.[1] Also in the 108th Congress, Representative Zoe Lofgren, Democrat from California, introduced a similar DMCA reform bill, co-sponsored by Boucher.[2] These bills would have modified the basic ban on circumventing copy controls, allowing circumvention to aid otherwise legal activities such as fair use. There are mechanisms for winning temporary exemptions via a triennial hearing held by the Register of Copyrights, but despite some valuable victories for obviously fair uses, this procedure remains deeply problematic.[3] A generic fair use exemption would be far better for such fair users. The reform proposals also would have scaled back the antitrafficking provisions, allowing companies to develop and sell tools with substantial noninfringing uses. In short, the bills would have tethered charges of illegal circumvention to charges of infringement, and they would have applied the *Sony* standard[4] to the development and distribution of tools capable of circumvention. Like Sony's Betamax video recorder, companies would be able to develop circumvention devices that are capable of substantial noninfringing uses.

The DMCA would be quite different if such a reform had passed. For instance, the law still would have forbidden hacking DVDs en route to selling bootlegged copies; in addition to the civil and criminal penalties for infringement, even a reformed DMCA would have retained civil

---

[1] Digital Media Consumers' Rights Act of 2003, H.R. 107, 108th Cong. (2003); Digital Media Consumers' Rights Act of 2005, H.R. 1201, 109th Cong. (2005).

[2] Benefit Authors without Limiting Advancement or Net Consumer Expectations (BALANCE) Act of 2003, H.R. 1066, 108th Cong. (2003).

[3] DeCherney, "From Fair Use to Exemption;" Herman and Gandy, "Catch 1201;" Sender and DeCherney, "Defending Fair Use."

[4] *Sony Corp. of America v. Universal*, 442. The court held: "the sale of copying equipment . . . does not constitute contributory infringement if the product is . . . capable of substantial noninfringing uses."

and criminal penalties for circumvention by would-be bootleggers. If Boucher's reforms had passed, however, the DMCA would have allowed a consumer to hack the DRM on a legally purchased DVD to transfer the movie to her laptop – an activity that is illegal (but common) today. Technology firms also would have been permitted to develop and sell circumvention devices under such a reform, as long as these tools were capable of substantial noninfringing uses. Since DRM systems generally prevent some noninfringing uses,[5] most circumvention tools are likely capable of substantial noninfringing uses. This would have been quite a legal shield for would-be makers of circumvention devices, spreading the tools to circumvent DRM from the dark corners of the internet into the open – and even onto the shelves of big box retailers.

If these reforms had passed, the DMCA would have been changed into something much less frightening for the likes of Ed Felten and Dmitry Sklyarov. Legal threats against encryption researchers under such a regime would be less frequent and less likely to succeed. This might not be enough to comfort researchers, however. Indeed, given the current law's exemption for encryption research,[6] Felten likely would have prevailed had the Recording Industry Association of America (RIAA) actually sued – rather than merely threatening a suit. Yet that is little comfort for an individual facing a legal threat from a major industry trade group. Since the court's dismissal of Felten's suit, no researcher has faced similar legal threats for academic encryption research. If passed, the reforms would have further increased any such researcher's odds of success in court, although even a remote threat of a suit is often adequate to discourage certain activities. As Felten explains, "For me and my colleagues, *probably* wasn't enough. Even a 99% chance of getting to keep our houses and savings wasn't enough. Nor should it be."[7]

If the potential difference for academic researchers would have been important but small, the impact of such a reform on for-profit activities would have been enormous. There is a night and day difference between the two legislative strategies for somebody in Sklyarov's situation – researching encryption for academic purposes and turning this knowledge into a marketable product. Under a reformed DMCA, a firm like Elcomsoft would be much better positioned to take calculated risks in this circumstance, and, although the law might still prevent some technologies

[5] Netanel, *Copyright's Paradox*, 74–5.   [6] 17 U.S.C. § 1201(g).
[7] Ed Felten, "Revisionism," *Freedom to Tinker*, August 5, 2003, https://freedom-to-tinker.com/blog/felten/revisionism.

from coming to market, the odds would be much more favorable to technology firms and thus to their employees.

From the perspective of the strong copyright (SC) coalition, the proposed reforms would have substantially reduced its ability to use the DMCA to keep circumvention devices on the margins. Hundreds of thousands – if not millions – of people download and use software that circumvents DRM; as of this writing, the most common goal is to defeat the encryption on DVDs (and, increasingly, on Blu-Ray discs), but many other DRM systems are routinely targeted. Many other consumers, however, do not even know that such options exist. For many, circumvention devices such as DVD rippers are effectively unavailable until they appear in mainstream retail stores – if Best Buy does not sell it, it does not exist. Keeping circumvention tools out of these less technology-savvy consumers' hands may indeed preserve some revenue for the content industries.[8]

Outcome and Significance

DMCA reform garnered serious attention and support from virtually every significant member of the SFU coalition, and it drew substantial opposition from the SC coalition. The House Committee on Commerce and Energy held several hearings to discuss the bills in detail. Further, in the 109th Congress (2005–2006), the bill's thirteen bipartisan co-sponsors included House Committee on Energy and Commerce Chair Joe Barton, giving it instant credibility.

Although the kerfuffle over the Hollings bill revealed the judiciary committees' belief that they should get first crack at copyright issues, the commerce committees – which have jurisdiction over the regulation of consumer goods such as electronics – also have a legitimate role to play once copyright becomes a tool for regulating technology. This opens the door to venue shopping for both sides. In general, the judiciary committees have been quite hospitable to the SC coalition, whereas the commerce committees have proven friendlier to the technology industries and thus more skeptical of DRM regulation. Barton's chairmanship sharpened this divide.

Despite the substantial push, the reform proposals all died in committee. The motion picture, recording, and proprietary software industries

---

[8] In particular, children's movies undoubtedly sell many extra copies because many parents don't know how to make backup copies – leaving them to pay full price to replace copies that got lost, damaged, or smeared with jam. Doctorow, *Content*, 8–9.

provided stiff opposition, as did their many allies in Congress. Congressional members of the SC coalition helped limit Barton's influence by isolating discussion of the bills to his committee. Each of the other three proposals discussed in detail in this study were subject to hearings in both the Commerce and Judiciary committees in either the House or Senate (or in both); in contrast, neither judiciary committee held a hearing on any of the DMCA reform bills. Even in Barton's committee, the proposal never came to a vote. Despite the low ceiling set for the DMCA reform proposals, however, these efforts represent a watershed moment in the DRM policy debate. For the first time, the SFU coalition was on the offensive and gaining some traction. The effort may have stalled, but it shows how seriously the coalition had grown by the mid-2000s.

THE BROADCAST FLAG

The 2000s saw a number of proposals for further expansion of copyright's reach in regulating technology. As discussed earlier, the Hollings bill was among them. Another proposal of note was the 2005 Digital Transition Content Security Act,[9] which would have prevented the redigitization of analog content.[10] Although these and other proposals drew some attention, the proposal that came closest to passage sought to impose a DRM system called the "broadcast flag" on digital television (DTV) receivers.[11] This proposal was the result of sophisticated negotiations between multiple industries and other stakeholders. After a rulemaking, the Federal Communications Commission (FCC) passed a broadcast flag mandate,[12] but the in *American Library Association v. Federal Communications Commission*, the DC Circuit Court of Appeals struck it down as exceeding the FCC's regulatory reach.[13] The decision noted that Congress might give the FCC the jurisdiction, and legislation to do so made some headway in Congress. The DTV flag even had enough momentum that the

---

[9] Digital Transition Content Security Act of 2005, H.R. 4569, 109th Cong. (2005). This proposal to close the so-called "analog hole" was not strictly a DRM proposal, but because analog outputs represent a potential weakness in DRM schemes, it is a closely related subject.

[10] Gillespie, *Wired Shut*, 197.

[11] Ibid., 193–222. Gillespie briefly discusses the other contemporary proposals before embarking on a detailed examination of the technology and politics of the broadcast flag generally.

[12] *In re* Digital Broadcast Content Protection, 18 FCC Rcd. 23,550 (2003) (codified at 47 C.F.R. pts. 73, 76) ["FCC Flag Order"].

[13] *American Library Association v. FCC*.

proponents of a far less developed proposal – for a similar flag mandate on high-definition (HD) radio receivers – tried to piggyback on the DTV proposal. The failure of these efforts was also a clear sign of the SFU coalition's growing political impact.

Bottling Digital Broadcasts

Consumers have long been able to record broadcast radio and television, first with analog tape, and now with digital recording devices. This ability has long caused anxiety for the content industries. Even though copyright holders have tried to sue manufacturers of home recording technology, the *Sony* case recognized home taping as at least potentially noninfringing; in that case, the court recognized as fair use those instances when consumers record television programs and watch them later.[14] Because the FCC sets the technology standards for broadcasting, content owners are unable to impose DRM unilaterally on over-the-air broadcasts. To impose a DRM scheme on broadcast material, they would need the government to include at least the potential for DRM into the broadcasting standards.

The transition to digital broadcasting increased copyright holders' anxiety over home recording; digital recordings of digital broadcasts are better than digital or analog recordings of analog broadcasts. Yet this transition also offered a unique opportunity to limit home recording beyond the technical limits imposed by analog technology. Motion picture studios[15] seized this opportunity, hoping to recreate the success of the relatively sealed environment offered by DVD distribution. Their best political weapon was the threat to withhold content; without tight DRM, they argued, they would withhold their high-value content from broadcasting, thus sabotaging the transition to DTV broadcasting.[16]

---

[14] *Sony Corp. of America v. Universal*, 442–56.

[15] As movie studios are also core sources of TV shows, their concern is the protection of made-for-TV programming, as well as that of feature films. Also, the dichotomy between studios and broadcasters is for the most part between divisions within the same companies rather than between separate companies. Each of the major national broadcasters and most of the most successful TV programming studios exist as divisions of still-larger media conglomerates. See, e.g., Scott, "The Other Hollywood."

[16] Gillespie, *Wired Shut*, 200. The studios threatened that they would withhold desirable, recent films from broadcast, and broadcasters threatened not to transmit HD versions of their content. Only the threat to withhold feature films had even a patina of credibility. Movie studios have other substantial revenue streams that could be threatened – DVD sales, pay and basic cable licensing, and so on – whereas broadcasters rely almost exclusively on advertising revenue. Thus, a decision by broadcasters to withhold high-quality

The studios' best shot at imposing a flag mandate was adding DRM capabilities into the standards for DTV. They reached out to the persuadable technology (PT) division – in particular, the consumer electronics industry – and built an interindustry coalition to develop a mutually acceptable technical solution. This DRM system could then serve as the basis for a government mandate. There was no political will for encrypting content at the source, so the next best choice was to force a mandate that all tuners encrypt content before passing it along to other media devices. Tarleton Gillespie explains the system:

> Digital broadcasts would be accompanied by a mark that indicated whether the owner of that content would permit it to be redistributed or not. Any digital tuner that transformed this signal into a displayable form would be required to check for and honor this flag. If the content was flagged, the tuner would allow it to be recorded only in specified formats – formats that would preserve the broadcast flag if that copy were passed to another device . . . after encrypting it using one of a limited set of authorized encryption technologies.[17]

In this way, only authorized forms of reuse would be allowed. This would have curtailed consumers' ability to record and reuse broadcast media.

In 2001, Fox Broadcasting Company first proposed the DTV broadcast flag technical standard and began building an interindustry coalition. This effort was organized as the Broadcast Protection Discussion Group (BPDG), including representatives from the major motion picture companies, as well as "consumer electronics corporations, . . . information technology and software companies, . . . companies specializing in existing forms of copy protection, . . . and consumer and public advocate groups."[18] Despite initial, vocal objections by some participants – in particular, nongovernmental organizations (NGOs) – the process was reasonably smooth. "The premise of the flag and how it would work was already agreed upon at the start, or agreed upon by enough of the major players that critics could be pushed aside."[19] Even groups that actually opposed the flag mandate continued to participate, seeking a role in steering the process.

versions of TV programs would have almost no identifiable benefit other than the cost savings of not upgrading production facilities and broadcast towers.
[17] Gillespie, *Wired Shut*, 202.   [18] Ibid., 203.
[19] Ibid., 204.

Although important differences remained,[20] the BPDG presented the DTV flag proposal to the FCC as reflecting unanimous interindustry agreement. In November 2003, with all the industries on board and the only real opposition coming from the NGOs, the FCC passed a rule implementing the broadcast flag as a required standard for DTV receivers.[21] The rule was to take effect July 1, 2005.

Lowering the Broadcast Flag

In 2004, a coalition of four NGOs and five library groups filed suit to stop the broadcast flag rule from taking effect. Among NGOs, Public Knowledge led the charge, joined by the Electronic Frontier Foundation, Consumers Union, and Consumers Federation of America. Library groups included the American Library Association (ALA), Association of Research Libraries, American Association of Law Libraries, Medical Library Association, and Special Libraries Association. In May 2005, the Washington, D.C. Circuit Court sided with the petitioners, holding that the FCC had exceeded its jurisdiction.[22] The FCC may regulate receivers, but the three-judge panel unanimously held that the current statute does not grant the FCC the "authority to regulate receiver apparatuses after the completion of broadcast transmissions."[23] This decision prevented the flag requirement from ever taking effect – just two months before the regulation would have been implemented.

The court ruling left open the possibility for congressional intervention; if the FCC needed congressional authorization, a new law could provide it. In May 2006, then-Senator Ted Stevens introduced an omnibus telecommunications reform bill.[24] One section would have authorized the FCC to adopt a broadcast flag mandate, permitting the Commission to reenact its 2003 ruling.[25] This was part of the subtitle known as the Digital Content Protection Act of 2006.[26] The bill was the subject of congressional hearings and a relatively high volume of attention, but the

---

[20] The most divisive issue was on the question of how new encryption schemes would be approved – the process for certifying devices to handle content after it had been encrypted. Gillespie, *Wired Shut*, 206–10.
[21] FCC Flag Order.   [22] *American Library Association v. FCC.*
[23] Lee, "The Audio Broadcast Flag System," 411.
[24] Communications, Consumer's Choice, and Broadband Deployment Act of 2006, S. 2686, 109th Cong. (2006).
[25] Ibid., § 452.   [26] Ibid., §§ 451–454.

broadcast flag was only part of the cacophony of debate over the bill, which passed committee but never came up for a final vote in the Senate.[27]

Stevens' efforts stalled in part owing to the remarkable groundswell of public demands that network neutrality be part of any comprehensive telecommunications reform act,[28] although other forces of opposition also slowed the bill. Among those forces were members of the SFU coalition, who opposed the flag mandate. In particular, NGOs such as Public Knowledge and the EFF came out in full force against broadcast flag proposals in both the House and Senate.[29] With the FCC's decision having been overturned, industry voices such as the Consumer Electronics Association – who had participated in the BPDG discussions, although in part seeking a more permissive system – became important voices of opposition to the broadcast flag mandate in Congress.[30]

It is unclear whether these forces alone could have stopped either the whole bill or a stand-alone broadcast flag bill, but the SFU coalition was emboldened by the court's ruling, and opposition to a flag mandate was sustained and powerful. The nonprofit and library groups were pivotal in slowing the proposal's momentum; had they not participated heavily, the flag mandate would have become law. Their role in the successful

---

[27] The Stevens bill, S. 2686, passed the Senate Committee on Commerce, Science, and Transportation as H.R. 5252, which was the number assigned to the telecommunications bill authored by Joe Barton (R-TX) that had already passed the House on a vote of 321 to 101. Communications Opportunity, Promotion, and Enhancement Act of 2006, H.R. 5252, 109th Cong. (2006). Had the Stevens bill passed the Senate, this change would have enabled a conference committee to work out the substantial difference between the two proposals.

[28] Hart, "The Net Neutrality Debate," 418; Lisa Caruso, "Outmanned, Outfoxed, Outspent," *National Journal*, August 12, 2006; Daniel W. Reilly, "The Telecom Slayers," *Salon*, October 2, 2006, http://www.salon.com/2006/10/02/slayers/.

In the interest of full disclosure, I have long been a public advocate for network neutrality.

As member of the network neutrality movement, it is modestly self-serving to credit that movement – rather than the many other political forces that came to bear – for stopping the Stevens bill. That caveat in mind, support for net neutrality was a roadblock of at least some importance, although it might not have been sufficient to stop the bill's passage.

[29] E.g., *Content Protection in the Digital Age: The Broadcast Flag, High-Definition Radio, and the Analog Hole: Hearing Before the Subcomm. On Telecomms. & the Internet of the H. Comm. on Energy & Commerce*, 109th Cong. 21 (2005) (statement of Gigi B. Sohn, President, Public Knowledge); ibid., 77 (letter from Fred von Lohmann, Senior Staff Attorney for Intellectual Property, Electronic Frontier Foundation). Both groups also posted copious amounts of oppositional materials on their websites.

[30] Ibid., 33 (statement of Michael Petricone, Vice President of Government Affairs, Consumer Electronics Association).

suit is the most obvious impact, but consider also their seeming success in turning the electronics industry against the mandate. During the BPDG process, the electronics industry's concerns were primarily about preserving marketable functions (e.g., the capacity to shift recorded programs to a user's computer), and they expressed little public objection to the idea of a flag mandate. The outcome of the *ALA* ruling, as well as what was undoubtedly a strong push from NGOs,[31] emboldened the consumer electronics industry – a key portion of the PT division – to become full-fledged opponents of a flag mandate. By drawing the electronics industry into the opposition, the SFU coalition added more political pressure than it could have mustered on its own.

Few Salute the Audio Flag

Although the DTV broadcast flag nearly became law, proposals for a digital radio flag gained much of their viability from piggybacking on the DTV flag effort – nevertheless, proponents abandoned them in their infancy. No similar interindustry coalition developed a radio flag, and even members of Congress who supported the DTV flag were often opposed to the audio flag. Despite this, it was contained in two bills, and the similarities between the proposals – strategically employed by audio flag proponents – gave it at least a patina of credibility.

In addition to permitting the FCC to mandate the DTV flag, the Stevens bill also included an audio flag provision, albeit a much more prospective one than the DTV flag authorization. If the Stevens bill had passed, the DTV authorization would have directed the FCC to begin a rulemaking process specifically to implement its original 2003 mandate, albeit with minor modifications.[32] The audio flag authorization would have given the FCC the power to implement a similar rule, but only if a similar interindustry process had led to substantial agreement within eighteen months; otherwise, the Commission was to report back to Congress.[33]

---

[31] This study did not find public evidence of such coalition building, but it would have been irrational of the NGOs not to attempt to persuade the electronics industry to weigh in against the flag mandate. Additionally, it would be consistent with the literature. Persuading would-be allies to one's way of thinking is a vital inside-the-Beltway policy tactic, and it is often the case – and certainly so here – that NGOs are more strident in their positions than their potential allies in industry or government. See Paul A. Sabatier and Hank C. Jenkins-Smith, "The Advocacy Coalition Framework," 130; Jenkins-Smith, St. Clair, and Woods, "Explaining Change."

[32] Communications, Consumer's Choice, and Broadband Deployment Act of 2006, S. 2686, 109th Cong. § 452 (2006).

[33] Ibid., §§ 453–454.

Also in 2006, Representative Mike Ferguson introduced legislation granting the FCC the authority to require audio flag compliance for digital radio tuners.[34] Whereas the audio flag provisions of the Stevens bill would have required a substantial interindustry consensus, the Ferguson bill made no such stipulation; it simply granted the Commission the authority to impose an audio flag mandate. Although the omnibus Stevens bill had a great deal of political muscle behind it and was close to passage, the much more targeted Ferguson bill never gained much traction. For instance, many members of Congress who supported the DTV mandate stated explicitly that they did not think the audio flag mandate was a good idea. The lack of a preexisting interindustry agreement weighed heavily against its passage.

Another factor also weighed against the audio flag proposal: the recording industry has a substantially diminished capacity to withhold content from broadcasters. Broadcasters seeking to use movies and TV shows must negotiate with copyright holders on a work-by-work basis, giving both industries a reason to work together to avoid a negotiation showdown.[35] In contrast, terrestrial radio stations are in a much less precarious position when it comes to getting licenses to broadcast content. The statutory list of the exclusive rights of copyright holders[36] grants no general right of public performance for sound recordings; there is an exclusive right of performance for sound recordings that applies to digital audio transmissions,[37] but a separate exemption makes clear that this does not apply to digital broadcasts by FM stations.[38] In short, sound recording copyright holders get no royalties from and have no leverage over terrestrial broadcasters.[39] Not only do record companies not try to stop radio airplay, they strongly encourage it – so much so that it has led to the practice of record companies paying large sums to get their songs on the radio.[40]

There is an exclusive right of public performances of musical compositions,[41] so all broadcasters must negotiate royalty terms with

---

[34] Audio Broadcast Flag Licensing Act of 2006, H.R. 4861, 109th Cong. (2006).

[35] Broadcasting content is a public performance, and the copyright holders for "motion pictures and other audiovisual works" enjoy an exclusive right to control their public performance. 17 U.S.C. § 106(4) (2006).

[36] Ibid., § 106. [37] Ibid., § 106(6).

[38] 17 U.S.C. § 114(d) (2006).

[39] Anderson, "'We Can Work It Out,'" 73–4.

[40] Eric Boehlert, "Pay for Play," *Salon* (March 14, 2001), http://www.salon.com/2001/03/14/payola_2/.

[41] 17 U.S.C. § 106(4).

these copyright holders – generally songwriters or their heirs. Yet such licensing agreements via royalty collecting societies (American Society of Composers, Authors, and Publishers [ASCAP], Broadcast Music Inc. [BMI], and Society of European Stage Authors and Composers [SESAC]) are a long-established mechanism for collecting reasonable royalties for songwriters.[42] As the Audio Home Recording Act (AHRA) debate illustrated, music publishers' digital copyright strategy is based on royalty collection rather than DRM mandates. As such, publishers did not make even an idle threat to withhold licenses from broadcasters. With no music industry threat to withhold content, the audio flag proposal was treated with little urgency.

CONCLUSION

Like the DMCA reform bills, the audio and DTV broadcast flag bills provide excellent opportunities to see the SC and SFU coalitions in action. Both efforts warranted substantial attention from all interested parties, but each coalition was strong enough to stop the other's proposals from becoming law. In particular, the failure of the broadcast flag proposals further highlights the growth of the SFU coalition. Without its focused resistance in the courts and in Congress, the broadcast flag mandate would have become law. That the broadcast flag has already been swept into the dustbin of history is a remarkable victory for a coalition that was, by all rights, just getting started.

---

[42] See Anderson, "'We Can Work It Out,'" 93. Anderson writes approvingly of "the rate of 3% to 5% of revenue that all radio broadcasters pay to music publishers and songwriters through their licenses with ASCAP, BMI, and SESAC."

Part II

Political Communication in Key Digital Rights Management Debates, 1989–2006

6

Communicating in Congress

Even relative to the many other issues that it considers, the U.S. Congress plays an especially central role in the politics of copyright. One reason is that copyright is exclusively a matter of federal rather than state law.[1] Another is that copyright depends very little on administrative branch enforcement. Except for criminal copyright cases, which involve administrative agencies such as the Federal Bureau of Investigation (FBI) and Immigration and Customs Enforcement (more on the latter's role in Chapter 11), administrative agencies have little opportunity to shape the impact of the copyright statutes. Congress does delegate some decision-making authority to the Copyright Office, but that office is part of the Library of Congress and thus part of the legislative branch, and its decisions are generally regarding relatively small-scale issues such as royalty rates. Thus, once a copyright bill becomes law, it is up to judges to apply the law and set precedent about its meaning. Because federal judges are not supposed to be open to direct political influence (and, despite limitations to this principle, are clearly less easily influenced than members of Congress), this leaves the U.S. Congress as a singular destination for copyright advocacy. This makes the political action easier to locate for copyright than for most issues.[2]

[1] 17 USC § 301(a). Although this is true of copyright per se, state law also plays a role in many cases that are actually questions of copyright. For instance, many copyright holders have used contracts, "signed" by consumer actions, such as opening a labeled plastic wrapping or clicking to indicate agreement, to carve out exclusive rights that exceed those defined in federal copyright law. Importantly for the purpose of this study, these contracts are often enforced via DRM technologies such as encryption and watermarking, backed by Title I of the DMCA.

[2] On matters from air pollution to collective bargaining to education, statutes are brought to life – or neglected – by administrative agencies that determine whether and how the government will enforce the law. These and many other issues are also questions of state

Congressional hearings are a vital source of data for studying the legislative process, serving a number of purposes for both legislators and scholars. They are reliable indicators of congressional interest in policy issues,[3] and they also serve to measure which groups have access to policymakers.[4] Hearings also serve as vehicles by which committees choose what information is sent to the larger chambers.[5] Finally, committees use hearings strategically to redefine issues and claim jurisdiction away from other committees.[6] Of course, most policy advocacy happens outside the hearing rooms, but as the formal record of the state of a given debate, hearings are a rather good proxy for the whole of the advocacy.

In *Digital Copyright*, Jessica Litman observed that those who support stronger copyright protection generally, and strong prohibitions on circumventing digital rights management (DRM) specifically, have long enjoyed greater access to policymakers. The results reported in this chapter provide more formal reinforcement for these observations; among the total population of congressional members across all periods under study, a solid majority called for stronger copyright laws. Yet I also find that this advantage eroded over time, and in the latest period – 2003 to 2006 – those calling for expanding fair use even enjoyed a slight advantage. This change in the direction of copyright advocacy, as well as major changes in the groups represented at the witness table, suggest that the copyright policy subsystem has undergone a substantial shift over the past two decades.

Using LexisNexis Congressional, I found seventeen relevant congressional hearings within the three time frames under study.[7] Across these

[2]nd local law, leaving advocates on many issues to fight political battles in legislative bodies, administrative agencies, and courts on multiple levels of government.

[3] Jones and Baumgartner, *The Politics of Attention*, 21.

[4] Leyden, "Interest Group Resources."

[5] Diermeier and Feddersen, "Information and Congressional Hearings."

[6] Talbert, Jones, and Baumgartner, "Nonlegislative Hearings."

[7] This was based on a search for hearings from the three time frames (1989–92, 1995–98, and 2003–06) with the word "copyright" but not the word "appropriations" in the description. This retrieved 128 hearings. A second coder and I agreed 100 percent (Krippendorff's $\alpha = 1.0$) about which hearings were relevant. Throughout the study, all coded variables were checked with a second coder before full sets were coded, and they all earned α of at least .80. Readers who want more details on my method and even more details about my findings can see an exceptionally detailed account in my dissertation, although I also welcome any questions that remain. To spare those readers who care little for such details, I've chosen to elide a great deal here; this includes the reporting of α scores for the remaining variables. The same goes for some of the more mundane aspects my findings, such as a list of the titles, dates, and document counts for each hearing.

seventeen hearings, there were a total of 660 documents, 435 of them relevant to one of the DRM debates. This adds up to a lot of information gathered from hearings on DRM regulation. The beliefs about copyright expressed in these hearings say a lot about the politics of copyright.

DECADES OF CALLS FOR STRONGER COPYRIGHT

Taken together, the congressional hearings across all three periods under study were significantly biased in the direction of calling for stronger copyright law. Out of all 435 documents, 241 (55 percent) called for stronger copyright, whereas 29 (7 percent) were neutral or mixed, and 165 (38 percent) pushed for stronger fair use. This is a net advantage of seventy-six more documents supporting the strong copyright (SC) position than the strong fair use (SFU) position. If this were an election, one would say that the SC coalition had won in a landslide. Unlike an election, though, this imbalance does not mean that the SC side had more broad-based support. Rather, it shows each committee leadership's perception of who has earned a seat at the witness table; this matters in ways that I discuss later in this chapter, as well as in Chapter 11.

I also scored each document on a copyright viewpoint scale, from 1 (supports SC) to 3 (supports SFU). For those documents that did not take one of these two positions, I scored the DRM-relevant paragraphs to get a more nuanced score, so not every document scoring between 1 and 3 is exactly 2. Still, because the vast majority of documents do take a clear position, the distribution looks like two columns with a few small piles of bricks in between, as shown in Figure 6.1.[8]

---

[8] A statistician would describe the distribution as highly non-normal – which is just a technical term for saying that these data can be hard to work with. A normal distribution would have most of the documents in the middle and few at the extremes – the classic curve shaped like a bell. SAT scores offer a fine example. For each section, the average (mean) score of about 500 is also near the most common score (median). In contrast, very low scores (near 200) and very high scores (near 800) are very rare. This makes it very easy to compare SAT scores among groups of students. The *U.S. News* rankings of colleges provide an example: a school's selectivity is determined in part by the average SAT score of the students who enroll there.

In contrast to such neat analysis, the non-normal data I use here are harder to use, and a lot of the standard statistical analyses can be inconclusive or misleading. For instance, the mean score for Congressional documents is 1.83, but the median is 1; thus, the "average" document is far from typical. Therefore, I look at the data from a lot of angles, such as looking at the ratios of SC documents to SFU documents. For readers who are not trained in statistics, I will try to explain everything in plain English.

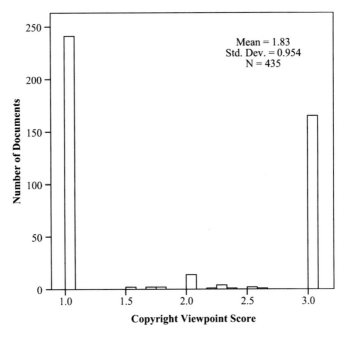

FIGURE 6.1. Distribution of Copyright Viewpoint Scores, Congressional Documents

Virtually everybody who participated had an opinion in the SFU or SC camp. As is surely the norm in most congressional debates, few hearing participants joined the action to express a middling viewpoint. Government officials accounted for nearly all of the twenty-nine neutral or mixed documents; congresspersons generated twenty-two, and appointed government officials, such as officials from the Copyright Office and the Patent and Trademark Office, authored three of the other seven. Even among the congresspersons and other officials, however, most did take sides – and most sided with the SC agenda. Congresspersons made SC arguments (forty-three documents) more than twice as often as SFU arguments (twenty documents). Documents from appointed federal officials were even more reliable in their SC allegiance, with twenty-eight such documents, compared to just two SFU documents. This represents a net total of forty-nine more SC documents than SFU documents, which is a solid majority (65 percent) of the seventy-six document advantage for the SC coalition across all documents from all participants.

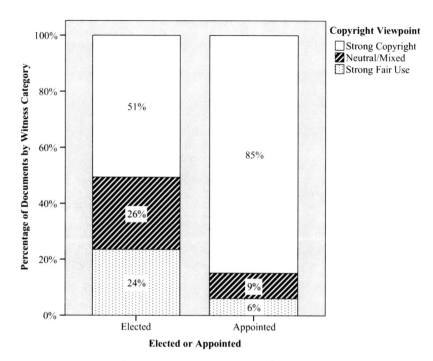

FIGURE 6.2. Copyright Viewpoint, Congressional Documents by Elected and Appointed Officials

Figure 6.2 shows how government officials tend to favor the SC side; the graphed area of each column represents all documents authored by elected (left column) or appointed (right) government officials, and each column is divided to illustrate the share of SC, neutral, and SFU documents authored by each witness type.

Over the period studied, most congresspersons and nearly every federal bureaucrat in pertinent offices were reliable members of the SC coalition, at least as regards DRM policy. With such explicit support for the SC coalition, it is unsurprising that committee leadership arranged hearings that tended to favor greater regulation of DRM.

SHIFTING TOWARD FAIR USE

The SFU coalition began to make substantial inroads into the congressional record over the course of the study. By the 2003–2006 period, SFU documents outnumbered SC documents. Figure 6.3 shows this change over time.

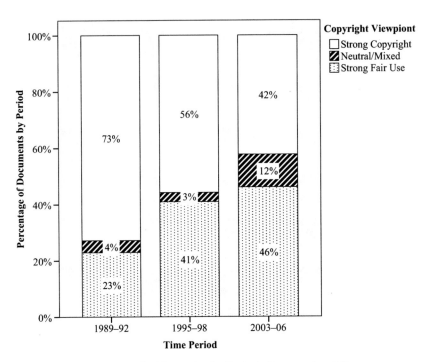

FIGURE 6.3. Copyright Viewpoint by Period, Congressional Documents

This shows how the debate over copyright has shifted a great deal over time. In the first period, SC documents outnumbered SFU documents by 86 to 27 – a ratio of 3.19:1. In the 1995–1998 period, this advantage was 86 documents to 63, a much-reduced ratio of 1.37:1. By the 2003–2006 period, there was a reversal; there were 69 SC documents and 75 SFU documents, for a ratio of .92 SC documents per SFU document. This points to a major change in the copyright debate over this time. Among documents taking sides, a document was 2.33 times more likely to call for SFU in the second period than in the first. Such documents in the third period were 1.48 times more likely to support SFU than in the second period – and 3.46 times more likely in the third period than in the first. In other words, the balance of copyright viewpoints was more than three times more favorable to the SFU position in the last period than in the first, a substantial change.[9] The contrast is even sharper when looking

---

[9] Statisticians have a system of tools to help explain how big a change really is – whether it is actually big enough to care. These are tests of effect size. I give a brief overview here, but for a more thorough, accessible introduction, see Coe, "It's the Effect Size." Even if a result is statistically significant – meaning that we are fairly sure that it is not a result that

just at speeches given in person by congresspersons and witnesses. Because in-person testimony is an even more effective means of communicating with policymakers – or, at minimum, an even clearer indication of access to policymakers – this suggests even more fundamental realignment in

is caused by sampling error – it may not mean much practically. To measure whether the difference really matters, we need to know how different the groups are, relative to how variable the measure is within each group. In statistical terms, we compare the averages between the two groups, relative to a measure called the "standard deviation," or SD for short. If the data are normally distributed, about two-thirds of a population will be within 1 SD of average. If most of the members of a group are near the average, the SD will cover just a small part of the overall range of values; if many members are far from the average, the SD will be larger and cover more of the range of values. For instance, in the 2011 scores for the Critical Reading section of the SAT, the average (mean) score was 497 and the SD was 114 points, so about two out of three test takers scored within 114 points of 497, or from 383 to 611.

Effect size measures the difference between each group's average, relative to the standard deviation. For studies in the social sciences, Cohen's "A Power Primer" helps us spot three groups of effect sizes: For an effect size d that is about .2, the effect is small, "but not so small as to be trivial" (p. 156). If d is about .5, the effect is medium, or fairly noteworthy. At $d = .8$ and above, an effect is notably large – bigger than is typically reported in the social sciences.

Again, SAT tests are a great example. One might wonder whether it is worth the potentially large sums to send one's high school-aged student to an expensive test prep class. Although these classes can cost as much as a serviceable used car, one study found that they generally lead to an average score improvement of just 15 points per section. John Hechinger, "SAT Coaching Found to Boost Scores – Barely," *Wall Street Journal*, May 20, 2009, http://online.wsj.com/article/SB124278685697537839.html. This would represent a meager effect size of approximately $d = .13$. On Cohen's scale, this effect is pretty trivial.

Effect sizes are easiest to calculate using data that spread out across a range. For this study, that means using the average copyright viewpoint, on a scale that ranges from 1 (SC) to 3 (SFU). For each time period, these were: 1.50 (1989–92; $SD = .84$), 1.85 (1995–98; $SD = .98$), and 2.05 (2003–06; $SD = .95$). For the difference between the first and second periods, the effect size, d, is .38, which Cohen (1992) describes as a small- to medium-sized effect. The difference between the second period and the third, $d = .21$, is a small but nontrivial size. The difference between the first and third, $d = .61$, represents a medium to large effect size.

Because these data have such an abnormal distribution – most of the data piled up in two columns at each end of the scale, as in Figure 6.1 – I also report some other calculations of effect sizes that are based on ratios between SC and SFU documents. In "A Simple Method for Converting an Odds Ratio," Susan Chinn sets out how to calculate a d-like effect size score using ratios. Using these measures, the d-like effect size for the difference between the first and second period is .47 (nearly a medium size). The difference between the second and third periods is $d = .22$ (small but not trivial), and the difference between the second and the third is $d = .69$ (medium to large). These are very similar to those found using the copyright viewpoint scale; although neither method is ideal (one incorrectly assumes a normal distribution, the other ignores neutral documents), it is rather reassuring that the two kinds of measures suggest very similar results.

TABLE 6.1. *Copyright viewpoint of congresspersons' documents over time*

Time period	SC	Neutral	SFU	Total documents	Mean score (1 = SC, 3 = SFU)
1989–1992	12	2	–	14	1.10
1995–1998	10	5	6	21	1.81
2003–2006	21	15	14	50	1.87
Total	43	22	20	85	1.73

the copyright debate.[10] Although it has taken the better part of two decades, the SFU coalition has reason to be encouraged by this degree of progress.

ALLIES IN CONGRESS

Members of Congress are crucial allies for policy coalitions; without at least a few allies in Congress, no coalition will gain much traction in advancing desirable legislation or stopping undesirable bills. At the start of this study, only the SC coalition had congressional allies, but each successive period saw the SFU coalition add allies in Congress. Over time, members have taken an increasingly active role, and their rhetoric has moved toward the SFU side. Table 6.1 shows this change.

The "Total Documents" column highlights how congresspersons' contributions to the debate have risen dramatically over time. The total number of relevant documents per period grew much less rapidly, so this rise in congresspersons' speeches and written submissions has also increased

---

[10] From 1989 to 1992, there were forty-seven relevant speeches – whether from the witness table or the congressperson's chair. Of these, thirty-seven were SC, two were neutral, and just eight were SFU speeches, for a ratio of 4.62 SC speeches per SFU speech. From 1995 to 1998, there were thirty-one SC speeches, four neutral, and twenty SFU, or 1.55 SC speeches per SFU speech. In contrast, the period from 2003 to 2006 saw twenty-six SC speeches, eight neutral, and thirty-two SFU speeches, a ratio of .81 SC speeches per SFU speech. Relative to the first period, a speech in the second period was 2.98 times more likely to call for stronger fair use. A speech in the third period was 1.91 times more likely to call for stronger fair use than in the second period and 5.70 times more likely than in the first. These convert to d-like effect sizes of .60 (first vs. second period), .36 (second vs. third), and .96 (first vs. third), suggesting medium, small-to-medium, and quite large effect sizes, respectively.

Using the copyright viewpoint scale measures suggests similar results for effect size. Those scores are $d = .49$ (first vs. second), $d = .31$ (second vs. third), and $d = .83$ (first vs. third).

their relative share of documents, which started at 12 percent, rose to 14 percent, and jumped to 31 percent.

This rise in congressional expression of opinion reflects the shift in DRM politics, from legislation by consensus to a more contested process. The Audio Home Recording Act (AHRA) was a relatively easy move for Congress; once the industries agreed on the bill's specifics, it only required congressional ratification rather than extended analysis. The opening statements in the first Senate hearing on the bill are instructive.[11] Senators Inouye, McCain, Gore, and Burns took turns congratulating two of the three affected industries – electronics and recording – for reaching a compromise, then encouraging them to further amend the deal to appease the third industry, music publishing. John Breaux, the fifth and final member to speak, said, "I am here to learn as much as anything else" and offered no specific opinions on the bill at all. In the next Congress, once the music publishers' demand for royalties was included in the bill, members generally described the bill in terms ranging from generally to exceptionally supportive. Representative Alex McMillan described it as a "win-win-win proposition" supported by an unusual level of agreement.[12]

Since then, the debate has become far more contested, congresspersons have jumped into the fray, and some members have begun to express SFU positions. Although most members supported the anticircumvention provisions of the Digital Millennium Copyright Act (DMCA), Rick Boucher in particular repeatedly expressed SFU views during that debate. For instance, he argued that banning circumvention devices would not be necessary to comply with the World Intellectual Property Organization (WIPO) Copyright Treaty and would create "a reluctance to bring promising new technology to market."[13] Although Boucher authored five of the six congresspersons' documents in this period, Representative Cliff Stearns also joined the opposition. The latter argued for a more moderate version of the bill that would "balance the necessary needs of the content community ... with the legitimate concerns of the manufacturing community ... and with the needs of the educational network of schools and

---

[11] *Digital Audio Tape Recorder Act of 1990: Hearing Before the Senate Subcommittee on Communications of the Committee on Commerce, Science, and Transportation*, 101st Cong. (1990).

[12] *Digital Audio Recording: Hearing Before the House Subcommittee on Commerce, Consumer Protection, and Competitiveness*, 102nd Cong. 2 (1992).

[13] *H.R. 2281, WIPO Copyright Treaties Implementation Act; and H.R. 2180, Online Copyright Liability Limitation Act: Hearing before the House Subcommittee on Courts and Intellectual Property*, 105th Cong. 192 (1997).

libraries in our nation."[14] Although he did not author a relevant hearing document on the point, Representative Scott Klug also fought to limit the reach of the DMCA's anticircumvention provisions as the bill was moving through the 105th Congress.[15] In addition to the substantially more mobilized opposition from those outside Congress, having even a few Representatives arguing for copyright moderation made a real impact, for instance, in helping to carve out the exceptions that became part of the final bill.

By the period of 2003–06, even more members of Congress were staking out a decidedly pro-SFU position. In particular, House hearings to consider the DMCA reform proposals saw several members strike out against what they described as overly broad DRM regulation. In the opening statements of just one such hearing before a House Commerce subcommittee,[16] five different members spoke out in favor of such a reform. Jan Schakowsky argued, "the DMCA was drafted with such broad strokes that it swept away the fair use provisions of the copyright law and now is being abused by those who want to squelch competition in areas wholly unrelated to copyright."[17]

The SC coalition is usually the first to invoke the rhetoric of property rights, but the SFU coalition also has a powerful property rights argument,[18] and members started to make this argument in supporting the Boucher reform proposal. Joe Barton, then-Chair of the full House Committee on Energy and Commerce, invoked the pro-SFU rhetoric of property rights to argue for copyright moderation, worrying that DRM regulations strip users of their property rights over their computers and personal copies of media such as DVDs.[19] Next, Representative Darrell Issa expressed concerns about the *321 Studios* case, which applied the DMCA to stop the sale of a software program that circumvents the DRM on DVDs. Although 321 Studios' DVD copying software may or may not have struck the proper balance between the right to protect copyrighted works and the consumer's right to make fair use of those works, the court ruled that their sale of a tool to circumvent DRM was illegal regardless;

---

[14] *The WIPO Copyright Treaties Implementation Act: Hearing before the House Sub-committee on Telecommunications, Trade, and Consumer Protection*, 105th Cong. 9 (1998).
[15] Herman and Gandy, "Catch 1201," 146–7.
[16] *Digital Media Consumers' Rights Act of 2003: Hearing Before the Subcommittee on Commerce, Trade, and Consumer Protection*, 108th Cong. (2004).
[17] Ibid., 3.   [18] Herman, "Breaking and Entering."
[19] *Digital Media Consumers' Rights Act of 2003: Hearing Before the Subcommittee on Commerce, Trade, and Consumer Protection*, 108th Cong. 4 (2004).

enabling mostly or even exclusively fair use is not a defense to charges that one violated Section 1201. Issa described this interpretation of the statute and this ruling in particular as "an obvious problem" in need of a remedy.[20]

After a few words of opposition from several members, Representatives Rick Boucher and John Doolittle also spoke out in favor of DMCA reform. Although Boucher had opposed the strong language in the DMCA from the beginning, Doolittle had been a supporter. By 2004, however, he recanted, saying in part, "I didn't grasp what the real issues were at stake in this DMCA at the time that it came before the House. I have a better handle on it now and I think we went way overboard as a Congress in enacting that legislation. It needs to be corrected."[21] This is remarkable humility and honesty by Doolittle – and yet another sign of the major shift in the debate over DRM. In just the opening statements of this one hearing, the efforts to reform the DMCA had more clear congressional allies (five) than all efforts to moderate the DMCA as it was being crafted (three). These five were a substantial portion of the SFU allies in Congress – in addition to them, I also identified pro-SFU documents by Representative Zoe Lofgren and Senator John Sununu – and they were still outnumbered by SC allies. Yet this surge in SFU allies in Congress represents a profound change in the dynamic of the debate. It also suggests that the SFU coalition has, over time, helped raise congressional awareness that DRM mandates do come with important costs – that the SC coalition's mantra of protecting the creative industries presents an incomplete picture. To effect such a change, the members of the SFU coalition had to gain access to policymakers, and that access has come with major changes in the roster of people at the witness table.

REPRESENTATION IN CONGRESS

Some of the groups that participate in the copyright debate are quite at home in the halls of Congress, whereas other groups are rarely heard there. Simply counting participation from various sectors provides a fairly reliable indicator of whether a set of documents will lean toward stronger copyright or stronger fair use because most groups are fairly reliable in their coalition membership. Music, movie, publishing, and proprietary software companies support the SC position in general and the call for

[20] Ibid., 5.   [21] Ibid., 13.

strong bans on DRM circumvention in particular. Meanwhile, librarians, educators, consumers, free software activists, and public interest groups generally support the SFU position and the call for little or no DRM regulation. Electronics manufacturers are also reasonably friendly to the SFU coalition, but unlike the other sectors, they are better described as part of the persuadable technology sector than core members of the SFU coalition. In the early history of the debate over DRM, none of the core SFU groups had much access to policymakers, and even electronics manufacturers had far less preferential policymaker access than content industry groups. The story of the evolving debate over DRM policy is largely a story of those core SFU groups' increasing access to the attention of policymakers.

Who Participates and How Often

I saw the witnesses as breaking into eleven categories.[22] Figure 6.4 documents the representation for those in each category among all congressional documents.

Among all categories, the media sector (123 documents) and the technology sector (113 documents) were far and away the most frequently represented groups. The media sector includes industries such as movies, recorded music, radio and television broadcasting, newspapers and other periodicals (except trade publications dedicated to technology), and books. This also includes people with media jobs – such as musicians, actors, producers, directors, and writers – a few of whom were brought in to testify, to give a human face and some celebrity power to the SC coalition's arguments. The technology sector includes industries such as consumer electronics, software (including video games), and computer hardware, as well as technology periodicals. Firms that develop and sell DRM technologies, such as Macrovision and Digimarc, are also included here, as are groups that develop and sell DRM circumvention technologies, such as 321 Studios.

The media and technology sectors include the for-profit industries with the most at stake and the most capital to invest, and their very heavy participation reflects that these issues can have large financial impacts on each. Still, it is remarkable how heavily these industries dominated the

---

[22] As with all such divisions, the splits here are not platonic forms but somewhat subjective. Still, the breaks here are fairly clean, and the important results would not look very different if another sensible division were used instead.

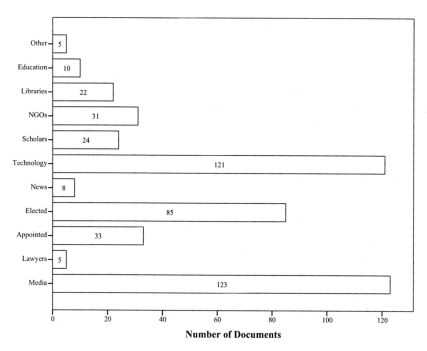

FIGURE 6.4. Document Count by Sector, Congressional Documents

hearings. Removing those documents generated by members of Congress (eighty-five documents) and appointed government officials (thirty-three documents) leaves 317 documents authored by those outside government, and the media and technology sectors authored 236 of these 317 documents – a remarkable 74 percent of the total.

This leaves several sectors that are not seeking higher profits. Nongovernmental organizations (NGOs) contributed the next most frequently, with thirty-one documents. Examples include Public Knowledge, the Electronic Frontier Foundation, the Digital Future Coalition (DFC), and the Progress and Freedom Foundation.[23] The only remaining sectors

[23] Unsurprisingly, many participants described their policy positions as being in the public's best interest, but most participants have direct ties to one or more of the other sectors described here. With just two exceptions, only groups that had no direct ties to other sectors were coded as NGOs. (The NGOs do generally accept funding from industry donors, as well as from ordinary people and foundations, but they are sufficiently independent from industry funders to warrant a separate category.)

This policy subsystem has few "Astroturf" groups, or faux public interest groups that are really funded and controlled by industry players. The industry groups that participate generally identify themselves as such. Two groups in this study could reasonably

with at least ten appearances are scholars (sixteen documents) and librarians (fourteen documents). Educational institutions and groups (except as represented by scholars) participated just twice on their own, although several did back the DFC and thus could be described as having participated a bit more meaningfully.

Three groups appeared more rarely: representatives of legal associations and other unaffiliated lawyers (five documents), news articles submitted for the hearing record (eight documents), and participants who fall into none of the above categories (five documents). With such small numbers, these groups are excluded from further analysis here.

Coalition Allegiances of Groups

It matters who appears in congressional hearings because different sectors have different loyalties and agendas. This can be quantified by examining the share of documents from each sector that support a given rhetorical position. Figure 6.5 illustrates the share of each major sector's documents that took each position in the debate. For simplicity's sake, all nonprofit sectors – scholars, NGOs, libraries, and educational institutions – have been collapsed into one category, "nonprofit" actors.

Several of these sectors proved to be very clear members of one of the two coalitions. The media sector and appointed officials were quite reliably in the SC coalition, with 80 percent and 85 percent of their respective documents calling for strong DRM regulation. In contrast, 90 percent of the nonprofit groups' documents called for less DRM regulation. All three groups had less than 10 percent of their documents in the neutral category. In the debate over DRM policy, these groups are the rhetorical anchors at the far ends of the spectrum. In contrast, members of Congress and the technology sector were relatively split. Among congresspersons' documents, a slim majority (51 percent) advanced an SC position, 26 percent were neutral, and 24 took an SFU stance.[24] The technology sector

be described as representing both nonprofit and other sectors: the Digital Future Coalition (DFC, representing nonprofit, technology, scholars, libraries, and education) and the Chilling Effects Clearinghouse (nonprofit and scholars). The former is a coalition of multiple groups, including several true NGOs, and the latter has a track record of soliciting input and participation from the general public; this is not true, for instance, of the consumer electronics-driven Home Recording Rights Coalition, which is really a consumer electronics industry group. Both the DFC and the Chilling Effects Clearinghouse are coded as NGOs, which best describes their mission and operations.

[24] Totals equal 101 percent due to rounding error.

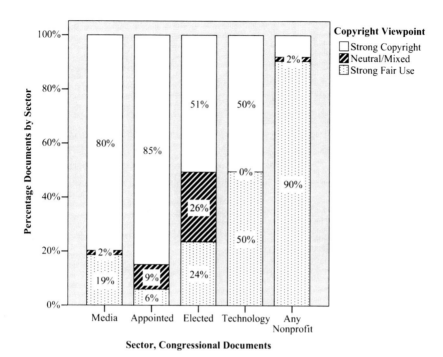

FIGURE 6.5. Copyright Viewpoint by Major Sectors

was almost perfectly divided; among 113 documents, 57 were in the SC camp and 56 were in the SFU camp.

The combination of sector representation and the allegiance of each sector helps explain the SC coalition's legislative successes, including the successful passage of the AHRA and DMCA. The media and technology sectors dominated the hearings, framing the debate as being primarily of concern to for-profit industries. This would be a recipe for gridlock if these sectors were diametrically opposed, but they are not; although the media sector is the anchor of the SC coalition, the technology sector is divided and more open to compromise. This is a reflection of technology companies' rational interests in copyright; as long as each company gets the exemptions it needs to do business, regulations of DRM technology seem less objectionable. The resulting legislative language thus reads like a contract between industries. Jessica Litman describes this process in some detail, in particular as it occurred during negotiations over the DMCA.[25] If these sectors are the only organized participants in

[25] Litman, *Digital Copyright*, 122–45.

the discussion, DRM regulation can continue to expand, leaving space only for those exceptions for which the technology sector has successfully fought.

There is another reason the technology sector is not much of a counterbalance to the media industry: the substantial diversity of business models within the technology sector. As a heterogeneous group of companies, the sector is of two minds about copyright law. Some companies – and some divisions within larger firms – are primarily in the business of selling copyrighted software, such as operating systems, productivity suites, entertainment software, and high-end creative software. For many of them, DRM and regulations against hacking it are important business tools. Obviously, DRM vendors are also quite happy to see laws requiring the implementation of their products or making it illegal to tamper with them; the former automatically increases sales, whereas the latter increases these products' perceived efficacy[26] and reduces the need to out-engineer every would-be circumventor with a broadband connection. Other companies and divisions sell mostly hardware; they generally see DRM regulations unfavorably. For obvious reasons, companies selling DRM circumvention software are also in favor of loosening or eliminating the rules governing circumvention and the marketing of circumvention devices. Finally, note that some of the world's largest technology companies – Sony and GE are particularly vivid examples – have also gotten into (if not necessarily stayed in) the media business. For these companies, the policy interests of their various divisions can be like a microcosm of the copyright debate as a whole, with the content divisions furiously supporting stronger copyright and the consumer electronics divisions seeking mostly to ensure that new copyright laws do not prevent their business models. Those within the technology sector who push against the growth of copyright have thus been fighting the war on two fronts, both within their own ranks and against strongly driven interests in the media sector. Combined with the SC coalition's ability to appease various technology interests with specific exemptions and concessions, this is an exceedingly difficult battle to win. If the battle is between the media and technology sectors, it is a recipe for repeated expansions of copyright.

---

[26] There is some considerable debate as to the degree to which various DRM deployments actually do reduce infringement, a difficult thing to measure; this study takes no position on this empirical question.

Changes in Representation and Shifts in Allegiance

As the DRM debate evolved, some groups had an increasing presence in the hearing record, and the technology sector moved closer to the SFU coalition. The most important change in representation was the nonprofit sectors' sharply increased participation in each successive period, both in absolute numbers and in relative share. In the first time period, nonprofit actors authored just eight documents, compared to forty-eight documents by the media sector and twenty-four by the technology sector. By the second period, there were nineteen nonprofit documents, thirty-seven media sector documents, and fifty-eight technology sector documents. By the period from 2003 to 2006, nonprofit groups had reached virtual parity, contributing thirty-six documents – compared to thirty-eight for the media sector and thirty-one for the technology sector. This is a substantial growth in visibility for the nonprofit sectors,[27] owing largely to the creation of SFU-oriented NGOs. First came the DFC. As discussed in Chapter 3, the DFC was essentially formed in opposition to the ideas that formed the core of the DMCA's anticircumvention provisions. The DFC authored five documents in the middle period and three in the latest period. Public Knowledge has had even more success gaining access to the hearing record.[28] From 2003 to 2006, Public Knowledge authored or co-authored thirteen documents (one co-authored with the DFC), more than one-third of all documents by nonprofit actors. The birth and growth of SFU-supporting NGOs was a major part of the shift from a strong pro-SC bias in the early 1990s to a rough balance between the two coalitions in the mid-2000s.

Another force in the shift toward more pro-SFU participation was the movement of the technology sector toward the SFU camp. It was strongly in favor of the 1992 AHRA, viewing it as a compromise that would allow members of the sector to sell digital audio recording devices, and 83 percent of the technology's sectors documents from the first period

---

[27] A document authored by a person or group in one of these sectors – media, technology, or any of the nonprofit sectors – was 1.67 times more likely to be authored by a nonprofit actor in the second period relative to the first, 2.06 times more likely in the third than the second, and 3.43 times more likely in the third than the first period. These convert to d-like effect sizes of .28, .40, and .68 – effects that are small but not insignificant, small-to-medium, and medium-to-large in size – respectively.

[28] In the interest of full disclosure, I interned with Public Knowledge in 2006, and I sought out Peter Jaszi, the driving force behind the DFC, for consultation on this research project. In both cases, I did so having already come to the conclusion that they were important players in the DRM debate; these numbers justify that conclusion.

(20 of 24) were in support of this expansion of DRM regulation. In the debate over Title I of the DMCA (from 1995 to 1998), however, 57 percent of technology sector documents (33 of 58) were in the SFU camp, and 61 percent of documents (19 of 31) from 2003 to 2006 supported the SFU position. Since resource mobilization is such a vital part of policy advocacy, and since the technology sector has access to a much larger pool of capital than the nonprofit sectors, the technology sector's movement toward stronger fair use is of vital importance to the SFU coalition's chances for successful outcomes. This shift has undoubtedly been due to a mix of persuasion from core SFU groups – especially NGOs – and some technology industry actors independently concluding that the SC agenda is mostly against their best interests. Regardless of the mix of causes, the effect of this move toward SFU allegiance has been to get a more SFU-leaning mix of views before Congress and, undoubtedly, to slow the SC coalition's ability to pursue its agenda.

Changes in other sectors have also helped push the mix of opinions toward the pro-SFU end of the scale. Scholarly participation rose, doubling from the first period (five documents) to the second (ten) and holding steady (nine) in the last period. Yet the influence of scholars has probably been more foundational than political – more significant for what is said outside Congress than in. The deluge of SFU-leaning public scholarship has undoubtedly helped build the broader movement, including much of the momentum and ideology behind SFU-leaning NGOs, but their participation in Congress is too light to suggest this degree of influence. As discussed earlier in this chapter, members of Congress have also voiced SFU-leaning opinions with greater frequency over time. Where public scholarship has been a leading indicator of the SFU movement, the increasing number of congressional allies has been a trailing indicator. The increasing frequency with which pro-SFU witnesses are invited to testify and congresspersons' increasing willingness to support their views are both signs that the voices of stronger fair use have reached a critical mass of perceived legitimacy in Congress.

CONCLUSION

During the debate over what became the 1992 AHRA, Congress heard almost exclusively from the voices for stronger copyright. This meant heavy doses of input from the recording and music publishing industries, members of the media sector that anchor the SC coalition. By the mid-2000s, however, legislative hearings were evenly split between the SC and SFU coalitions. Several members of Congress moved squarely into the SFU camp, at least on the question of DRM regulation. This was undoubtedly in large part due to the creation and mobilization of more substantial pro-SFU forces outside Congress. Spurred on in part by SFU-leaning scholars, SFU-supporting NGOs have sprung up and grown into a central part of the debate over copyright in general and the regulation of technology in particular. Due, in some part, to these NGOs' persuasion, many technology industry actors have also moved toward the SFU position – as have a small but important group of congresspersons.

The evolution of the opinions expressed in Congress lines up with the changes in policy outcomes. The SC coalition has had an increasingly difficult time advancing its legislative agenda, and it has even had to confront a meaningful if ultimately doomed push to scale back the reach of the 1998 DMCA. Thanks to these changes in the policy environment, the overall tone in the relevant congressional hearings moved from strongly supportive of the SC position to relatively neutral. This is a recipe for gridlock, and, so far, that is exactly what has happened. From the perspective of the SFU coalition, at least, this is a positive development.

7

Communicating in Print

In addition to trying to communicate with policymakers directly, policy actors have also long sought to take their case to the voting public via the news media. Not every policy actor seeks media coverage; some prefer a less visible role, a luxury for those who have more direct access to policymakers. In the copyright debate, since the strong copyright (SC) coalition enjoys a larger share of support from policymakers, that coalition has little incentive to seek news coverage of their proposed changes. In contrast, the strong fair use (SFU) coalition has relatively less support from policymakers – and, in their opinion at least, are advocating positions that better line up with the public interest. Thus, the SFU coalition has every incentive to seek greater press coverage in an effort to pressure policymakers based on perceived or actual public opinion. Before the web, news media coverage was almost the only way to reach a large segment of the population, barring an expensive option such as direct mail. Although the web has risen in political significance, offline news outlets – or, at least, the news institutions that predated the web and are still distributed in part via offline means – are still quite valuable to policy actors.

The number of news outlets that could possibly run a story has exploded in the last twenty years, but not all news outlets carry equal value for advocates. Despite the fracturing of the news environment and television news' continued role as the top news source for the typical voter, major national newspapers – especially the *New York Times* and *Washington Post* – still serve a central role in the discussion of national policy issues. Elite papers, and the *Times* in particular, serve as benchmarks for other media to determine what counts as the news of the day.[1] Also, policymakers use the amount and tone of coverage to gauge public opinion,[2]

---

[1] McCombs, *Setting the Agenda*, 113.   [2] Mutz, *Impersonal Influence*, 51–3.

and policymakers themselves are particularly likely to read the *Times* and *Post* to decide which issues and frames are growing in importance.[3] Both newspapers also make large investments in the coverage of national policy issues generally and science and technology specifically, "with a large and prestigious staff of science writers and editors.... Given their influence, both papers are primary targets of media lobbying by various political actors."[4] In tracking mainstream news coverage of national technology policy, then, the *Times* and *Post* are natural choices. Other media are also important. In particular, the media industry and technology industry press also have a lot to say about copyright, and these messages percolate out into the debate, a role I discuss in this chapter and the one that follows. Still, since the *Times* and *Post* play such a central role in covering national policy issues, the coverage in these papers is a rather good indicator of the degree to which the SFU coalition has brought the debate over digital rights management (DRM) regulation out of the halls of Congress and into the offline news environment more generally. There has been a rather low volume of coverage of DRM policy – especially when compared to the deluge of articles covering digital copyright in other ways. The coverage has moved subtly toward the SFU position, and the sectors that consistently support the SFU position have become more frequent news sources over time, but the low volume of coverage limits the political value of these changes. Even industry publications have been fairly quiet on these issues.

LOW VOLUME OF NEWSPAPER COVERAGE

The *Post* and *Times* each featured a modest number of articles that discussed the specific DRM policy proposals of the day. The *Times* had a total of thirty-six articles across all three periods (1989–92, 1995–98, 2003–06), and the *Post* had just twenty-two. Table 7.1 shows these totals, as well as the numbers by time period.

Spread across four debates and twelve years, these figures show that both newspapers regularly covered DRM policy debates but did so sparingly – just enough so that their daily readers might get a basic overview of each debate. However, this is not because either paper thought copyright to be an unimportant issue; both had a great deal of coverage of copyright in general. According to LexisNexis, over the

---

[3] Kingdon, *Agendas, Alternatives, and Public Policies*, 60.
[4] Nisbet and Huge, "Attention Cycles and Frames," 19.

TABLE 7.1. *Newspaper coverage by period*

Number of relevant articles (Total copyright-related articles)	*New York Times*	*Washington Post*	Total
1989–1992	16 (177)	5 (107)	21 (284)
1995–1998	6 (530)	7 (366)	13 (896)
2003–2006	14 (1,000)	10 (431)	24 (1,431)
Total	36 (1,707)	22 (904)	58 (2,611)

same periods, the *Times* had 1,707 articles that were about copyright to some degree, and the *Post* had 904.[5] Especially compared to the wealth of input at congressional hearings, this is a fairly sparse amount of coverage. Newspaper editors clearly think many items related to copyright are of interest, but they do not see the legislative debates over DRM regulation as being of particular public interest. Although I did not count them specifically, the larger sets clearly included hundreds of articles about infringement via digital technologies – the very concerns that led to the proposal and adoption of the DRM regulations studied. For instance, from 2003 to 2006, the *Times* featured 193 stories with "copyright" in the headline, lead paragraphs, and indexing terms and one of the following terms in the body of the story: "bittorrent," "bit torrent," "grokster," "napster," "peer to peer," "peer-to-peer," and "p2p." Likewise, the *Post* had 88 such stories.

Both newspapers treated concerns about the digital transmission of copyrighted content as a subject of substantial concern, but both failed to provide extended coverage of some of the most important policies that resulted from these concerns. This shortfall is most apparent in the context of the 1998 Digital Millennium Copyright Act (DMCA). As early as 1994, the Patent and Trademark Office publicly signaled that the administration would push for something like the DMCA. The negotiations leading up to the 1996 signature of the two World Intellectual Property Organization (WIPO) treaties featured an extended international debate over the future of copyright law in the digital age. The DMCA represents the most profound change in copyright law since 1976, and Title I of the DMCA has profoundly reshaped copyright law. In the four years leading

---

[5] This is as measured by whether LexisNexis said an article had the word "copyright" in the headline, lead paragraphs, or search terms. Although these figures are thus limited by the accuracy of the database's categorization, I read each article myself, searching for DRM policy-related articles, and I was struck by how few articles were not really about copyright (i.e., "false positives").

up to its passage, the *Times* and *Post* ran just thirteen stories between them on the issue. One *Post* article, set aside because it had too little relevant content, even described the anticircumvention provisions of the bill as "relatively noncontroversial."[6]

Major daily newspapers are too thin on detailed policy information for any citizen who wants to learn much detail about the debate over specific digital copyright proposals. This is understandable from the viewpoint of the newspapers. As general-interest publications, they can only spend so many column inches on any issue, and issues that are technically complicated and not likely to have massive society-changing impacts will not likely receive much attention. Even on technically complicated issues in which large portions of the public have expressed strong opinions, from mercury pollution to network neutrality, coverage is undoubtedly too light to satisfy those who wish for greater public interest. Still, it is notable that coverage did not grow much over time, even as copyright coverage in general saw roughly a fivefold increase.

To understand why DRM coverage stayed flat as copyright coverage blossomed, consider what one author identifies as the criteria for what determines the newsworthiness of a given event: timeliness, relevance to the audience, the audience's potential identification with an event, the degree of conflict involved, and sensation.[7] Under these or any similar set of criteria, the DRM policy debate rarely involves newsworthy events. The general public has little perception that encryption is relevant to their day-to-day lives; this study is conducted in the belief that it plays an important role in shaping the media environment, although even I must concede that this is an indirect impact for most people. Few DRM-related events offer chances for audience identification; for instance, most people would have a hard time sympathizing with encryption researchers who do not follow specific lines of research due to vague legal threats. In the context of policy debates, the newsworthiness of a conflict is generally indexed to visible political figures, meaning that the press generally covers political issues and perspectives that are debated by political elites – and only those issues and perspectives – regardless of public opinion.[8] Until the recent past, the degree of high-level political conflict around copyright has been fairly low; congresspersons on the strong fair use (SFU) side of the debate have always been rare and never included the top

[6] Mike Mills, "Bill Attacks Copyright Minefield: House Subcommittee Considers Authors' on-Line Rights," *Washington Post*, May 15 1996, C1.
[7] Schultz, "The Journalistic Gut Feeling," 196–8.
[8] Bennett, "Toward a Theory."

congressional leadership of either party. Finally, DRM regulation rarely involves sensational events. This relatively low newsworthiness for the DRM debate contrasts sharply with a well-covered issue in copyright: the music industry's strategy of legal action against peer-to-peer users. These legal machinations often create discrete, timely news events that are sensational, create a potential sense of identification in many readers, and have obvious relevance to millions of internet users. Little wonder that Recording Industry Association of American (RIAA) suits received so much more coverage than DRM legislation, even though the legislative decisions still stand and while the music industry has stopped pursuing new defendants.

This is not to say that there are no newsworthy events that relate to DRM regulation; the legal threats against Ed Felten's research team and the arrest of Dmitry Sklyarov are two such examples. For the SFU coalition, these were valuable opportunities to communicate with the public about the perils of the DMCA, but these opportunities are rare for exactly that reason; they must be initiated by a copyright holder. This behavior can reasonably be cast as bullying, so, paradoxically, copyright holders have a long-term strategic interest in pursuing few legal cases. The current situation favors the strong copyright (SC) coalition: the threat of legal action prevents the development and sale of DRM circumvention devices in the mainstream commercial market, and it scares many researchers and tinkerers away from reverse-engineering research, but it does so without garnering widespread public attention. Thus, copyright holders can do a lot to keep this issue out of the newspapers simply by not giving the SFU coalition a sensational story line to pitch. From 2000 to 2002, the Felten and Sklyarov stories merited thirty-three total stories in the *Times* and *Post* – substantially more than the combined twenty-four DRM policy-relevant stories from 2003 to 2006.[9]

---

[9] One might ask whether this undermines the methodological choice to focus on DMCA reform debate beginning in 2003, but the Felten and Sklyarov incidents were hardly the spark for an immediate congressional push to reform the law. Of twenty-one copyright-related hearings between the start of coverage of Felten's story (November 2, 2000) and the end of 2002, only one meets this study's standards for relevance to the DMCA reform debate. The title of the 2002 hearing, *Consumer Benefits of Today's Digital Rights Management (DRM) Solutions: Hearing Before the Subcommittee on Courts, the Internet, and Intellectual Property of the House Committee on the Judiciary*, 107th Cong. (2002), hardly suggests an impending revolt against the DMCA.

Because there was still no substantial movement in place to turn these incidents into political momentum, the Felten and Sklyarov stories served more as inspiration for such capacity building.

A MOSTLY BALANCED COPYRIGHT VIEWPOINT

In addition to being infrequent, newspaper coverage was mostly balanced. A slim majority of articles included at least some representation of each coalition's side in the debate. Out of fifty-eight total articles, thirty were neutral or mixed, sixteen supported the SFU position, and twelve took the SC view. This reflects the journalistic practice of presenting both sides of political conflicts, which is caused by "the fear of appearing biased, [and] which leads to a formulaic 'he said, she said' reporting style."[10] Nearly a century of journalists' self-identification as objective – itself a strategic reaction to skepticism of the press[11] – has pushed mainstream news outlets toward the middle on all conflicts for which there are at least two well-represented sides. The coverage also looks mostly balanced when using the copyright viewpoint score for each article. Where a score of 1 represents SC and 3 represents SFU, the mean score for all articles is 2.11.[12]

The two papers were not identical but were each mostly neutral in their coverage. Of thirty-six articles, the *Times* ran eight SC, eight SFU, and twenty neutral articles, a perfectly balanced distribution among the three categories. Of twenty-two articles, the *Post* ran four SC, eight SFU, and ten neutral or mixed pieces. Across all articles, the *Times'* mean viewpoint score was 2.03, and the *Post's* mean score was 2.24.[13] The number of articles per paper is perilously low – a few articles still could have made a big difference – but, based on these figures, the *Times* looks almost exactly balanced, whereas the *Post* had a modest pro-SFU bias.

Coverage was reasonably balanced during each period, but there was a meaningful shift over time; papers' coverage moved from leaning modestly toward the pro-SC position to a modest pro-SFU position. Table 7.2 shows how many articles took each position for each period.

This change is also clear when comparing copyright viewpoint scores. Where a score of 1.0 represents the SC position and 3.0 represents SFU, articles from 1989 to 1992 had an average score of 1.81. In contrast,

[10] Jamieson and Waldman, *The Press Effect*, 168.

[11] Schudson, *Discovering the News*, 122.

[12] Standard deviation (SD) for all articles is .72; for those that did not take a position ($M = 2.08$), it is .27. One can use effect size measurements – described in the footnotes from the previous chapter – for a rough measure of whether these deviations from perfect neutrality are meaningful. (To have a population with which to contrast these articles, I imagine a group of articles with the same SD but a mean viewpoint score of 2.) Doing so, the measure d for all articles is a genuinely trivial .15, although for articles that do not take a position, $d = .30$, a small to medium effect. Taken together, I think these correctly suggest a small but distinct bias toward the SFU message across all periods.

[13] For the *Times*, $SD = .71$; for the *Post*, $SD = .73$.

TABLE 7.2. *Rhetorical categories by period*

Number of articles per category	Strong copyright	Neutral/ mixed	Strong fair use	Total
1989–1992	9	6	6	21
1995–1998	2	7	4	13
2003–2006	1	17	6	24
Total	12	30	16	58

for 1995–98, the average was 2.29, and for 2003–06, it was 2.28.[14] The majority of coverage conveyed both sides of the debate for each time period, but coverage in each period had a decided slant – a bias ranging from a relatively small pro-SC bias (1989–92) to a medium-sized pro-SFU bias (1995 onward).[15] Because the direction of this bias changed over time, the contrast between periods is even more substantial.[16]

The degree of change after the first period correctly suggests the under-lying change in copyright politics that I have been identifying throughout this book. In the first period, there was almost no mobilized opposition to the proposals that became the Audio Home Recording Act (AHRA); news coverage reflected this dearth of skeptics. By the second period, DMCA opponents, such as those organized within the Digital Future Coalition, were successfully engaging the media to a degree that the coverage leaned toward the SFU message. By the third period, the SFU coalition was even better organized, and it successfully engaged in media outreach to a degree that not only continued to pull newspapers subtly toward the SFU position, but also likely contributed to the rebound in coverage.

SECTOR REPRESENTATION IN NEWSPAPER COVERAGE

The representation of sectors in newspaper coverage of the DRM debate is similar to that in Congress. Many articles quoted more than one sector; the 58 included articles quoted a total of 101 sectors. As in congres-sional hearings, the best-represented groups are the media sector and the

---

[14] The SD for each period, respectively, was .85, .70, and .52.

[15] Using the same assumptions described in note 12, the bias for each period is as follows: for 1989–92, $d = .22$; for 1995–98, $d = .41$; for 2003–06, $d = .54$. These would represent small, nearly medium, and medium effect sizes, respectively.

[16] Contrasting the first and second periods, $d = .60$. Comparing the first and third, $d = .68$. Both are medium to large effect sizes. The second and third periods are so similar that $d = .02$, a truly trivial effect size.

technology sector. The media sector, including interests such as the recorded music and motion picture industries, were quoted in twenty-eight articles. Likewise, technology industry sources, representing firms such as consumer electronics manufacturers, computer manufacturers, and software firms, appeared in twenty-six news articles. Nongovernmental organizations (NGOs) appeared in thirteen articles, good enough for third place. Elected (nine articles) and appointed (eight) government voices also appeared with relative frequency.

Scholarly voices (six) and others (five), such as ordinary consumers, appeared just a bit more often than lawyers (three) and librarians (three).

As the DRM debate became more contentious, this increasingly heated exchange was also reflected in newspaper coverage. The change is palpable even when comparing individual articles, which became more likely to quote multiple sectors over time – and thus more likely to quote opposing voices in the same article. From 1989–92, the average article cited just 1.24 sectors. This rose slightly, to 1.46 from 1995–98, but in the last period, it jumped to 2.33 sectors per article. The increasing rancor over DRM policy is reflected in a ramped-up effort by competing coalitions to gain access to these major newspapers. Over time, some groups have enjoyed increasing access to newspapers. See Figure 7.1, which highlights the changes over time for those sectors with at least six total appearances.

The stacks are quite different in total size because of the differences in total articles (21, 13, and 24), as well as sectors quoted per article (1.24, 1.46, and 2.33). Of greater interest, though, is the changes in proportional representation enjoyed by each sector. The technology and media sectors enjoyed high relative representation across each period. Technology sources appeared in twelve out of twenty-one articles (57 percent) in the first period, three of thirteen (23 percent) in the second, and eleven of twenty-four in the latest period (46 percent). Likewise, across each period, media sources were quoted in nine (43 percent), five (38 percent), and fourteen articles (58 percent). Especially within such a small number of articles, these changes are unremarkable.

In contrast, appointed officials, members of Congress, and NGOs saw their representation increase substantially. Appointed officials went from unquoted in 1989–92 to appearing in two of thirteen articles (15 percent) from 1995–98 and six of twenty-four articles (25 percent) in 2003–06. Congresspersons were quoted just once in the first period (5 percent), but this rose to three (23 percent) and then five articles (21 percent). Finally, NGOs saw a dramatic rise in the last period, from just two

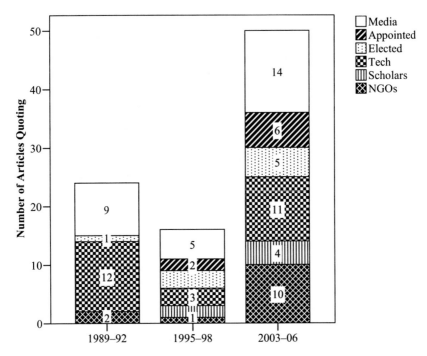

FIGURE 7.1. Newspaper Articles Quoting Select Sectors by Period

articles in the first period (10 percent) and one article in the second (8 percent) to ten articles (42 percent) in the latest period. The gains for these sectors relative to the technology and media sectors is made even clearer in Figure 7.2.

This graph presents the same data as Figure 7.1, but instead of a simple count of the number of articles citing each sector, it stretches each period's data upward to fill up the graph. This makes it easier to assess how each sector performed, relative to other sectors, in a given period. The media and technology sectors have lower relative visibility over time because of the increase in other groups' visibility. Nongovernmental organizations, congresspersons, and appointed government officials have all increased from near silence in newspaper coverage to meaningful participation. The affiliations of quoted sources reflect the broader change in coverage over time. Leading up to the AHRA, newspapers created the impression that DRM policy was primarily a private discussion between the media and technology sectors – albeit, with consumers' desire to adopt digital audio tape (DAT) decks held hostage. Increasingly, however, DRM has been

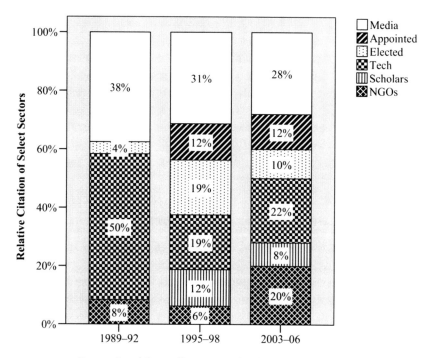

FIGURE 7.2. Proportional Sector Representation in Newspaper Articles by Period

portrayed as a policy issue that matters to the broader public, one that is worthy of participation by congresspersons, appointed officials, and civil society groups.

The upswing in the appearance of appointed officials is in part due to the topic of the broadcast flag. Many voices from the Federal Communications Commission (FCC) chimed in, both debating the merits of the Commission's flag mandate and defending the agency's jurisdiction to impose it. In contrast, the upswings in congressional and NGO participation are the result of people who have deliberately publicized the issue of DRM policy. The congressperson at the forefront of the effort to reform Title I of the DMCA is Representative Rick Boucher (D-VA), although the 2003–06 period also saw important support – including support in the media – from House colleagues including John T. Doolittle (R-CA) and Zoe Lofgren (D-CA). Likewise, Public Knowledge, a Washington, D.C. nonprofit advocacy group founded in 2001, has contributed substantially by serving as a regular source in news stories – appearing in five of the twenty-four relevant articles from 2003–06, as well as contributing dozens of the other articles about other copyright issues.[17] The Electronic Frontier Foundation (EFF), formed in 1990, has also served an increasingly visible advocacy role on DRM policy since the passage of the DMCA; it appeared in one 1995 article and four articles from 2003–06, and it also appeared in dozens of other copyright-related articles. By repeatedly reaching out to the media and being readily available when reporters call, these two NGOs have made major contributions to reshaping coverage of copyright. They help raise questions of the broader public good, and this has been an important if subtle boost to the voices calling for stronger fair use.

A VARIED ROLE FOR INDUSTRY PRESS

For the reasons described above, this study focuses on the *Times* and *Post* as a proxy for the coverage of DRM policy among general-interest news outlets. This leaves out an important if much less widely read group of publications: industry trade press outlets in both media and technology.[18] Coverage in these outlets reaches a small sliver of the population, but a much larger share of each outlet's audience is likely to care about copyright. In this way, the trade press can provide information about policy issues to the constituents who would be easiest to mobilize into action. As with the elite newspapers, though, trade press coverage of the DRM debate was rather slender in some of the outlets I studied, and the variance is consistent with the overall results of this study. Unlike the *Times* and *Post*, not all of the trade press sources in LexisNexis are indexed as far back as the beginning of the AHRA debate – not least because some of the sources have been created in the years since. Yet the database has good enough coverage to make a fair assessment of the broadcast flag and DMCA reform debates.

To quantify how the trade press covered the debates from 2003 to 2006, I studied seven very to reasonably well-known sources in media and

---

[17] I interned for Public Knowledge in the summer of 2006, but I did so as a volunteer, and the organization has never paid me for any services.

[18] In discussing my dissertation, Bill Rosenblatt correctly pointed out that, by not studying trade press coverage of the issue, that study had something of a blind spot. Bill Rosenblatt, "Roots of the Online Upheaval of SOPA/PIPA," *Copyright and Technology*, May 13, 2012, at http://copyrightandtechnology.com/2012/05/13/roots-of-the-online-upheaval-of-sopapipa. With a sincere thanks for his critique, I saw fit to include a brief discussion of the print media trade press coverage here. As will become clear in the next chapter, I already had reason to engage a fuller discussion of the role of the trade press online in the next chapter.

technology. Three (*Billboard*, *Daily Variety*, and *Hollywood Reporter*) are important entertainment industry periodicals. Since the technology world is a bit more diverse, I included two news outlets (*Information-Week* and *Network World*) that are sources for information technology (IT) news, as well as a consumer electronics periodical (*Consumer Electronics Daily*) and another with a focus on telecommunications (*Communications Daily*).[19] Despite using a less labor-intensive search strategy than that used for the *Times* and *Post*,[20] I was able to get a reasonable estimate of the frequency of coverage in each outlet, especially as compared to each other. The results are laid out in Table 7.3.

The differences across publications are staggering. The three content industry trade outlets have modest coverage and a modest pro-SC bias. *InformationWeek* and *Network World* had modest coverage, but each had a high level of pro-SFU bias – running more pro-SFU articles than neutral articles. The other two titles had modest pro-SFU bias, with incredibly comprehensive coverage. *Communications Daily* had sixty-five total articles, with roughly two-thirds being neutral articles but a ratio of almost 3:1 pro-SFU articles among those with a clear bias. *Consumer Electronics Daily* had thirty-eight total articles, and their coverage was similarly mostly neutral but with a modest pro-SFU bias.

---

[19] Although not definitive, LexisNexis indexing is a fair indicator of a trade publication's relative importance. I chose several among those indexed that I know to carry at least some weight in their relative sectors. Although readers may have good reason to quibble about individual sources that are included or excluded, the results are a fair representation of how the broader trade press covered these debates. For *Consumer Electronics Daily*, coverage is from January 5, 2004, onward; all six other titles are covered since before 2003.

[20] With the *Times* and *Post*, I personally examined every document for which "copyright" was a keyword or in the headline or lead paragraph, thus identifying every single article related to any of the four DRM debates I studied. Doing so for seven additional publications – none of which has the kind of political significance of a major daily paper – would be more than is required to illustrate the point of this section. Thus, I used keyword searches for each of the two debates from the 2003–06 period.

For the broadcast flag search, I looked for articles with (broadcast! w/10 flag) – that is, any derivation of the word "broadcast" within ten words of "flag" – anywhere in the article and at least two appearances of the word "copyright" anywhere in the article. For the DMCA reform search, I used the following Boolean string:

(dmca OR (digital millennium copyright act)) AND atleast2(copyright) AND (drm OR (digital rights management) OR tpm OR (protection measure) OR encrypt! OR lock!)

This strategy may have meant a few missed articles in total across all seven publications, but considering that trade publications are especially likely to use the terms of art – as opposed to general-readership papers, which might express the same ideas with less technical terminology – the number is likely very low.

TABLE 7.3. *Relevant articles and rhetorical categories by trade press publication*

Periodical	Strong copyright	Neutral/ mixed	Strong fair use	Total
Billboard	2	6	0	8
Hollywood Reporter	2	5	0	7
Daily Variety	1	9	1	11
Information Week	0	1	3	4
Network World	1	1	11	13
Communications Daily	5	46	14	65
Consumer Electronics Daily	4	25	9	38
Total	15	93	38	146

The differences across industry rags is probably in some measure idiosyncratic, a reflection of each publication's audience, although they also suggest the different political strategies across industries, which have already become clear by this point in the study. The idiosyncratic component is probably the best explanation for the wide variation in coverage. The media and IT titles seem to have substantial readership by those in the industry, outside of management; this even includes those who are not industry professionals, although this is most likely for *Billboard* and less so for the other four titles. For such a mix of readers, light coverage of policy matters makes sense. In comparison, *Communications Daily* and *Consumer Electronics Daily* seem to have readerships that are more concentrated among upper management, thus warranting these publications' much more detailed policy briefings with a specific eye toward how it will affect these industries. In other words, for these publications, the amount of coverage is probably more a sign of each publication's audience within an industry than it is of an industry's political position.

Although the amount of coverage is idiosyncratic, the degree of overt bias is more consistent with the rest of the study's findings. As is clear from congressional hearings and the political history of these issues, the content industry, telecommunications industry, and consumer electronics (CE) industry have long felt either modest (CE) or high levels of comfort (the other industries) in taking their case directly to policymakers. Each of these industries is also well-represented by a specific trade group that has its members' exact interests at heart. Thus, there is no general need to mobilize readers, and mostly balanced coverage is the order of the day for trade press coverage. The pro-SFU portions of the IT sector, however, have long felt that their place at the table in Washington, D.C., is hardly guaranteed. Software companies have founded trade groups, such as the Business Software Alliance (BSA) and Entertainment Software Association (ESA), to advocate for stronger copyright. Even larger IT sector lobbying organizations, such as the Information Technology Industry Council, generally push for stronger copyright – despite membership rosters with companies like Google and eBay, which face more copyright headaches than copyright revenue. This probably explains the very high degree of bias in *Network World* and *InformationWeek*. Especially in the mid-2000s, these readers' interests were not being addressed by well-heeled lobbyists, and they were thus less likely to take policy developments as something to be dealt with by professional lobbyists. Thus, these publications were only reflecting the ethos of the strongly pro-SFU technology press more generally, although much more of that coverage was happening online in places that do not have corresponding print publications. I discuss this in more detail in the next chapter.

CONCLUSION

Across all periods, newspaper coverage has been mostly balanced. Over time, however, newspapers have moved substantially in the direction of the SFU coalition. This has undoubtedly stemmed in large part from the concerted efforts of a few policy actors. Sympathetic congresspersons, especially Representative Rick Boucher, and NGOs such as Public Knowledge and the EFF, have helped reshape the newspaper dialog around DRM policy. They have contributed to the overall rise in the number of sectors quoted per article, adding to the perception that DRM policy is the subject of meaningful political debate in which the broader public has an interest. Because these elite newspapers help set the parameters for legitimate policy debate, this development is an indicator of the success of the SFU coalition's offline communication strategy.

The pro-SFU bias surely reflects greater efforts by the SFU coalition to get coverage for specific policy issues – and each coalition's relative efforts reflects each group's rational interest in seeking public attention to the specifics of the DRM debate. The SC coalition neither needs nor wants a high level of attention paid to policy specifics. Especially relative to the SFU coalition – but even relative to most other industries – the SC coalition has a very well-funded, well-connected operation in Washington. Rather than appealing for broader public support, they can and do simply communicate their wishes to policymakers. Because copyright has not historically been an issue of deep interest to the public, keeping the debate quiet benefits those who are best positioned to win desirable outcomes through direct lobbying. Even if they wanted to mobilize action by the tens of thousands of employed in the entertainment industries, SC advocates could get at least as much traction by turning to the trade press. Although I did not conduct a formal content analysis of the trade press on this count, an informal examination turned up little evidence of such a call to action – even, for instance, when broadcast flag legislation was pending in Congress.

In sharp contrast, the SFU coalition has always been outspent and much less well-connected in the Capital. Thus, they have every incentive to seek new venues, including the court of public opinion. As described in the previous chapter, this has meant an escalating involvement by the commerce committees, where technology interests have more traction. In the context of the public media, it implies exactly what this chapter's results suggest: the SFU coalition is seeking to expand the conflict to include the broader public in the discussion. As the SFU coalition has formed and grown, it has undertaken more media outreach, and the results show their growing presence.

Although these changes over time are important, the most significant finding of this chapter is that newspapers do not provide much coverage of DRM policy debates – an average of only a little more than seven articles per topic per paper. This is probably a fair representation of the topic's newsworthiness for a general readership, but it is not enough to enable even daily readers to follow the intricacies of the policy debates at hand. Thus, although the thin coverage is an understandable editorial decision for a general-interest newspaper, it leaves SFU advocates with little hope of achieving broader public engagement around DRM policy through news coverage alone. Even among the trade press, coverage has been surprisingly light, except for those periodicals targeted at upper management. If SFU advocates seek broader public engagement on the policy specifics, the old-fashioned route is to convince the press that the legislative battles are a key part of the copyright story; empirically, this has not worked out.

In terms of the media environment, the period of this study contains a radical change: the mass adoption of the internet. By the mid-2000s, every successive year saw millions more U.S. households adding broadband internet connections. Political activists of all stripes were emboldened by the newfound power of the internet to sidestep old media gateways and shape policy outcomes. The limits of the general purpose newspaper and limited-audience print publication were beginning to dissolve as obstacles that could keep advocates from reaching a broader public. Especially as a coalition that is largely populated by internet enthusiasts, the SFU coalition quickly embraced the web as an important vehicle for expanding the scope of the conflict over DRM policy.

8

The Copyright and Digital Rights Management
Debate Online

In a world without online political advocacy, the strong fair use (SFU) coalition would have faced long odds in its efforts to communicate its message. True, it made substantial inroads in Congress and even drew increasingly favorable – albeit sparse – newspaper coverage of the legislative debates, as well as relatively detailed, sympathetic coverage from the technology trade press. Yet the strong copyright (SC) coalition's much greater financial support for regular lobbying made it unlikely that the SFU coalition could ever make much of a policy impact without a broader appeal to a mobilized public. Further, the infrequency of policy-specific coverage in newspapers made such an appeal virtually impossible through that medium. These factors, combined with the SFU coalition's general comfort with and even enthusiasm for internet use, made that coalition an obvious candidate for taking to the web early and often to make its case. That is exactly what happened. As I show in this chapter, SFU-aligned websites were far and away the dominant voice in the online copyright debate.

Demonstrating the decidedly pro-SFU flavor of the online discussion – at least, demonstrating such dominance in the era before the Stop Online Piracy Act (SOPA) blackout – is something of a challenge. Unlike newspapers and congressional hearings, no carefully curated, centralized database of web content exists. Even search engine companies, with hundreds of the brightest engineers in the world at their disposal, struggle with the problem of identifying and sorting all of the relevant content on the web that might be related to a given topic. Thus, unlike in previous chapters, I'll say a good bit about my research methods here, although this will be with an eye toward helping the reader understand what these results mean. As is true throughout this book, social scientists seeking a fuller explanation, or even hoping to use some of these methods, can

120

see more extensive explanations elsewhere.[1] These choices are not definitive, but they reflect a set of strategies that seemed to work well. First, I identified those websites that are at the center of the online debate over copyright. Once I had those in hand, I searched individual sites for relevant pages and analyzed them using the same tools I used to analyze congressional hearing documents and newspaper articles. I explain a bit about each method before discussing what I found.

THE COMMUNITY OF WEBSITES DEBATING COPYRIGHT

Rather than doing a general web search for what anybody might say about copyright and digital rights management (DRM), I sought to identify a community of websites that are relevant – that regularly participate in the copyright debate and are valued enough to earn links from other members of the community. After all, most policy advocacy happens within policy communities – groups of policy actors that interact regularly around a given issue.[2] To understand online issue advocacy around DRM policy, then, it seemed most sensible to identify the sites of actors who are members of the relevant policy community. As the January 2012 blackout shows, a coalition that wants to reach the general public for a specific period can be wildly successful if it draws in sites with a much broader audience, but these lightning-in-a-bottle scenarios are rare. Further, for them to even happen around niche issues such as digital copyright law, it is quite likely essential that they follow the early lead of a well-built infrastructure of online advocacy around the issue in question. I discuss this in more detail in Chapter 12.

Mapping the Community of Copyright-Debating Websites

To identify the group of sites that are invested in the copyright and DRM debate – and, with that community identified, to find its more important members – I looked to the hyperlinks between websites. Each link from one site to another is in many ways a vote for the linked site – much like an academic citation, it literally says to the reader, "For more information on this topic, we suggest you go *here*." Although an author may link to (or quote) a document as part of a refutation rather than

---

[1] Herman, "The Battle over Digital Rights Management;" Herman, "Taking the Copyfight Online."

[2] Sabatier and Jenkins-Smith, "The Advocacy Coalition Framework."

an expression of agreement, to do so is at least a statement that the referred-to document is worth refuting. Much as frequent academic citations demonstrate scholarly authority, a high number of incoming links demonstrate online authority. This view of authority is at the core of Google's PageRank algorithm, as well as central to much of the research on the network structure of the web.[3] Further, most websites tend to link to other sites on similar topics, creating clusters of related websites, within which the same patterns of linking help establish commonality and relative authority within each community.[4]

To identify the more authoritative sites at the heart of the online copyright debate, I used a tool called the Issue Crawler,[5] which was developed by Richard Rogers[6] and has since been used by other scholars.[7] To use the crawler, the user enters a list of websites that are already known to be members of a target community; these become the "seed" websites. The crawler then visits the seed websites, searching for hyperlinks to still other websites. Any new website that has incoming links from at least two of the seed websites is added to the list, and the crawler repeats the process. The results are a list of up to one hundred sites,[8] each of which has at least two hyperlinks from other sites in the community.

The crawler produces a color map of interlinked websites, and this map says a great deal about the relationships between the included websites. Each site is represented by a circle; the larger the circle, the more incoming links from other included sites. Also, sites' circles are placed near or far depending on how often links to each site appear together on another site. Thus, if many other sites link to both Site A and Site B, then the circles for both A and B will be near each other. In contrast, if no sites that link to A ever link to Site C, then the circles for A and C will be far apart. The crawler also produces a list of each website that was included, ranked by how many incoming hyperlinks each received from the other sites. Each set of results is one "crawl." For an example of a map depicting the results of one crawl, see Figure 8.1.

---

[3] Barabási, *Linked.*   [4] Benkler, *The Wealth of Networks,* 12–13.

[5] Govcom.org Foundation, "Issue Crawler," http://issuecrawler.net.

[6] Rogers, *Information Politics.*

[7] Bruns, "Methodologies for Mapping;" Farrall and Delli Carpini, "Cyberspace;" Xenos and Bennett, "The Disconnection in Online Politics."

[8] The default settings were two rounds of crawling (finding sites linked from the seed websites, adding these to the set, and crawling these and the original seed sites to produce final results) and a limit of 100 sites included in results. These are recommended for identifying an issue network, which was my goal. The default is now one iteration, although the user is still free to choose two or three.

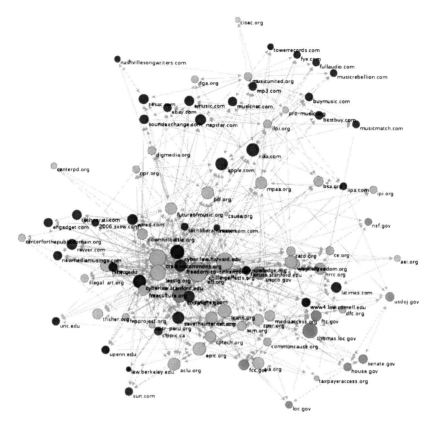

FIGURE 8.1. Issue Crawler Map of Online Copyright Debate, November 2006

This map represents all ninety-five sites from the web crawl conducted November 2006. It represents the SFU coalition and the SC coalition, and it even represents the substantial separation between the two groups. Sites break fairly cleanly into two groups: the SFU group on the bottom, and the SC group on the top.

The SFU coalition dominates this map, anchored by the large group of closely linked, large circles that are clustered just to the bottom left of the graph's center. The high number of sites and the tightness of their connections are responsible for the poor readability in that region of the map; site labels and linking arrows are on top of one another. (Readers may find the version on the supplementary website somewhat more usable on this count, since one can click on each circle to find out which site it represents, as well as the number of incoming and outgoing hyperlinks.) The largest circles in this group represent the high number of incoming links for Lawrence Lessig's site, as well as for three pro-SFU nongovernmental organizations (NGOs) – the Electronic Frontier Foundation (EFF), Creative Commons (CC), and Public Knowledge. Several peripheral sites orbit around this center, located to the left, right, and bottom. Sites ending in .org (roughly thirty in total) dominate this whole SFU area. Starting with the Copyright Office site in the center of this cluster and spreading rightward, there are ten sites ending in .gov. A total of eight .edu sites are scattered across this area, as are thirteen .com sites.

Between the SFU cluster in the lower portion of the graph and the SC coalition in the upper portion is a relatively large gap with few sites. This correctly suggests the wide differences between these groups of organizations; linking websites effectively declared that there are two kinds of organizations, and this is the space between them. In the upper portion of the graph are fewer sites with smaller circles, and they are less densely linked. The eighteen .com sites make up a majority of the nodes, and eight to eleven .org sites (depending on which sites one includes) make up the balance. The number of .com sites is proportionally much higher than in the bottom portion of the map; in the SFU region, .com sites represent less than 25 percent of sites, whereas, in the SC region, they represent at least 60 percent of sites.

Although the numbers examined in full detail later in the chapter illustrate this definitively, even a first-impression glance at this map correctly suggests that the SFU coalition has more websites in this network, and the most linked-to sites are in the SFU coalition. The SFU coalition is better represented and much more heavily interlinked. This map begins to show what this chapter shows definitively: that the SFU coalition has made a substantial investment in building a community of sites that make its case.

Adding Up a Year of Results

The web changes constantly, so a single crawl can be influenced by short-term events – a single op-ed in a newspaper, technical issues limiting a website's functionality, a short-term push to generate link traffic to a given site, and so on. To counteract this, I ran thirteen crawls, one per month from October 2006 to October 2007. This period roughly corresponds to the tail end of the debates over Digital Millennium Copyright Act (DMCA) reform and the broadcast flag. In the 13 sets of results, 210 web domains (e.g., publicknowledge.org) appeared at least once; of these,

TABLE 8.1. *Top ten web Crawl results by mean rank*

Rank	Organization/Individual	URL	Mean rank
1	Creative Commons	creativecommons.org	1.77
2	Electronic Frontier Foundation	eff.org	2.38
3	Free Software Foundation	fsf.org	3.85
4	Lawrence Lessig	lessig.org	6.69
5	Center for Democracy and Technology	cdt.org	14.46
6	Public Knowledge	publicknowledge.org	16.00
7	Thomas, Library of Congress	thomas.loc.gov	18.54
8	Stanford Center for Internet and Society	cyberlaw.stanford.edu	18.77
9	Consumer Project on Technology	cptech.org	21.31
10	Berkman Center for Internet and Society	cyber.law.harvard.edu	22.69

78 appeared in a majority of crawls (at least 7). Table 8.1 lists the top ten, sorted by average rank across all thirteen crawls.[9]

Much like the single Issue Crawler map shown in Figure 8.1, this list tells the reader that the SFU coalition is much more at the center of the online debate. Even those with a basic familiarity with the debate will know that the EFF, the Free Software Foundation, Public Knowledge, and Lawrence Lessig are well-established SFU advocates. The Center for Democracy and Technology, as well as the Stanford and Harvard cyber-law centers, are well-respected venues that host a great deal of discussion on copyright; these groups are not as clearly pro-SFU in principle, but in practice they each have a distinct pro-SFU leaning. The Consumer Project on Technology, which has now evolved into Knowledge Ecology International, is another regular voice on the pro-SFU side of many copyright debates.

Creative Commons itself has little to say on copyright legislation, but serves rather as a hub for content creators who wish to make a binding

---

[9] The most-linked site for a given crawl is ranked number 1; for any months a site is not included, I assigned it the rank of 99. I used ranks to compare websites rather than incoming hyperlinks because the total number of total links returned in a given crawl varies wildly.

public commitment to enforce fewer (if any) of their rights as copyright holders. This is highly consistent with the SFU message of freer circulation of information, and many sites in the SFU coalition license their content under CC licenses. The default HTML code for using a CC license on one's website embeds a CC logo that links back to the CC website. Thanks to this widespread use of CC licenses among the online participants, that site was often the top site in results. The only site in the top ten that does not at least lean toward the SFU message is the Library of Congress's Thomas database of federal legislation, an important reference for legislative debates on any issue at the national level.

Ordering sites based on their mean or median rank comes with one important disadvantage: the loss of a tremendous amount of data. The difference between first and second is unlikely to be the same as the difference between the thirty-ninth and fortieth. Other scholars have found that the distribution of links between websites follows "a 'winners-take-all' power-law distribution, where a few successful sites receive the bulk of online traffic."[10] This is true for the web as a whole, as well as within communities of related websites. For a community such as the copyright debate, this means the top-ranked site is likely to have substantially more in-links than even the fifth or tenth site. It also means that, as measured by the number of incoming hyperlinks, the difference between the first- and second-place sites will likely be a good bit larger than the difference between the ninth- and tenth-ranked sites, and much more substantial than the difference between thirty-ninth and fortieth.

The Issue Crawler results exhibited a clear winner-take-all distribution.[11] This was true despite the relatively small number of sites; unlike

---

[10] Hindman, Tsioutsiouliklis, and Johnson, "'Googlearchy,'" 1.

[11] My statistical training is not adequate to assess whether the distribution is, strictly speaking, a power law. For a somewhat accessible (at least, accessible to those with an intermediate understanding of statistics) primer on the distinction, see "Twitter Followers Do Not Obey a Power Law, or Paul Krugman Is Wrong," *Luminoso Blog*, February 9, 2012, http://blog.lumino.so/2012/02/09/twitter-followers-do-not-obey-a-power-law-or-paul-krugman-is-wrong/. For those who want a more detailed understanding (and have a decidedly more advanced understanding of statistics), see Aaron Clauset, Cosma Rohilla Shalizi, and M. E. J. Newman, "Power-Law Distributions in Empirical Data," *SIAM Review*, 51, No. 4, 661–703. In addition to the Luminoso post, Shalizi also wrote a somewhat more accessible introduction to and summary of the paper on his personal blog: "So You Think You Have a Power Law – Well Isn't That Special?," *Three-Toed Sloth*, June 15, 2007, http://masi.cscs.lsa.umich.edu/~crshalizi/weblog/491.html.

It is not particularly important whether these data are best summarized by a power law per se versus some other exponential function. As Shalizi recommends, "Ask yourself whether you really care. Maybe you don't. A lot of the time, we think, all that's

the broader web, it is realistic to imagine ninety sites linking to each other with relative equity, but this is decidedly not what happened. In a typical crawl, the top site had about 1.4 times as many incoming links as the second-ranked site, 2.7 times more links than the fifth-ranked site, and 3.0 times more than the tenth-ranked site. More dramatically, the typical crawl saw the top-ranked site draw about fifty times more incoming links than the fortieth-ranked site. In contrast, the fortieth-ranked site typically had about 4.2 times more links than the eightieth-ranked site. In other words, the typical difference between first place and fortieth was over ten times greater than the typical difference between fortieth and eightieth. This is to say nothing of the hundreds of sites that link into this population but were not included because they had not won enough incoming links.

Faced with such a steep drop-off in link share from the top few sites, I needed to use a measure that accounts for the disproportionate authority given to the top sites. For this, I developed a measure based on each site's typical share of incoming hyperlinks – an "adjusted share of incoming links" or, more simply, "link share."[12] This is calculated so that the sum of all seventy-eight included sites is 1.0. Table 8.2 provides a list of the top ten websites by link share; combined, they earned a remarkable 62.6 percent of the incoming link traffic. The top site, CC, had an inlink share of 14.3 percent.

---

genuine[ly] important is that *the tail is heavy*, and it doesn't really matter whether it decays linearly in the log of the variable (power law) or quadratically (log-normal) or something else."

What matters in this study is the rapid drop-off between the top sites and the rest, and I believe I can document that fairly quickly, with rather elementary statistical methods. On the website supplementing the book, readers can find a log-normal plot of websites' shares of hyperlinks. Figure 8.2 is the normal-normal plot, which means I have not transformed either of the variables. To create the log-normal plot, I just took the natural log of each site's share of hyperlinks. The resulting plot is still not a straight line, but it is much, much closer.

Against Shalizi's express recommendations – but in a fair representation of my statistical knowledge and the limited importance of using exactly the right tool for this particular analysis – I have run a linear regression of the log-normal plot. (Shalizi claims this crude technique "makes the baby Gauss cry.") This produces an R Square of .970, versus .458 for the normal-normal plot – meaning that the log-normal plot is, at a minimum, a great deal more linear than the normal-normal plot. While this crude technique does not sort out which type of function best summarizes the data, it does provide a quantified illustration of the rapid decay from the top-ranked sites to the rest. Which is a really complicated way of saying that the online copyright debate is, as expected, yet another winner-take-all distribution of online attention.

[12] For more, see Herman, "The Battle over Digital Rights Management," 262–4.

TABLE 8.2. *Link share among top ten sites*

Rank	Organization/Person	URL	Adjusted mean inlink share
1	Creative Commons	creativecommons.org	.143
2	Electronic Frontier Foundation	eff.org	.094
3	Free Software Foundation	fsf.org	.088
4	Lawrence Lessig (Stanford Law School) et al.	lessig.org	.058
5	Center for Democracy & Technology	cdt.org	.056
6	Computer Professionals for Social Responsibility (Peru chapter)	cpsr-peru.org	.044
7	Consumer Project on Technology	cptech.org	.041
8	Future of Music Coalition	futureofmusic.org	.036
9	Media Access Project	mediaaccess.org	.034
10	The Fair Use Network	fairusenetwork.org	.031
	Total Link Share for Top Ten Sites:		.626

As with the top ten list based on average rank, the top sites based on link share are also a list of SFU advocates and sympathizers; in the latter case, this is true of all ten sites. This is even more remarkable in the context of the highly unequal distribution; not only do all of the top ten sites support the SFU agenda, they have nearly twice as many incoming links as the other sixty-eight sites combined. Although these numbers illustrate the winner-take-all distribution rather well, a graphical representation may do even better. Figure 8.2 does just this. It shows the rank and link share of every site, ordered from the most-linked site on the left to the least-linked site on the right.

The top few sites each enjoy a vast share of all link traffic, whereas roughly the bottom three-fourths of the sites each have a very small share of the links. The top-ranked site, to the far left, is the only site above 14 percent. The second- and third-ranked sites hover near 9 percent, part of a very steep drop among the top ten. The slope becomes far less steep as one approaches the bottom of the rankings; after roughly the twentieth-ranked site, the difference between any two adjoining sites becomes negligible. Those familiar with Chris Anderson's description of the "long tail" will recognize this shape.[13] Although most of these sites

[13] Anderson, "The Long Tail."

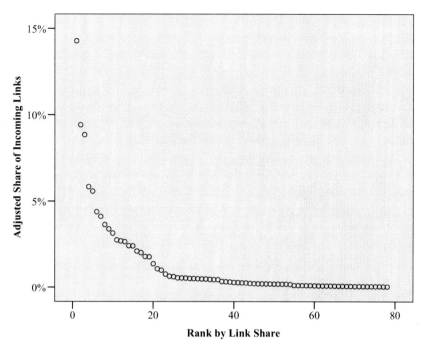

FIGURE 8.2. Link Share of Included Sites, Most-Linked to Least-Linked

are in the long tail, relative to the whole web, within the community, the short head is dominated by core SFU advocates.

Combined with what most readers already know about the copyright debate, the Issue Crawler results start to highlight the dominant position of the SFU coalition online. No matter how one creates the list of top sites – by average rank or by link share – the sites in the top ten are almost all SFU advocates. Further, none of the well-known SC advocates are well-linked in the online space. Whether sorted by mean rank or link share, the Recording Industry Association of America (RIAA), the Motion Picture Association of America (MPAA), and Business Software Alliance (BSA) each did no better than thirty-ninth. These groups carry outsized power in Washington, D.C., but online, they are not especially well-respected members of the community. A key reason is that they do not participate to a meaningful degree in the online debate. Each of these groups' sites had few if any links to SFU sites; instead, they used their links to direct visitors to legal places to buy copyrighted works. Still, these SC industry groups each received several links from SFU sites, reflecting SFU groups' attempts to rebut the SC groups' claims. For example, in 2002, the MPAA had posted an FAQ page on the broadcast flag; in response, the EFF posted a line-by-line response.[14] In my searches for documents relevant to the debates over the broadcast flag and proposed DMCA reforms, I found not one site from any of these three SC groups linking to an SFU group, showing that they feel no need to use their websites to rebut SFU groups' arguments. By not engaging with SFU groups, these SC industry groups became marginal players in this online space. Likewise, SFU groups were certainly only motivated to link to and discuss SC industry groups' sites because of the offline lobbying prowess of the latter.

Although the results based on the Issue Crawler alone are instructive, they are not by themselves definitive as to the contents of the online debate. To make well-founded conclusions about content, I needed to gather a meaningful set of these sites' relevant content, then analyze it using the same rubric I had used for the offline debate.

FINDING AND ANALYZING RELEVANT ONLINE DOCUMENTS

The Issue Crawler helped identify the community of websites that are debating copyright online; looking at the results across thirteen monthly crawls, seventy-eight different sites appeared in a majority of results. I chose to focus on these sites, but I still needed a way to identify specific documents relevant to the copyright debate. By "document," I mean an item posted online with a unique web address, such as a blog post, position paper, or mission statement. Most of the results were in HTML format; those in other mostly text formats, such as Word or PDF files, were also included, but video and audio (both fairly rare) were excluded. Every included site discusses several other issues, so it was necessary to find more narrowly tailored content to analyze. I also wanted to have a sense of which sites had produced a high volume of relevant content and which were less vocal. To accomplish these goals, I turned to site-specific Google searches. For instance, to identify the documents the MPAA had placed online that relate to the broadcast flag debate, I searched for:

copyright (audio OR video OR radio OR broadcast) flag site:mpaa.org

I chose these search terms after carefully testing several options, a process I detail elsewhere.[15] The result of this search showed that the MPAA

---

[14] Electronic Frontier Foundation, "Consensus at Lawyerpoint: MPAA FAQ on Broadcast Flag," July 4, 2002, http://bpdg.blogs.eff.org/archives/000148.html (dead link, visited April 1, 2008; on file with author).

[15] Herman, "The Battle over Digital Rights Management," 128–41. To summarize: I tested search terms based on searches of the U.S. House website, trying to find search terms

had hosted seven documents related to the broadcast flag debate. Using a similar process, I decided on this search term for the DMCA reform debate:

> copyright (dmca OR "digital millennium copyright act") (boucher OR encrypt! OR 1201 OR hack! OR DRM OR "digital rights management") site:mpaa.org

This search also retrieved seven relevant documents. I repeated this process for each of the seventy-eight sites that appeared in a majority of the monthly web crawls. I did all of the searches within a few days, saving each relevant page in a stable form such as PDF or HTML; this nearly eliminates concerns about the web changing during the much longer process of analyzing each document.

In total, I found 915 relevant documents – 321 resulting from searches for the broadcast flag debate, and 594 for searches concerning the DMCA reform debate. These were mostly in the core years for these two policy debates. Out of 771 documents with an identifiable year, most were in 2003 (142 documents, or 18 percent), 2004 (66, 9 percent), 2005 (131, 17 percent), or 2006 (172, 22 percent). Because documents were retrieved in 2007, there were 82 documents (11 percent) from that year, as well as 178 from previous years (23 percent). Among other things, this shows that the sites in the DRM debate had a remarkably long memory, including fourteen documents from the 1990s. It also supports the view that the period from 2003 to 2006 was the core time for these debates, with a ramping-up year (eighty-two documents, 11 percent of the total) in 2002 and a ramping-down year in 2007.

Thanks to the much larger number of sites advancing the SFU agenda, as well as each coalition's rational internet strategy, I expected the online

that maximized relevant results and pushed them to the front of the search results. Using these test searches, I estimated that these well-targeted searches of individual websites would rarely have more than about forty relevant documents, and relevant results would almost always be within roughly the first 100 results. Even if these estimates do not apply to other studies – for instance, surely there are sites that have hundreds of relevant documents on a given issue – they may provide a good guideline for how deeply to probe an individual website before giving up, as well as how many documents to include from them before allowing them to take over the dataset.

For searches with a limited number of results, the last page of results generally includes the statement, "In order to show you the most relevant results, we have omitted some entries very similar to the [number] already displayed. If you like, you can repeat the search with the omitted results included." For the broadcast flag searches, I also chose the search option to "repeat the search with the omitted results included." This was not necessary for DMCA reform searches.

debate to have a decidedly pro-SFU bias. Even relative to this expectation, however, I was surprised by the strength of the bias. Of 915
documents, 733 took a strongly pro-SFU stance (80 percent). Another
ninety-four were neutral or mixed (10 percent). Just eighty-eight documents (10 percent) took a strongly pro-SC stance. Pro-SFU documents
outnumbered pro-SC documents online by eight to one. This heavy
pro-SFU bias was also consistent with the types of actors who went
online to make their cases.[16] Of the 915 online documents, scholars
were responsible for 319 (35 percent) and NGOs for 283 (31 percent),
nearly two out of every three online documents. Other SFU-leaning coalitions such as libraries (seventy-eight documents, 9 percent) and online
news sources such as *Wired* (fifty-three documents, 6 percent) also made
notable contributions. The SFU-leaning parts of the technology sector
accounted for most of that sector's eighty-five documents (9 percent
of all relevant web documents), with seventy-one of those documents
(84 percent) taking the pro-SFU position and just eight (9 percent)
taking the pro-SC position. The media sector (thirty-two documents,
3.5 percent of the total) and appointed government officials (also thirty-
two documents, 3.5 percent) were the only other reasonably vocal groups
online, and they were practically silent compared to their proportions in
congressional hearings.

The pro-SC coalition obviously has adequate resources so that, if they
thought it was important, they surely could have posted far more than
eighty-eight relevant webpages or other documents. Instead, they made no

---

[16] Of 915 web documents, ninety-one actually included the voices of more than one sector.
To simplify this analysis, for each of these documents, I categorized it as belonging to the
sector of the site hosting it. This particularly affected news sites (28 of 53 documents),
with the bulk of the rest of the multisector documents found on scholarly websites (31
of that sector's 319 documents) and NGO websites (21 of 283 documents). Counting
sectors using the same method as for newspapers would provide a slightly different
picture of the online visibility of a few sectors – in particular, the media sector (55
appearances vs. 32 documents for which they can claim primary or sole responsibility),
appointed officials (46 vs. 32), and elected officials (29 vs. 11) would seem to have
been marginally more meaningful participants in the online debate. Yet this would be
giving them too much credit for online advocacy; these extra appearances are more the
result of true online communicators seeking them out and putting the results online.
Stories appearing on the *Wired* website alone account for eleven of the twenty-three
extra appearances by the media industry, five of fourteen for appointed officials, and
twelve of eighteen for elected officials. Returning reporters' phone calls and appearing
on multisector panels that later wind up online (another major source of multisector
documents) are decidedly not efforts at online communication. Thus, here and in the
next chapter, I use exclusive sector coding to tabulate online sectors and to compare
these results to offline sector representation.

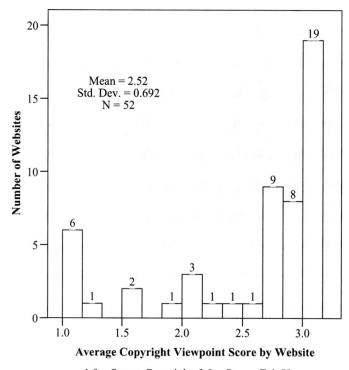

FIGURE 8.3. Mean Copyright Viewpoint Score by Website

serious investment in discussing these policy debates online. This becomes especially clear when comparing the numbers of pro-SC and pro-SFU sites, as well as the number of documents per site in each coalition.

BLOGGING FOR FAIR USE: MORE SITES, MORE TO SAY

Combined with the results from the Issue Crawler, the content analysis helps paint a fairly complete picture of the debate online. Of the seventy-eight included sites, fifty-two had at least one relevant document and were thus analyzed further. I then calculated the mean copyright viewpoint score for each of these websites. Figure 8.3 shows the heavily pro-SFU skew of the population of websites. On this copyright viewpoint scale, where 1.0 represents the SC position and 3.0 the SFU position, the average (mean) site had documents with a mean score of 2.52, and the median site had a mean score of 2.87. Of the fifty-two sites with at least some relevant documents, just nine sites (17 percent) were clearly in the pro-SC camp – which I define as having a mean viewpoint score between 1.00 and 1.60. Another five sites (10 percent) had a more neutral average score of between 1.60 and 2.40. This leaves the bulk, thirty-eight sites (73 percent), with a clearly pro-SFU score above 2.40.[17] The most common mean score is actually 3.00, with nineteen of the fifty-two websites (37 percent) earning this score by posting only pro-SFU messages.

As noted, the top sites are nearly all strong SFU supporters, and the much larger base of SFU allies surely contributes to this outcome; since sites are more likely to win links from allies, the larger base of supportive sites in the SFU coalition makes it fairly likely that the top sites will generally support the SFU agenda.

Although the larger number of SFU allies contributed to the core SFU groups' prestigious online positions, this is not the entire explanation. An additional important factor was the SFU groups' much more vocal online participation. In particular, a few sites had disproportionately high volumes of content specific to the DRM debates. Figure 8.4 shows this distribution. Of the seventy-eight sites that were searched, twenty-six sites (33 percent) had zero relevant documents, eleven sites (14 percent) had one document apiece, and another nineteen sites (24 percent) had between two and ten documents. In contrast, a handful of sites were brimming with a very detailed discussion of these issues. The EFF had more relevant documents (eighty-one documents, 9 percent of the total) than the fifty least-prolific sites combined (seventy-two documents). Four more sites (wired.com, berkeley.edu, freedom-to-tinker.com, and ala.org) had more than fifty.[18] The ten sites that produced the most relevant information combined for 543 documents, or 59 percent of the total. Of these ten sites, nine were very solidly pro-SFU, with mean viewpoint scores of 2.78 or higher. Only the U.S. Copyright Office, which hosts documents authored by members of both coalitions created during their proceedings to determine exemptions to the anticircumvention provision of the DMCA,[19] had both a high number of documents (forty-four)

---

[17] I sorted sites by mean copyright viewpoint score. On a scale of from 1 to 3, where 1 = SC and 3 = SFU, nine sites had a mean score below 1.6, five sites had mean scores between 1.6 and 2.4, and 38 sites had mean scores over 2.4.

[18] House.gov is not included in this list of websites with the most relevant documents. For the purpose of focusing on the online debate *as differentiated from* the congressional debate, I only included documents that were not online reproductions of hearing documents. This left six relevant documents, and these had a mean valence of 2.472.

[19] Information on how to participate, as well as every document and oral statement submitted as part of this record, is available at http://copyright.gov/1201. For an analysis

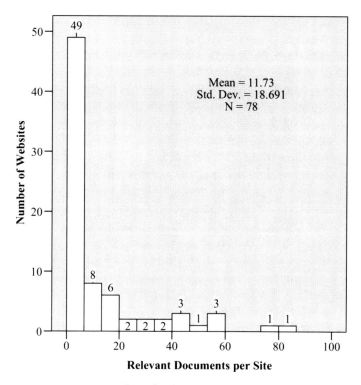

FIGURE 8.4. Number of Relevant Documents per Website

and a relatively neutral viewpoint score (2.08). No SC-allied site had more than twenty documents, and only two pro-SC sites had ten documents: the MPAA (fourteen documents, mean viewpoint score of 1.00) and the now-defunct Progress and Freedom Foundation (eighteen documents, mean viewpoint score of 1.57). The RIAA had just one relevant document; it did not even post the documents it had already prepared for congressional hearings. Not only did the RIAA not think it worthwhile to participate actively in the online debate, it did not even make the time to add materials that illustrated its arguments in the offline debate.

The SFU coalition not only has a lot more online allies than the SC coalition, it also has a great deal more to say about specific legislation than any of the SC-affiliated sites.

of the legislative history of these proceedings and the first two rounds, see Herman and Gandy, "Catch 1201."

A BRIEF UPDATE

On the time scale of social scientific research, results that are several years old are considered part of the process. Relative to the speed with which the web evolves, however, results from 2006–07 are already rather old. This is not to say that they are invalid or even that we cannot be confident that the results still hold. A similar full-scale study carried out today would find very similar results on the important variables of coalition allegiance and sector participation. The SFU coalition still has far more allied sites posting far more relevant documents online every year. SFU sites still get far more incoming links from other regular participants in the online copyright debate. The SFU message is still carried primarily by NGOs and scholarly groups. Still, some notable changes have taken place in the online space, and these are worth recounting.

To better identify and analyze the changes in the online copyright debate, I ran another crawl in early January 2012.[20] The map for this crawl, as well as for crawls from 2010, 2011, and later in 2012, is available on the website. Fortuitously, Yochai Benkler used a similar tool developed at Berkman – Media Cloud[21] – to conduct very similar, detailed analysis of the network of sites in the copyright debate at several points in time from the fall of 2010 until after the SOPA strike.[22] In a twenty-minute conference presentation – the video of which is online – Benkler walks the audience through select details and important changes of each iteration of the map. His findings are remarkably similar to those here, although he also offers valuable details and many additional insights along the way. The point of this update is not to repeat what Benkler says in his talk, but to provide an in-depth update of the findings of this chapter. For the sake of this update, I focus on the January 2012 crawl as illustrative of the continued validity of the study's core findings, although I also highlight important changes.

---

[20] I made two methodological changes taking advantage of the Crawler's newly improved computing power and my access to more complete information. First, instead of two rounds of crawling (iterations), I used three. The Crawler is now more capacious, so three rounds of crawling is now a more appropriate, proportional use of resources. Second, for starting sites ("seeds"), instead of the original five sites, I used the seventy-eight sites included in the majority of crawls from 2006 to 2007.

[21] Hal Roberts, "Overview of Media Cloud Methods," *Media Cloud*, May 1, 2011, http://blogs.law.harvard.edu/mediacloud2/2011/05/01/overview-of-media-cloud-methods/.

[22] Benkler, "The Networked Public Sphere."

Newly at the Top: Social Networks and Government Sites

Among the more obvious developments, the years since 2006 have seen the stratospheric rise of social networks as an important means of connecting with other people and finding information on the web. In particular, Facebook and Twitter have taken a central role in many people's online lives. As such, these sites have also become very important hubs for disseminating information from niche communities into broader public awareness. The crawler results reflect this change. As of January 2012, CC had been bumped down to the second most-linked site in the network, with the new top site being Twitter. Other social sites Facebook (number 4 in the rankings), YouTube (12), and AddThis.com (a site for feeding content into social media networks, 14) also had prominent positions. Even Flickr (24) and MySpace (31) showed up in the results. These sites can all be used to send a variety of messages, but among users of social media, the SFU coalition has far more allies than does the SC coalition. This would be demonstrated rather clearly during the January 2012 SOPA strike, the day of which saw millions of tweets about SOPA,[23] but it was already fairly clear even to the casual observer well before this point. As with the web generally, the SFU coalition has done more to communicate its message via social media, and these networks have made it even easier for sympathizers to spread these messages to an even broader population.

The new rankings show continued high marks for other SFU allies with previously top sites. Beside CC, this also includes EFF (now 8), Harvard's Berkman Center (11), and Public Knowledge (18). These numbers are notably lower than in 2006–07, but this is not at all because they have been displaced by SC-allied sites. In addition to the rapid rise of social sites, the other substantial change is a sharp increase in the share of links going to official government sites. Several are at least potentially relevant, including the Copyright Office (5), the White House (6), the Library of Congress (15) and its legislative database (thomas.loc.gov, 13), and the U.S. Patent and Trademark Office (16). Although the inclusion of these government sites makes sense, many other government sites that are clearly not relevant are also high in the rankings. These include USA.gov (3), recovery.gov (9), regulations.gov (10), and grants.gov (17).

---

[23] Fight for the Future, "The January 18 Blackout/Strike in Numbers," *SOPA Strike,* http://sopastrike.com/numbers (last visited June 12, 2012).

To understand this, the norm among government sites is that they link to other government sites almost exclusively – even though many nonstate sites link to government sites. This gives state-sponsored sites a substantial built-in comparative advantage in measures of hyperlinks to sites; the links from many sectors point to government sites, but government sites do not often link back out to sites in other sectors. In the earlier crawls, these government sites had not included enough links to other government sites to leverage this norm and dominate the rankings like this. Thus, this collective rise in the rankings is a hint that government agencies have become more web-savvy in the intervening years – both in finding relevant content on other agencies' websites and linking to it, and in linking to other government sites more generally. In any case, sites like USA.gov are obviously not relevant to the debate over copyright. Since nearly all of the government sites in the newer results were also featured in earlier results – just with lower rankings – this shift does not mean a change in the overall balance of SFU- versus SC-leaning sites or much difference in those coalitions' relative prestige in the online rankings.

Strong Fair Use Still Strong Online

Combined with social media sites (now four of the top twenty), government sites (ten of the top twenty) have clogged the top of the 2012 rankings, making the results less obvious than before but not substantially different. By setting government sites aside, however, it becomes clear that the SFU coalition still has a rather dominant position atop the rankings. The top twenty sites from the January 2012 crawl, excluding government sites, are listed in Table 8.3.

In addition to the top-twenty SFU allies already identified, other notable SFU allies with respectable rankings include the Free Software Foundation (fsf.org, 25), American Library Association (ala.org, 27), the Chilling Effects Clearinghouse (chillingeffects.org, 29), and the Center for Democracy and Technology (cdt.org, 30). The Electronic Privacy Information Center (epic.org, 23) is also ranked highly, and although its interest in copyright is modest, it is aligned with the SFU coalition on the right to circumvent DRM in the interest of protecting user privacy; thanks to its presence at the congressional hearings on the DMCA, users have the right to circumvent DRM to protect their personal information.[24] Likewise, worries about SOPA have pushed the Wikimedia Foundation (Wikipedia,

---

[24] 17 U.S.C §1201(i).

TABLE 8.3. *Top twenty web Crawl results, excluding government sites, January 2012*

Rank excl. gov't	Overall rank	Organization/Company	URL
1	1	Twitter	twitter.com
2	2	Creative Commons	creativecommons.org
3	4	Facebook	facebook.com
4	7	Adobe	get.adobe.com
5	8	Electronic Frontier Foundation	eff.org
6	11	Berkman Center	cyber.law.harvard.edu
7	12	YouTube	youtube.com
8	14	AddThis	addthis.com
9	18	Public Knowledge	publicknowledge.org
10	20	New York Times	nytimes.com
11	23	Electronic Privacy Information Ctr.	epic.org
12	24	Flickr	flickr.com
13	25	Free Software Foundation	fsf.org
14	26	Vimeo	vimeo.com
15	27	Amer. Library Assn.	ala.org
16	28	Wikimedia Foundation	wikipedia.org
17	29	Chilling Effects Clearinghouse	chillingeffects.org
18	30	Ctr. for Democracy and Technology	cdt.org
19	31	MySpace	myspace.com
20	32	Internet Corp. for Assigned Names and Numbers	icann.org

28) squarely into the SFU camp, at least on internet liability issues. Although the Internet Corporation for Assigned Names and Numbers (ICANN, 32) seems not to have taken an official position on issues such as SOPA, a search of its website shows many anti-SOPA positions taken by affiliated individuals. Vint Cerf, former chair of ICANN, took a very public stance against SOPA.[25] Thus, of the top twenty nongovernmental sites, eight are core SFU allies and three are loose allies. Six more are

[25] Declan McCullagh, "Vint Cerf: SOPA Means 'Unprecedented Censorship' of the Web," *CNet News*, December 15, 2011, http://news.cnet.com/8301-31921-3-57344028-281 /vint-cerf-sopa-means-unprecedented-censorship-of-the-web/.

social media sites that are undoubtedly being used far more heavily for sending SFU-leaning messages than SC-leaning messages. The remaining three sites are either sources of information (*New York Times*, 20; video sharing site Vimeo,[26] 26) or software that helps users view online content (Adobe, 7). In short, the SFU coalition is still in the driver's seat of the online copyright debate, dominating the top of the rankings of nongovernment sites.

Likewise, the SC coalition still has few allied sites, and these have comparatively low rankings. The RIAA (riaa.com, 41) and MPAA (mpaa.org, 69) still have middling rankings. Notable losses in SC allies ranked in crawler results were the Business Software Alliance (bsa.org) and the Progress and Freedom Foundation (pff.org). The BSA did not earn enough links to be included, and the PFF "closed its doors on October 1, 2010."[27] In a notable change, the MPAA started participating more heavily in the online debate, posting dozens of relevant results.[28] This change in strategy was far more reactive than proactive; it only became serious about this once the SOPA debate was garnering lots of online publicity. The RIAA's site had just twelve relevant results; this may be twelve times

---

[26] One might quibble with listing YouTube as a social networking site but listing Vimeo as merely a platform for distributing content. Founded in 2004, Vimeo has much of the social networking capability of YouTube, and many people only use YouTube to watch or upload videos, so it would be defensible to include or exclude both sites from any list of social networking sites. This distinction is based on my informal understanding of the sites' respective usage patterns; it seems fairly clear that, relative to Vimeo, YouTube is used far more for social networking and has much more of a history of social networking. This probably explains why one particularly well-known summary of the literature on social networking sites – boyd and Ellison, "Social Network Sites" – excluded Vimeo and included YouTube in its list of major social networking sites.

[27] Progress and Freedom Foundation, http://pff.org (last visited May 11, 2012).

[28] A Google search of their site for "Stop Online Piracy Act" (in quotes) claimed to have found about 290 results that were not obviously duplicates. Google search ("stop online piracy act" site:mpaa.org) (May 11, 2012), at http://google.com.

   Initial results listed "about 520 results," but if one tried to see all of them, Google cut the list to 290, excluding the others as "very similar." Even this shorter list, however, still included multiple versions of relevant documents – so much so that the actual number of relevant documents is surely several dozen, not several hundred. Without manually examining each document, a precise number is hard to give, but adding in the title of one blog post ("Engineer Looks at the Facts on Anti-Piracy Bills") to the search supposedly retrieves twenty-three nonredundant results. Another search with the basic terms plus an obscure phrase from another post ("This follows a letter Abrams wrote in May that affirmed") retrieved six supposedly nonredundant results. Thus, the figure of 290 is many times too large.

   All other sites included here were searched using the same search terms, and reported figures are for searches excluding highly similar results – that is, the number Google thinks one might possibly want.

as many results as it had during the mid-decade period (just one), but, considering the tidal wave of attention to the issue, this hardly shows a public relations strategy making full use of the web. The only remaining vocal SC ally online was, somewhat surprisingly, the American Society of Composers, Authors, and Publishers (ascap.com, 78). In earlier results, the site had not even been included. It barely made it into the 2012 results – the list included seventy-eight sites, with ASCAP dead last – but it was probably included in the newer results because it was fairly vocal around SOPA, both before and after the blackout. The same Google search of ASCAP's site found roughly twenty-seven relevant results, a notable contribution. The only other potentially allied sites were three content industry sites: the Copyright Clearance Center (copyright.com, 51), CD Baby (cdbaby.com, 76), and Magnatune (magnatune.com, 84). None of these had any SOPA-relevant results.

Although the MPAA ramped up its contribution and the RIAA and ASCAP increased their contributions, these paled in comparison to the total results on SFU coalition sites. A quick search of four SFU-allied sites – the EFF, the Berkman Center, Public Knowledge, and the American Library Association – showed that each had several dozen relevant documents. Although a full analysis of all relevant documents on each site is beyond the scope of this brief update, it is already fairly clear that a large majority of the relevant web documents discussing SOPA have a very strong pro-SFU bias. Even the site of the music industry's most important magazine, *Billboard* (billboard.com, 62), covered the SOPA strike sympathetically. In two relevant articles, one began with, "You know the protest against the Stop Online Piracy Act (SOPA) has gone mainstream when the headline of the Drudge Report on Wednesday morning reads, 'Hands Off the Internet!'"[29] The other cited nearly a dozen solo artists and musical groups who had come out against SOPA.[30] Neither cited a single pro-SOPA source or identified any arguments in favor of SOPA. Thus, a full analysis of sites debating SOPA would put even *Billboard* in

---

[29] Glenn Peoples, "Protest Against Anti-Piracy Bills Goes Viral," *Billboard*, January 18, 2012, at http://www.billboard.com/news/sopa-blackout-sites-include-google-wikipedia-1005907752.story/news/sopa-blackout-sites-include-google-wikipedia-1005907752.story.

[30] Emmanuelle Saliba and Devon Maloney, "Trent Reznor, Amanda Palmer, OK Go Among Artists Cosigning Anti-SOPA/PIPA Open Letter," *Billboard*, January 19, 2012, http://www.billboard.com/news/trent-reznor-amanda-palmer-ok-go-among-artists-1005926152.story/news/trent-reznor-amanda-palmer-ok-go-among-artists-1005926152.story.

the category of SFU allies. When the music industry's most visible magazine is on the other side of the issue, it is clear that the SC coalition was
too late to the online debate and had lost the online public relations war,
hands down.

Technology News Sites: A Fair Use Echo Chamber

One less obvious but still notable development is the inclusion of
more technology news sites, broadly conceived. In the earlier crawls,
Wired.com was the only such site. *Wired* is not in the newer results, but
Slashdot.org (43), BoingBoing.net (46), Reddit.com (53), and Digg.com
(78) are. Each of these is an aggregator blog, meaning that they post links
to countless things online that are of interest to the authors and their
readers. Each thus produces a torrent of posts – many per day – largely
covering technology, science, and media. By linking to many interesting
things that appeal to a certain segment of readers, aggregators can become
very popular as a starting point for exploring the web – *Reddit* describes
itself as "The Front Page of the Internet" – and each of these four sites
has attracted very large audiences.[31] Yet this same role means that they
are not core members of any one community, including the copyright
debate, and thus each gets a middling relative share of links from core
copyright-debating sites.

Although not reflected by relatively high numbers of incoming links
from this specific community of sites, aggregator sites play a valuable role
in the copyright debate, and each of the four included here has a strong
pro-SFU bias. During most of the period from 2003 to 2006, *BoingBoing*
co-editor Cory Doctorow was also working for the EFF, and he continues
to be an active advocate for less copyright law. Thanks primarily to
Doctorow's posts, *BoingBoing* has always been a source of regular posts
about issues in digital copyright, which almost always include links either
to SFU allies' web pages or to news coverage of the issue that buttresses the
SFU position. The other three technology news sites in the newer results –
Slashdot, *Reddit*, and *Digg* – are user-generated. Users submit stories that
are then voted on by other users, and if other users collectively decide
the submission is of high enough quality, it gets placed on the front page,
bringing the story to the attention of the sites' hundreds of thousands of

---

[31] As of June 11, 2012, Alexa.com identifies *Reddit* as the 53rd-ranked site in the United
States, with still-lofty rankings for *Digg* (218), *BoingBoing* (1,333), and *Slashdot*
(1,172).

users. Placement on one of these sites also guarantees countless other links on other websites, further amplifying a story's visibility. This function is at the core of what Yochai Benkler calls the "attention backbone" of the internet.[32] To elaborate on his metaphor (and convert it into a simile), low-visibility sites are like the small nerve endings at one's extremities, whereas medium-visibility sites are like the larger nerves that can carry messages to one's spinal column – the core sites that can command the attention of a large share of the highly connected internet public. Benkler illustrates how this works with one specific example of how copyright information got carried from the internet's extremities to its backbone when Julian Sanchez at the CATO Institute wrote a blog post that took umbrage at the Chamber of Commerce's wildly inflated estimates of the annual cost of piracy:

> What Julian Sanchez at the CATO Institute does is, he goes to the [Government Accountability Office] critique of these numbers, and he goes through a very long post that links to the underlying stories – explains exactly who came up with them, what the sources are, links to other sources. Nobody links to CATO. CATO remains very small here. However, there is an attention backbone. Essentially what happens is *Techdirt* looks at CATO, and *Reddit* looks at *Techdirt* around this story. So essentially what we see is an attention backbone, where a particularly careful takedown of a core meme underlying the campaign gets stated in a place that continues to stay small and unlinked, but then gets transmitted over an attention backbone to the larger sites. So that's how things rise – even if they're not at the top to begin with – in a community of interest.[33]

There is no guarantee that any given story will follow this trajectory, but it is a great illustration of how it can and does work for untold thousands of stories that probably would not have garnered much publicity in the pre-internet era. In this case, a site that does not have great visibility, the CATO Institute (Alexa rank in the United States as of June 11, 2012: 14,835), runs a story with some solid original reporting. This gets picked up by a site that has respectably high but not backbone-level visibility, *Techdirt* (4,174). This then gets on *Reddit*, one of the most-visible sites in the world (53).

For many years, the internet has done very well at bringing unexpected waves of attention to countless topics first publicized on sites with low to medium visibility. In the metaphor of going viral, Patient Zero does not need to be preestablished as a thought leader. I saw this happen firsthand

---

[32] Benkler, "The Networked Public Sphere."   [33] Ibid.

when my recording of Ted Stevens' 2006 speech on network neutrality blew up, leading to the "Series of Tubes" meme. As an intern at Public Knowledge in the summer of 2006, I was recording the internet stream of the debate over a proposed network neutrality amendment to Stevens' massive telecommunications bill.[34] Those of us listening were shocked by the combination of Stevens' belligerence, incoherence, and lack of a sound understanding of even the basics of internet engineering. I thus made an MP3 of Stevens' speech and gave it to Alex Curtis, so that he could share the MP3 in a blog post for the Public Knowledge website (53,477).[35] Some of the sillier quotes were transcribed and posted on a *Wired* blog, *27B Stroke 6*,[36] which has since become *Threat Level*. (*Wired* is ranked number 385, although the *Threat Level* blog is somewhat less visible and was much less widely read then.) The story then appeared on thousands of sites, including *Digg*, *Metafilter*, *Slashdot*, and *BoingBoing*, and was even covered in the *New York Times*.[37] It was surreal, to say the least, to see an audio recording I had made become the news around which *The Daily Show* built an entire opening segment.[38] More than being surreal, though, it is a perfect example of how the internet's attention nervous system functions. This tendency has only grown more marked with the rise of social media.

As for the four attention backbone sites that are in the new results, each covers a range of topics with a different character, although each includes a very heavy dose of news on technology, science, and media. Each is also constantly posting links to SFU-aligned messages. In this way, rather than being core members of the copyright-debating community, they carry that community's message to the broader, technology-savvy public. When a core SFU group like the EFF, Public Knowledge, or the Berkman Center has a particularly newsworthy item, one or more of these sites' editors (*BoingBoing*) or users (*Reddit*, *Digg*, or *Slashdot*) will post it. If a story does get posted on one of these highly visible sites, that story then gets

---

34 Communications, Consumer's Choice, and Broadband Deployment Act of 2006, S. 2686, 109th Cong. (2006).

35 Tim Schneider, "Mr. Stevens' Wild Ride Through a 'Series of Tubes'," *Public Knowledge*, July 11, 2006, http://www.publicknowledge.org/node/521.

36 Ryan Singel, "Your Own Personal Internet," *Threat Level* (formerly *27 B Stroke 6*), June 30, 2006, http://www.wired.com/threatlevel/2006/06/your_own_person/.

37 Ken Belson, "Senator's Slip of the Tongue Keeps On Truckin' Over the Web," *New York Times*, July 17, 2006, http://www.nytimes.com/2006/07/17/business/media/17stevens.html.

38 "Headlines – Internet," *The Daily Show with Jon Stewart*, July 12, 2006, http://www.thedailyshow.com/watch/wed-july-12-2006/headlines – internet.

repeated by countless social network users and on thousands of other sites.

Even these results substantially understate the degree to which the technology news sector as a whole is biased toward the SFU coalition, as well as the degree to which these sites help carry that message to the broader public. *Wired*, *Reddit*, *Digg*, *Slashdot*, and *BoingBoing* are just a very small subset of a much larger group of well-trafficked technology sites that help circulate pro-SFU messages on a very reliable basis. Like them, literally every major online source of technology news that I know of is, to at least some degree, a reliable ally for carrying the SFU message beyond the SFU coalition's web cluster. Examples here (in addition to *Wired*) could be nearly endless, although a very short list might include sites like *ArsTechnica*, *CNet*, *Engadget*, *GigaOm*, *Gizmodo*, *PCWorld*, *TechCrunch*, and *Techdirt*. In particular, Mike Masnick has used the site he founded, *Techdirt*, as the outlet for the most detailed reporting available anywhere on SOPA, the Protect IP Act (PIPA), and related policy developments. Since the site has respectable online visibility, Masnick's incredibly strong pro-SFU message ricochets around the web. Although *Techdirt* is the most dedicated SFU ally, the site only stands out by degree of overt bias and frequency of coverage. I am aware of no important technology news website that does not post copyright-specific content with at least modest frequency, and each seems to have at least a modest leaning toward the SFU coalition. Especially in aggregate, these sites reach untold millions of readers every month – not only technology industry professionals, but millions of power users who come to learn about the industry and new technologies. Thus, although the audience share for core SFU allies' sites may range from solid to rather modest,[39] these groups' sites are not the primary means by which the public more broadly will hear their messages. Rather, it is through the online echo chamber of sympathetic sites, including especially the technology press – up to and including "The Front Page of the Internet."

CONCLUSION: A WEB OF STRONG FAIR USE MESSAGES

It would be hard to overstate the degree to which the copyright debate online is biased toward the SFU position. In the mid-2000s, pro-SFU sites

---

[39] According to Alexa.com, as of June 11, 2012, Creative Commons' site is ranked 2,717 in the United States. The ALA is 8,816, and the EFF is 10,000. Public Knowledge is much less-visible (53,477), although of these four sites, it is the most-read by policymakers and professional policy advocates in Washington, D.C.

outnumbered pro-SC sites by more than four to one, and this ratio seems to have risen in the years since. Further, there is much more pro-SFU information online than there is pro-SC information. An internet user can learn an incredible amount about the politics of copyright, and this is due mostly to SFU-leaning websites. These groups and individuals believe so strongly in online communication that they have effectively built an online echo chamber in which it becomes common sense that copyright should be scaled back rather than expanded. Within this mindset, those in the SFU coalition are simply right, and the fact that copyright is always getting stronger is a lamentable result of the SC coalition's Washington D.C., lobbying clout – clout that is so disproportionate that, in Lawrence Lessig's analysis, it corrupts policymakers' pursuit of the public good.[40]

Through 2006, it would have been fair to ask whether all this online advocacy was worth the effort. It is difficult to explain DRM regulations to average voters, let alone get them motivated to call their elected officials to demand DMCA reform. Yet other mechanisms are also likely at play that did make the effort worthwhile, even if only within this policy subsystem. First, although the SC coalition has long had plenty of resources for offline communication, the benefit of informal online coordination between SFU advocates is a real time and cost saver. It has been easier for these groups to align their messages, as well as to recruit other elites (such as scholars and policymakers) to their coalition. These online messages are read within the policy subsystem, and the information and arguments have shaped the debate in other media. One member of the SFU coalition reports that, on several occasions, policymakers and even opponents have responded to SFU allies' blog posts – doing so in conversations, while speaking at events, and even in formal confines such as congressional hearings. Even without thousands of calls from constituents to Congress, the SFU coalition's very heavy online advocacy has helped level the playing field in its favor.

Further, even though the copyright debate's moment of major public involvement had not yet come, this online work was part of a broader campaign of laying the groundwork for that day. By 2006, these sites' messages were already well-known and generally adopted by the opinion leaders at the forefront of the new digital information ecosystem. The technology press in general, and the online technology press in particular, cover new technologies with a decidedly "populist, pro-consumer viewpoint," which, in the case of DRM, means a decidedly "anti-DRM

[40] Lessig, *Republic, Lost*, 55–60.

tilt."[41] This is true of copyright coverage in general. Regular, sympathetic coverage from virtually the entire technology press has surely played a major role in the broader public dissemination of the SFU ideology, laying the groundwork for what became the SOPA strike. Thus, even the very stark results reported in this chapter probably understate the degree to which the internet is an echo chamber for the SFU message – which is remarkable, considering the findings.

Another mechanism is also probably at play, although this study does not use methods that can measure it: percolation into the broader population via two-step media effects, or the indirect effect of press coverage via communication through social networks.[42] Even though most people do not have a deep and abiding passion for new computing technologies, most know somebody who does; thus, most people probably know somebody who has been exposed to the highly pro-SFU coverage of copyright in the technology press. Because of their comparatively high level of knowledge on technology issues, these people can become opinion leaders on this topic among their family and friends, thus influencing many people's views on policy; after all, opinion leadership is often topically specific.[43] Thus, a user who wants to know about how copyright relates to internet communication – or one who seeks technical help with DRM issues, such as guidance in how to rip his or her DVDs to a hard drive – may turn to a friend or family member who is more knowledgeable, and that person will likely have gained a great deal of his or her information from highly pro-SFU online sources. Although this study does not measure the effect, it is surely another part of the process by which pro-SFU beliefs have percolated into mass consciousness to the degree that millions were ready to act during the SOPA blackout. In any case, this is an area meriting further study, both as regards the development of opinions on this specific policy, and in terms of how opinion leadership on policy issues works in the internet age more generally.[44]

---

[41] Bill Rosenblatt, "Roots of the Online Upheaval of SOPA/PIPA," *Copyright and Technology*, May 13, 2012, http://copyrightandtechnology.com/2012/05/13/roots-of-the-online-upheaval-of-sopapipa/.

[42] Katz and Lazarsfeld, *Personal Influence*; Katz, "The Two-Step Flow of Communication."

[43] Nisbet and Kotcher, "A Two-Step Flow," 333.

[44] On this count, the work by Nisbet and Kotcher, ibid., is a valuable study on the role of opinion leadership in the internet age, at least on the topic of climate change. As they note, however, "With few exceptions, the concept of opinion leadership has been investigated in the context of traditional forms of community and social interaction." Ibid., 339. Especially in the area of social networks, this is surely a model that is worth revisiting and adapting.

To the extent that the internet writ large has an opinion on copyright, that opinion is decidedly pro-SFU. This fits with the ethos of the people who have built the internet – the engineers, designers, content creators, venture capitalists, and so on – who did so with the explicit goal of sharing information. Additionally, the vast majority of the public has an interest in less copyright rather than more. Copyright is designed to limit access to works, giving copyright holders the opportunity to increase their market prices. Thus, the opposite of what copyright promises – more access at lower prices – is generally in the consuming public's interest, at least in terms of access to works that have already been produced. As long as copyright protections are effective enough that desired works will continue to be produced, it will be hard to mobilize the public to support further increases in copyright. Although the content industries are never satisfied with the level of protection, voluminous output by these very industries illustrates that, at least for the time being, copyright continues to be strong enough to incentivize the continued production of at least some categories of popular media works.[45] Further, the public loves new

---

[45] The media industries in general are actually far better off than their lobbyists would imply. For a detailed analysis, see See Michael Masnick and Michael Ho, *The Sky is Rising*.

  The movie industry in particular continues to see impressive growth in revenues. See Nate Anderson, "Piracy Once Again Fails to Get in Way of Record Box Office," *ArsTechnica*, February 23, 2011, http://arstechnica.com/tech-policy/2011/02/piracy-once-again-fails-to-get-in-way-of-record-box-office/. PricewaterhouseCoopers even predicts that the industry will see continued revenue growth through 2015. See Ben Child, "US film industry set for four years of strong growth, predicts report," *The Guardian*, June 14, 2011, http://www.guardian.co.uk/film/2011/jun/14/us-film-industry-growth-forecast.

  The music industry has seen real declines in revenue, though William Patry contends this is due primarily to the unbundling of music from albums into a market of singles. "The decline in CD sales and the increase in digital singles sales have nothing to do with piracy, and [are] instead a reflection of record companies' inability to continue their long-standing practice of forcing consumers to buy CDs and therefore albums." *How to Fix Copyright*, 68. Even then, paid album downloads grew 24 percent from 2010 to 2011, and global sales of downloads – albums and singles – increased 17 percent, leading music industry leaders to be optimistic for the future growth of total revenues. Mike Collett-White, "Music Sales Fall Again in 2011, but Optimism Grows," *Reuters*, January 23, 2012, http://www.reuters.com/article/2012/01/23/music-idUSL6E8CL0A720120123.

  Even though the movie and music industries constantly bemoan the difficulty of competing with free pirated content, they seem to be doing pretty well with it, even though their recent legislative agenda has mostly not been advanced. Even book publishers have overseen a slow but steady growth in revenue and traditional titles – not to mention the exponential growth in self-published titles. See Masnick and Ho, *The Sky is Rising*, 16–22.

technology, and this is doubly true of the technology industry professionals and power users who drive most of the online coverage of copyright. To the extent that copyright impinges access to new technologies or even specific features, this is a recipe for upsetting those who most desire these tools – and the online technology press is happy to blame the law and the content industries who pushed for it. In this way, the most technologically knowledgeable in society are the most likely to have the strongest opinions on copyright, and their opinions are the most likely to be pro-SFU. Although the resounding success of the SOPA blackout was a surprise for everybody, those who were surprised that strong opinions exist on the issue are clearly not following the online debate over the issue. If they were, they would have seen an endless deluge of messages supporting less copyright – and, in sharp contrast, a small trickle calling for more.

If there is one major media sector about which one should be genuinely concerned, it is probably newspapers, and that industry's decline in revenues is in almost no part due to copyright infringement.

9

Comparing the Online and Offline Digital
Rights Management Debates

Combined, the previous three chapters show that the online copyright debate is very different from the offline debate. The web is the strong fair use (SFU) coalition's home, although it has fought to achieve parity in Congress and even a minor advantage in newspaper coverage. In this chapter, I make a more formal, head-to-head comparison. Because each medium's documents were coded using the same rules, this comparison is fairly straightforward; the hard part was getting a set of online documents that represented the online digital rights management (DRM) debate. To ensure a truly fair comparison, I took the extra step of eliminating web documents outside the 2003 to 2006 time frame. This still leaves 511 online documents to analyze, more than plenty for a robust comparison with offline documents. In terms of both copyright viewpoint and the sectors represented, the differences are stark.

COMPARING COPYRIGHT VIEWPOINT

As discussed in previous chapters, newspapers and hearings during the 2003–06 period presented fairly balanced messages on DRM regulation. Of 163 congressional documents, 42 percent supported the strong copyright (SC) position, 46 percent the SFU position, and 12 percent a mixed or neutral position. Consistent with the journalistic norm of objectivity, newspapers were generally neutral (71 percent of articles), although of the seven that took a position, six (25 percent of the total) supported the SFU side. In sharp contrast, the web featured nearly all SFU documents. Of 511 web documents from 2003 to 2006, 82 percent advanced an SFU position, leaving just 10 percent neutral documents and 8 percent SC. Table 9.1 lays out the exact figures. These differences

TABLE 9.1. *Rhetorical categories by medium, 2003–06*

Rhetorical categories	Number of documents by medium			
	Congress	Newspaper	Web	Total
Strong Copyright	69	1	41	111
Neutral/Mixed	19	17	53	89
Strong Fair Use	75	6	417	498
Total	163	24	511	698

are obviously notable, representing a medium to large difference between categories.[1]

These figures already highlight the differences, but they may not adequately convey the relative shares of documents advocating each position in each medium. To better illustrate this difference, Figure 9.1 shows the relative distribution of documents taking each position across each medium. The difference between online and congressional documents is particularly stark. Among side-taking documents, a given web document is 6.2 times more likely to support SFU than is a given congressional document, a remarkably large difference.[2] For perspective on just how big this difference is, compare it to the most extreme partisan differences between two U.S. states in the 2008 presidential election.[3] A voter in Hawaii choosing between John McCain and Barack Obama was 5.2 times more likely to vote for Obama than a voter in Oklahoma – a sizable difference, to be sure, but still not as stark as the difference between congressional and online representations of the DRM debate.

Comparing media based on mean copyright viewpoint shows very similar results. Where 1.0 is the SC viewpoint and 3.0 the SFU viewpoint, congressional documents from this period averaged a nearly neutral 2.05. In contrast, newspaper articles averaged 2.28, and web documents averaged a highly slanted 2.75.[4] Newspapers and the web were substantially

---

[1] $\chi^2 = 189$, $df = 4$. (Two cells have an expected count less than 5, with a minimum expected count of 3.06.) The difference between media represents a medium to large effect size; Cramer's $V = .368$.

[2] This converts to a d-like measure of effect size of 1.01, which is an exceptionally large difference.

[3] This excludes Washington, D.C., in which 93 percent of voters chose Obama. Versus Oklahoma voters, a given D.C. voter was 25.8 times more likely to choose Obama. (Little wonder that so many Republicans oppose statehood for the District.)

[4] Standard deviations were as follows: For hearings, 0.95; newspapers, 0.52; the web, 0.59.

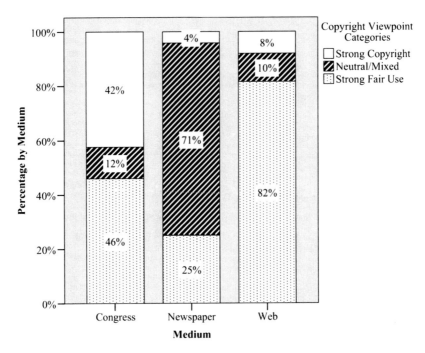

FIGURE 9.1. Copyright Viewpoint by Medium, 2003–06

different, each presenting a profound difference in how these two media represent the debate.[5] The substantial differences in average viewpoint scores affirms that web and congressional documents were even farther apart.[6] These differences highlight that members of Congress are hearing a profoundly different version of the debate than the one most accessible to the American public.

This sharp difference is certainly consistent with the major gap between public opinion and apparent congressional attitudes on copyright. Even in the period from 2003 to 2006, members of Congress were still more likely to take an SC stance during congressional hearings (21 of 50 hearing documents) than an SFU stance (fourteen documents). In contrast, the public has generally not been crying out for greater enforcement of copyright law. Since proposed copyright bills have not historically been highly visible, there is little survey data on exactly this question, but a

[5] Assuming equal variances ($F = .02$, $p = .883$), t equals 3.84 ($df = 533$, $p < .011$), a difference with an effect size ($d = .85$) that is large to very large.

[6] Noting the unequal variances ($F = 202.1$, $p < .001$), $t = 8.95$ ($df = 203.1$, $p < .001$), again with an unusually large effect size ($d = .89$).

survey run by Joe Karaganis of American Assembly at Columbia University is illustrative.[7] The survey reports that 70 percent of adults have copied music or video files – whether by copying files from discs in person or getting files online. Just 51 percent support warnings or fines for internet infringers – and even among the group that supports fines, 75 percent support a fine amount of $100 or less. Although this is not survey on DRM policy per se, it certainly suggests that most people take copyright infringement to be a relatively minor problem – and certainly not the kind of problem that would justify substantial restrictions on digital technology. This contrasts sharply with repeated congressional depictions of an epidemic of infringement and the need to do something to strengthen copyright. Even among those who supported DMCA reform or opposed one or both of the broadcast flag proposals, members often began their pro-SFU speech or written submission with a statement that infringement is indeed a major problem that must be addressed. In a 2004 hearing considering one proposed DMCA reform, Representative Joe Barton – one of the reform bill's co-sponsors – made a statement clearly in support of the bill. Even during this speech, however, Barton expressed the concern that digital technology "has posed many piracy problems for the content providers and for those of you that represent those interests I have very, very deep sympathy for the problems that you're facing against commercial piracy."[8] Indeed, this was typical across all of these hearings; even members who opposed the expansion of copyright or supported its contraction quite often expressed those beliefs in a broader context of concern about piracy. I cannot remember a single member of Congress expressing anything to the effect that infringement is not a major problem, and even staunchly SFU witnesses and submitters rarely questioned this premise.

Meanwhile, on the internet, values such as technological innovation, consumer rights, and freedom of expression were taken for granted, and the discussion was much more centered around the question of whether and how copyright law could be shaped to meet these goals. An Electronic Frontier Foundation (EFF) post about the broadcast flag was typical in expressing these priorities. In it, Senior EFF Intellectual Property Attorney Fred von Lohmann argued:

---

[7] Joe Karaganis, "Copyright Infringement and Enforcement in the US," November 2011, http://americanassembly.org/publication/infringement-and-enforcement-us.

[8] *The Digital Media Consumers' Rights Act Of 2003: Hearing on H.R. 107 Before The House Subcommittee On Commerce, Trade, And Consumer Protection*, 108th Cong. 4 (2004) (statement by Hon. Rep. Joe Barton).

Despite what Hollywood will tell you, this has nothing to do with Internet piracy. Instead, the broadcast flag is Hollywood's effort to control the future of TV technologies. If they get this technology mandate, Hollywood will be in a position to force innovators to negotiate before building new digital television products. Remember, these are the same companies that, in 1976, sued to impound the VCR and, today, will tell you that skipping commercials is stealing.[9]

Likewise, in a 2003 article in the *Communications of the ACM* that was posted on a site at Berkeley, legal scholar Pamela Samuelson argued, "The main purpose of DRM is not to prevent copyright infringement but to change consumer expectations about what they are entitled to do with digital content."[10] Online, there was no common acceptance of the need for and value of strong copyright enforcement. Online, the voices calling for strong copyright were the punch line instead of the assumed leaders. Unsurprisingly, the sectors that give rise to these voices were far less well-represented on the web than in hearings and newspapers.

COMPARING SECTOR REPRESENTATION

Not only do the three media differ sharply in copyright viewpoint, they also vary greatly in the types of actors that are represented. Among SC groups – especially the media sector and government officials – each sector's share of appearances in Congress and newspaper articles is larger than its online share. Likewise, among groups that support SFU – especially nongovernmental organizations (NGOs) and scholars – their online share is generally higher than their shares in either newspapers or hearings. As discussed in Chapter 7, newspaper articles were coded nonexclusively, as articles tended to represent more than one sector; this was especially true in 2003–06, when the twenty-four relevant articles had quotes from fifty-six sectors, or 2.33 sectors per article. In contrast, documents from hearings and the web were almost all best described as representing a particular sector, so in those chapters, I treated them accordingly. Nonetheless, to have an apples-to-apples comparison with newspapers, I included each sector represented in each document in hearings (175 sectors across 163 documents, or 1.07 per) and the web

---

[9] EFFector, Vol. 16, No. 5, February 20, 2003, http://w2.eff.org/effector/HTML/effect16
.05.html (dead link; on file with author).
[10] Samuelson, "DRM {and, or, vs.} the Law," 41.

TABLE 9.2. *Sector representation, proportional share, by medium*

| Sector | Proportional share by medium | | | |
	Congress	Newspapers	Web	Avg./Medium
Media	21.7	25.0	5.5	17.4
Congresspersons	28.6	8.9	2.4	13.3
NGOs	11.5	17.9	31.1	20.1
Scholars	5.1	7.2	34.6	15.6
Appointed Officials	5.0	10.7	3.4	6.4
Librarians	7.4	1.8	7.7	5.7
Technology	19.5	19.6	11.6	16.9
All others	1.2	8.9	3.6	4.6

(595 sectors, 511 documents, 1.16 per). I then normalized each sector's representation by medium, producing an adjusted share by medium. For instance, the media industry appears in 14 of 24 relevant newspaper articles, or 58 percent of articles. Divided by 2.33 sectors per article, the media sector's adjusted share in newspapers is 25 percent. These measures of adjusted share allow for useful comparisons across media. Table 9.2 lays out each sector's adjusted share for each medium.

As with the differences in views represented, undeniably large differences exist across media in representation of various sectors. The media sector had about a quarter of the share of congressional documents and newspaper articles, but just 6 percent of web documents. Likewise, congresspersons had nearly a third of congressional documents and some newspaper appearances, but they had just 2 percent of web documents. In contrast, the sectors at the core of the SFU coalition had much higher shares online than offline. Nongovernmental organizations had respectable shares in Congress (12 percent) and newspapers (18 percent), but these shares are small compared to their 31 percent share online. Scholars had small shares of hearing documents (5 percent) and appearances in newspaper articles (7 percent) but more than one-third of web documents. The differences between online and offline shares for these four sectors goes a long way toward explaining the differences in copyright viewpoint across these media.

The remaining sectors of interest were appointed government officials, librarians, and the technology sector. For appointed officials, the overall participation was expected to be low and was low in hearings and online, although newspaper appearances (six articles, 11 percent share) were a bit more common than expected. Librarians' participation was also low across all media: 7 percent of hearings, 2 percent in newspapers (i.e., one article), and 7 percent online. The American Library Association (ALA) is an important voice in the online debate; it hosted fifty-three relevant documents (thirty-four within the 2003–06 time frame – 6.7 percent of the 511 web documents in that window), all supporting SFU. Yet unlike NGOs and scholarly groups, with many sites each, the ALA was librarians' only voice online representing their views on DRM policy that was included as a regularly participating, authoritative site in the online debate.

The technology sector was one of just two (along with NGOs) that had double-digit shares across hearings (20 percent), newspapers (20 percent), and the web (12 percent). This intermedia visibility resulted mostly from the sector's diversity; it includes corporations that sell hardware, software, and services (e.g., IBM, Microsoft, Google) and their trade associations. These industry voices appeared in hearings and articles with a frequency rivaling the content industries. Technology industry groups also said a bit more online than did media groups. The Consumer Electronics Association posted twenty-eight relevant documents, and the Home Recording Rights Coalition added ten, which is notably more than the combined online presence of the Motion Picture Association of American (MPAA, six documents clearly dated from 2003 to 2006) and Recording Industry Association of America (RIAA, just one document).

The technology sector also includes many noncorporate actors that contributed to the online debate exclusively. For instance, the nonprofit Free Software Foundation provides the legal and logistical backbone for free software projects such as GNU/Linux; its site (ten documents) was the third most-linked site in the community. Computing Professionals for Social Responsibility (six documents) represents individuals in the technology sector. Finally, the Association for Computing Machinery (ACM) was a very vocal group, with forty-four documents. The group functions like an academic association, and many college faculty are members, but so are many private sector computer professionals; thus, it also counts as a technology group. With the exception of the ACM (mean score 2.85, nearly 100 percent SFU), all of these sites' documents took the SFU position. Although corporations were responsible for nearly all of the technology sector's participation in newspapers and hearings, these not-for-profit groups did most of the online advocacy. The only SC-allied technology trade group in the set, the Business Software Alliance, posted zero relevant documents online (of any date), but its representatives appeared in hearings and articles. Thus, the sector had high visibility across all three media, but not because many individual actors appeared in each medium. Rather, corporate voices sought more official channels, and nonprofit and scholarly voices took to the web.

CONCLUSION

The copyright debate looked very different depending on the medium through which it was viewed. Policymakers got a fairly two-sided view of the matter. Newspaper coverage leaned modestly toward fair use but had little coverage, thus preventing the SFU coalition from reaching the critical mass of public attention that might help unseat the current policy order. In contrast, the web debate was very one-sided. In particular, NGOs and scholars argued loudly against DRM regulation, providing the authoritative heart of the coalition's web cluster.

The one-sidedness of the web debate resulted from sharp differences in motivation and culture. Congresspersons are hardly the most tech-savvy group, and they already have access to each other and the news media, so they rarely discuss copyright online. Likewise, media companies have historically fared very well in Congress and can easily command press attention, so they have little more to gain online. Even were they to enter the online debate, they would only increase the visibility and legitimacy of the SFU coalition. It was apparently much more in their interests to continue to portray their opposition as morally suspect and beneath a serious response. Of course, this all changed in 2012, but based on the reasonable expectation that copyright would continue to be a low-visibility issue, their strategy was rationally the right move based on the information they had at the time. This is not to say that the SC coalition had no incentive to seek broader publicity. Quite the contrary, it was and remains engaged in a fight against online file sharing. However, this legal and public relations war mostly assumes current statutory law rather than challenging it. Thus, content industry advocates treated the issue as a matter of enforcement and public education – rather than a subject of legitimate public debate.

In contrast, the SFU coalition has incentives and culture that pushed and continue to push it toward maximum online engagement. Coalition members want to maximize sympathetic publicity and the visibility of specific policy debates; they know that, historically, conducting the policy debate primarily in Washington, D.C., leaves little chance to reduce the reach of copyright law or even to slow its advance. As a resource-poor coalition, SFU advocates have the most to benefit by decreasing communication costs. They are also attempting to use the web to reach ordinary citizens, and with little SC presence online, SFU voices have been able to carve out the medium as their own. Further, the SFU message appeals to the technologically savvy. The technology professionals, scholars, NGOs, librarians, and computer enthusiasts who drive the calls to limit copyright may be the most technologically adept multisector political coalition in history. For reasons of both political motivation and culture, then, it is natural for the SFU coalition to have a much heavier online presence. Given all of this, it is unsurprising that the web had a decidedly pro-SFU slant, especially relative to hearings and newspapers. Yet even relative to these expectations, the size of the differences between these media was truly remarkable. The web looked so utterly central to the SFU coalition strategy, and so anathema to the SC strategy, that the stage was clearly set for an internet-fueled avalanche of SFU activism.

Part III

The Present and Future of Digital Copyright and Digital Advocacy

10

The Digital Rights Management Debate Withers, 2007–2010

For nearly twenty years, digital rights management (DRM) policy was the single most visible issue in the debate over copyright in the digital age. By 2007, however, the issue was starting to garner less attention. Efforts to pass the broadcast flag stalled, and the strong copyright (SC) coalition quickly cut its losses and abandoned the issue. Digital Millennium Copyright Act (DMCA) critics continued to express their desire for change in the law, but they also came to accept that they would not be able to push through a major reform. The period from 2007 to 2010 was also marked by the growing acknowledgment by all parties that DRM has failed to slow – let alone stop – widespread infringement in any significant way. It is remarkable that the effort to reform the DMCA would wind down amidst the common acceptance that DRM, even as backed by law, has failed to prevent widespread infringement; yet that is exactly what happened.

DIGITAL RIGHTS MANAGEMENT FALLS SHORT

Digital rights management has never really provided a long-term solution to the problem of online infringement, but acceptance of this shortcoming has spread slowly. By the end of the new millennium's first decade, it became increasingly clear, even to those in the SC coalition and those outside the copyright debate entirely, that both DRM and the DMCA's anticircumvention provisions have fallen far short of their lofty expectations. The content industries should have seen this even before the bill was passed, but rather than admitting that they were wrong in the first place, they have subtly shifted their strategy away from DRM.

Digital Rights Management Fails, in Theory and Practice

Those who understand the technology behind DRM have long argued that DRM does not and will not present much of an obstacle to the dedicated infringer. Although far from the first, Cory Doctorow's 2004 speech to the Microsoft Research Group makes the definitive case.[1] In it, Doctorow explains why virtually all encryption-based DRM schemes are inherently vulnerable to circumvention. One need not understand Doctorow's argument – which requires a brief review of cryptography theory – to see that he is right. "DRM systems are usually broken in minutes, sometimes days. Rarely, months."[2] As new DRM schemes have been rolled out on purchased media – from DVDs to Blu-Ray discs, from iTunes Store downloads to the installation discs on professional-quality software packages – technologically sophisticated users have reverse-engineered each and posted their results online for all to see. Using these techniques, far less knowledgeable users can then help create and distribute unauthorized copies from their own originals. Thus, from *The Dark Knight* to Adobe Photoshop, users who want a copy but do not want to pay have many versions to choose from online.

Infringing copies and circumvention devices are widely available online, and this is not only because the technology to circulate them is now easy to use. It is also because the law against circumvention has the same enforcement problems as the law against infringement. Tracking down users who circumvent DRM and who traffic in software that facilitates circumvention – which are easily distributed on the internet – is no easier than tracking down users who traffic in infringing copies. Even if it were easier, only one willful infringer needs to break the DRM on one original copy of a given work; once just one unencrypted copy goes online, other users can rapidly reproduce thousands of pristine copies. In practice, massive online infringement only requires that a few dedicated infringers have the requisite circumvention software. If anything, it is easier to download decrypted copies than it is to decrypt one's own purchased copies. A normal computer on a typical cable modem connection can download infringing copies of dozens of films in the background with just a bit of user interaction upfront, whereas buying and making decrypted copies of the same number of films would require much more time and effort – to say nothing of the price difference.

---

[1] Cory Doctorow, "Microsoft DRM Talk," *Craphound*, June 17, 2004, http://craphound .com/msftdrm.txt.

[2] Ibid., § 1.

The unlikelihood of success with DRM should have been clear to the SC advocates who pushed for the DMCA. After all, they could have learned from the software industry's struggle with the same issues as far back as the 1970s and 1980s – long before the mass adoption of the internet. Despite what were then called "copy controls" on software (the term "digital rights management" had not yet been coined), it was relatively easy for would-be infringers to get access to either infringing copies of software or the software to circumvent copy controls.[3] Software developers found that their paying customers were inconvenienced by the copy controls – resulting in a substantial diversion of technical support resources – but commercial pirates were still stamping out thousands of copies for sale at bargain-basement prices. Circumvention techniques were also widely disseminated among those computer enthusiasts who had fewer scruples about trading in infringing files. Thus, the paying customers for these programs were inconvenienced at least as much as – and generally more than – those who were determined not to be paying customers. Software developers thus generally decided against complicated copy control systems for all but the most expensive software packages.[4] The norm became and remains the simple step of serial

[3] In an unfinished study I conducted in 2006 while an intern at Public Knowledge, I conducted phone or e-mail interviews with five experts in software or digital copyright who had been around long enough to have seen this firsthand. They were Jonathan Band, Daniel Bricklin, Daniel T. Brooks, John S. Erickson, and Edward W. Felten. They explained that, although software companies had hoped to use copy controls to stop the easy copying of software, most companies gave it up for most programs because it was ineffective at stopping dedicated infringers but quite good at inconveniencing paying customers. Although these results have not been the subject of any published studies with which I am familiar, the results are well-known among those who have been in the software industry for that long. If these experts were willing to answer my phone calls when I was a lowly intern, they surely would have been even more willing to share their thoughts with major content industry figures or government officials.

The key pre-DMCA case law on circumvention technology, *Vault Corp. v. Quaid Software*, did not add legal backing for these technology-based efforts to stop infringement. The court held that the circumvention software in question was legal because it also had substantial noninfringing purposes. Ibid., 262 (citing *Sony v. Universal*). Yet my brief research into the subject found little concern about *Quaid* in the software trade press at the time or in the memories of software engineers whose careers preceded the decision – let alone a shift in business strategy. Rather, most in the software industry had already abandoned all but the most basic copy controls before *Quaid*.

[4] One technique that has proven relatively resistant to circumvention is the use of hardware-based authentication devices, or "dongles." These devices are plugged into an available port on the user's computer – such as a printer port or, in more recent years, a USB port – and, without them, the software does not work. The encryption "key" is inside the dongle, and the dongle can usually be replaced only by paying a substantial amount to the software vendor – often only by purchasing another full copy

number authentication, although today some software requires one-time online authentication as well.

As with the software industry's trial with restrictive copy controls, the verdict on the strategy of protecting music and movies with DRM, and backing those DRM restrictions with regulations, is not encouraging for the copyright holders who pushed this strategy. As with the economic impact of infringement, the economic impact of legally backed DRM is difficult if not impossible to measure accurately; in the case of the latter, I am aware of no studies that even try. Yet if the goal has been to leave consumers with no choice but to obtain works through licensed channels, the available evidence suggests that this strategy has failed. Granted, there have undoubtedly been consumers who have purchased copies of works such as motion pictures because it was a bit harder to commit infringement – or because they were unable to make backup copies before their original media were lost or damaged.[5] On the other hand, restrictive DRM systems have also led several users who were previously uninterested in infringement to pursue illicit copies.[6] I am aware of no estimates of the size of each group – the number chased into purchases by DRM and the number chased into infringement out of frustration – but I suspect the economic impact of each is fairly insubstantial relative to the size of the affected industries. More troubling has been the negative impacts on noninfringing uses such as teaching, criticism and commentary, accessibility for the visually impaired, and the development of interoperable technologies.[7]

Especially as compared to the marginal user whose behavior has been affected by DRM, a huge number of users have continued to traffic in works that were released in DRM-restricted formats. Even a cursory search on any of the popular peer-to-peer trading sites lets one find nearly

---

of the software program. This leaves most would-be hackers reluctant to risk what could be a costly mistake in order to disassemble and reverse-engineer a copy control dongle. Even with the proliferation of USB ports, though, few applications use dongles today. For example, Apple's professional audio engineering software, Logic Pro, used a USB dongle through Version 7, but the company dropped the dongle in 2007 with Version 8.

[5] See Doctorow, "Microsoft DRM Talk," § 2.

[6] Ibid. See also Akester, "Technological Accommodation of Conflicts," 48–9, 58–9. In surveys with both ordinary college students and the visually disabled, Akester found people are more likely to go online and search for infringing copies because they cannot get the functionality they want from DRM-encumbered licensed copies.

[7] Electronic Frontier Foundation, "Unintended Consequences: Twelve Years under the DMCA," March 3, 2010, https://www.eff.org/wp/unintended-consequences-under-dmca.

any popular, recent movie. For any film that has already been released for the home video market, nearly all of the online copies are ripped from DVD and Blu-Ray discs – two formats that both use DRM. Most popular movies are even available in both formats, so users can even choose either high-definition quality or a smaller file size. This continued availability and popularity of infringing files, pulled directly from DRM-restricted media, is a powerful illustration of the failure of the DRM-and-DMCA strategy for curbing infringement. Even Bruce Lehman, the person most singularly responsible for the DMCA's anticircumvention provisions, has admitted that the strategy failed. At a conference in Canada, in 2007, he said, "our Clinton administration policies didn't work out very well," and "our attempts at copyright control have not been successful."[8]

The Failure of Digital Rights Management Was, Surprisingly, Surprising

The SC advocates who pushed for the DMCA's anticircumvention provisions knew that DRM technology is vulnerable to circumvention. Such knowledge was not only not a secret, the vulnerability of DRM was a core part of their argument. After all, if the technology by itself were adequate to prevent unauthorized access or use, no regulatory backstop would be necessary; knowing that circumvention is possible was part of the SC coalition's reasons for seeking to ban it. What is less clear, however, is why the SC coalition thought the law would be more enforceable than traditional copyright law. Such a belief would have been understandable if it did not foresee the then-looming end to the media world almost entirely defined by black boxes in living rooms. In that era – the era that was ending as the bill was heading toward passage – the DMCA could be effective, because a circumvention device is another stand-alone black box, and it would be easier to enforce the law against these boxes. In a media world where the computer plays an increasingly central role, however, a circumvention "device" often means software, and enforcing laws against forbidden software distributed online is as difficult as enforcing laws against forbidden copies of works distributed online.

If the SC advocates participating in the DMCA debate were to be surprised by a media world in which content is increasingly delivered to computers via the internet, their rhetoric at the time did not show it. As

---

[8] Quoted in Michael Geist, "DMCA Architect Acknowledges Need for a New Approach," March 23, 2007, at http://www.michaelgeist.ca/content/view/1826/125/.

discussed in Chapter 3, SC coalition members from Bruce Lehman to Jack Valenti predicted a future of internet distribution of media works. Yet it was not hard to see that the mechanism by which the DMCA would prevent rampant online infringement would have the same enforcement problems as the copyright laws already on the books. It is hard to imagine how the anticircumvention provisions' cheerleaders could all predict with such clarity both the shift toward online distribution and the exponentially greater enforcement problems for traditional copyright, yet fail so utterly to see the enforcement problems the new law would also face because of that same distribution system. I am not trying to insinuate that their support for the bill was disingenuous. Quite the contrary; I am arguing that we should all be genuinely surprised that they dedicated so much of their political energies to pushing the World Intellectual Property Organization (WIPO) treaties and DMCA through without apparently having asked the hard questions about whether doing so was the best use of their effort. This is most reasonably characterized as an example of what William Patry calls "a faith-based approach to copyright" rather than "an evidence-based approach."[9]

Quietly Backing Away from Digital Rights Management

The music and movie industries have hit many of the same obstacles that confronted the software industry with early attempts at what were then called "copy controls." As discussed in Chapter 3, these include the inefficacy at preventing wide-scale infringement, plus creating less-useful copies that reduce the value to customers and increase the cost of technical support. The music industry, in particular, has run into problems that forced a major retreat from DRM. The most notorious example was, in 2005, when Sony BMG released dozens of different albums on CDs that, when inserted into the CD drives of Windows computers, secretly installed malicious code on users' machines.[10] The type of software is called a "rootkit," which is software designed to hide its operations from both the operating system and the user. This rootkit was designed to prevent users from copying the music to their computers. Sony BMG quickly came to regret this decision, however, as it created real headaches for consumers and for the company. "Installed without users' knowledge or

---

[9] Patry, "How to Fix Copyright," 49.
[10] "Anti-Piracy CD Problems Vex Sony," *BBC News*, December 8, 2005, http://news.bbc .co.uk/2/hi/technology/4511042.stm.

permission, the rootkit exposed computers to substantive security threats that were quickly exploited. Sony immediately recalled millions of CDs and [faced] several lawsuits" from private users and state and federal agencies.[11] This is perhaps the most extreme example of DRM gone too far – tricking users into installing anticopying software on their computers, especially when said software is specifically designed to be extremely difficult to detect or uninstall. This was bad enough, but it was even worse that the software was sloppily engineered and exposed computers to security vulnerabilities. Sony reached expensive settlements with the Federal Trade Commission, dozens of states, and the plaintiffs in a class action suit.[12]

Much less dramatic but perhaps more telling has been the music industry's decision to drop its demand for DRM on tracks sold online. Before Apple could sell the first download on the iTunes Music Store in 2003, it took tremendous efforts from Apple and Steve Jobs himself to persuade record companies to participate in online delivery to any degree, and the promise of DRM protection was a key part of the pitch. Apple's DRM system, FairPlay, was a respectable compromise between the competing parties' interests. The record industry got reassurances that iTunes-downloaded music would be reasonably if not perfectly protected from widespread infringement. Consumers got a wide selection of cheap, legitimate music that, at least within Apple's ecosystem, played reliably. Apple won big by finally brokering a compromise that the two sides could live with – not due to sales in the music store itself, but because it fueled sales of Apple's highly profitable iPods.[13]

Yet in the iTunes Store (so renamed because it now sells more than music) and in online music sales generally, the trend has been toward DRM-free distribution. By late 2007 – just over four years from the store's launch – EMI, one of the big record labels, started letting Apple sell songs from EMI's catalog in "iTunes Plus" format, which has no DRM and higher audio fidelity. These songs sold at a premium – for $1.29 per track instead of the then-standard price of $0.99 – but they were an instant hit. Part of the strategy here is obvious: Charge extra for the convenience of

[11] Herman, "Breaking and Entering," 265.
[12] Robert McMillan, "Sony Rootkit Settlement Reaches $5.75M," *PC World*, December 22, 2006, http://www.pcworld.com/article/128310/sony_rootkit_settlement_reaches_575m.html.
[13] Andrew Orlowski, "Your 99c Belong to the RIAA – Steve Jobs: Apple Makes Nothing from iTunes Store," *The Register*, November 7, 2003, http://www.theregister.co.uk/2003/11/07/your_99c_belong/.

greater portability. Yet there were important competitive reasons as well, on at least three counts. First, although the iTunes Store made a dent in infringing downloading, it remained the case that millions of users continued to download infringing copies of music via P2P networks.[14] After four years, the industry began to realize that DRM restrictions on legitimate sales inconvenience paying customers while doing nothing to stop or deter dedicated infringers. Thus, iTunes Plus was at least partially an attempt to compete with the free offerings on P2P services by offering a more desirable product. Second, it helped break a logjam over pricing. Apple had long insisted that all tracks should have one low price: $0.99. Music labels accepted this at first, but once the store had proven successful, they began to push for higher prices on the hottest new tracks. Apple had refused, creating acrimony between it and the labels. With the additional value of higher quality DRM-free versions, however, Apple clearly believed that consumers would accept the higher price, and it has been proven correct; the iTunes Store sold over 16 billion tracks by late 2011.

A third motive was the desire by record labels to have more competition among internet music stores. By 2007, the music industry was quite concerned about the market dominance of Apple's iTunes Store. Apple's FairPlay DRM system makes it difficult for other MP3 players to play restricted music, and the iPod is engineered only to work with FairPlay DRM. On both counts, the DMCA makes it illegal for Apple's competitors to help their customers to get around these restrictions, creating a competitive problem of technology lock-in.[15] This helps prevent would-be aspirants to the throne from unseating Apple's dominance of both the MP3 player market and the online music market. Record labels were quite anxious about becoming too dependent on Apple, so they were intrigued when Amazon opened a DRM-free MP3 store in 2007. At the launch, Amazon secured the participation of two of the four major labels: EMI and Universal. By early 2008, all four major labels were onboard with Amazon, even as labels continued to insist on DRM in the iTunes store – or, in EMI's case, to charge a $0.30 premium for non-DRM versions.[16]

---

[14] Simon Aughton, *Online Music Stores Dent Teens' P2P Habit*, PC Pro (April 16, 2007), at http://www.pcpro.co.uk/news/110194/online-music-stores-dent-teens-p2p-habit#ixzz1plXECF68.

[15] Sobel, "A Bite Out of Apple?," 267–8.

[16] Antone Gonsalves, "Amazon Adds Fourth Major Record Label to DRM-Free Music Store," *InformationWeek*, January 10, 2008, http://www.informationweek.com/news/205602334?subSection=All+Stories.

This despite Amazon's selling these DRM-free tracks at or below the then-standard rate of $0.99 per song. Label executives who had previously insisted that DRM was the future were suddenly jumping on board with Amazon because, in the words of Warner Music Group chair Edgar Bronfman, Jr., "'We need some online competition' for Apple's iTunes Music Store."[17] Once the labels had proven their willingness to back away from the requirement for DRM, a DRM-free future for the iTunes Store was only a matter of time. By 2009, with the consent of all of the music labels, iTunes Store began to sell DRM-free music. On this count, the online sale of music went through roughly the same evolution as copy controls on software in the 1980s: the promise of infringement prevention gave way to the reality of real financial drawbacks, and the industry moved forward with less restrictive media as the norm.

The DRM on DVDs and Blu-Ray discs has not introduced the same service headaches or vendor lock-in to the home video market, due largely to the work of massive multi-industry bodies that have spent years developing technologies and business terms that can work (in principle) for all major media companies and all major electronics manufacturers. Thanks to this advance work before the deployment of DRM systems, the movie industry still continues to sell its wares in restricted formats. Thankfully for consumers, discs usually play on their intended home theater machines – that is, as long as the disc is not damaged and the disc and player have the same region code. Problems with region coding are not trivial; fans of movie genres that are generally released exclusively for other regions often have no legal way to play their movies.[18] Region coding has even caused at least one minor diplomatic faux pas, as when President Barack Obama presented British Prime Minister Gordon Brown with a gift of 25 DVDs of classic American movies. "When Brown sat down to watch one of them, he found he couldn't – because Obama had given

---

[17] David Kravets, "Like Amazon's DRM-Free Music Downloads? Thank Apple," *Wired*, September 25, 2007, http://www.wired.com/entertainment/music/news/2007/09/drm_part_one.

Apple also may have been trying to allay European regulators who were concerned that FairPlay served as a means of locking in customers. Ed Felten, "EMI To Sell DRM-Free Music," *Freedom to Tinker*, April 3, 2007, https://freedom-to-tinker.com/blog/felten/emi-sell-drm-free-music.

[18] One well-known problem genre on this count is anime movies and TV shows, which are often released for Japanese audiences only – or for U.S. and Japanese audiences, but not for other regional audiences, such as Europeans. Chikorita157, "Editorial: US Anime Industry and Corporate Media, What is the Problem?," *Chikorita157's Anime Blog*, February 17, 2010, http://chikorita157.com/2010/02/17/editorial-us-anime-industry-and-corporate-media-what-is-the-problem/.

him Region 1 DVDs, unplayable in Brown's Region 2 DVD player."[19] In practice, however, few viewers have problems with region coding, and other than this problem, DVD and Blu-Ray DRM restrictions are fairly unproblematic for most consumers. Incidentally, these successes show that multistakeholder negotiations in the marketplace can mean widespread acceptance for a DRM standard.

Thanks to the wide availability of DMCA-violating ripping programs, not only do would-be infringers face little difficulty, consumers of licensed copies do not have to pay twice to play the movies from their authorized discs on their personal computers – or phones, video players, or tablet computers. Further, although the movie industry continues to use DRM, it has effectively admitted that it can and will do little to use the DMCA to prevent the widespread distribution of ripping software online. The U.S.-based blog LifeHacker has featured posts that teach users how to rip both DVD[20] and Blu-Ray discs,[21] with no mention of a legal threat in response. Thus, even when a DRM system works fairly seamlessly and creates no competitive advantages for any one company, the DMCA-empowered strategy of keeping circumvention devices out of the hands of consumers is apparently no longer a top priority for the movie industry. In a marked shift from the early 2000s, when content industry lawyers were using legal threats to keep even the mere presentation of DRM-circumventing techniques out of conference panels, they have not threatened litigation against such sympathetic targets – apparently settling for keeping push-button circumvention devices out of major retailers. This is not to say that their industry groups have become willing to accept reforms limiting the reach of the DMCA's anticircumvention provisions. Quite the contrary – they have continued to fight even very limited attempts at reform.

BOUCHER'S EFFORTS END

Much as Patent and Trademark Office chief Bruce Lehman was the individual most directly responsible for what became Title I of the DMCA,

[19] Carlo Longino, "Obama's Gift to British Prime Minister Rendered Useless by DRM," *Techdirt*, March 19, 2009, http://www.techdirt.com/articles/20090319/1337464182.shtml.

[20] Jason Fitzpatrick, "Five Best DVD-Ripping Tools," *LifeHacker*, January 10, 2010, http://lifehacker.com/5444274/five-best-dvd+ripping-tools.

[21] Whitson Gordon, "The Hassle-Free Guide to Ripping Your Blu-Ray Collection," *Life-Hacker*, December 29, 2011, http://lifehacker.com/5559007/the-hassle+free-guide-to-ripping-your-blu+ray-collection.

former Representative Rick Boucher was the official most clearly associated with efforts to reform it. This was part of Boucher's broader efforts to advance policies that are in line with the strong fair use (SFU) agenda – efforts that have drawn commendation from others in the SFU coalition. The *Library Journal* recognized Boucher as its 2006 "Politician of the Year,"[22] and the advocacy group Public Knowledge honored him with a 2004 IP3 award, its highest honor.

In 2007, Boucher introduced a bill with a watered-down version of his DMCA reform proposals.[23] In his 2003 and 2005 bills, Boucher's proposals would have tied DMCA violations to infringement, meaning that circumvention for noninfringing purposes and technologies capable of substantial noninfringing uses would have been protected as legal.[24] In an effort to find something more politically palatable, Boucher wrote his 2007 bill such that it merely would have created a narrow list of exemptions to the basic ban on circumvention.[25] These exemptions would make a small dent in the DMCA, by providing the right to do a short list of specific things. These include the ability to circumvent the DRM on DVDs to show embedded high-quality clips as part of in-class lectures, or to circumvent the technology that locks cell phones to specific networks.[26]

---

[22] John N. Berry III, "Politician of the Year 2006: Rick Boucher – Fighter for Access," *Library Journal*, September 15, 2006, http://www.libraryjournal.com/article/CA637-0227.html.

[23] Freedom And Innovation Revitalizing U.S. Entrepreneurship Act of 2007, H.R. 1201, 110th Cong., § 3 (2007). Section 2, the other substantive section of the bill, would have instructed the court to remit damages for secondary infringement, "except in a case in which the copyright owner sustains the burden of proving, and the court finds, that the act or acts constituting such secondary infringement were done under circumstances in which no reasonable person could have believed such conduct to be lawful." Ibid., § 2(a). That section also would have encoded the *Sony* standard as follows: "No person shall be liable for copyright infringement based on the design, manufacture, or distribution of a hardware device that is capable of substantial, commercially significant noninfringing use." Ibid., § 2(b). Based on this section of the bill alone, this author was surprised that the proposal was allowed to die on the vine without a meaningful push from the persuadable technology division.

[24] Digital Media Consumers' Rights Act of 2003, H.R. 107, 108th Cong. (2003); Digital Media Consumers' Rights Act of 2005, H.R. 1201, 109th Cong. (2005).

[25] Freedom And Innovation Revitalizing U.S. Entrepreneurship Act of 2007, H.R. 1201, 110th Cong., § 3 (2007). The other substantive section, § 2, sought to reduce the scope of secondary liability for technology companies and, in findings where reasonable people might disagree about whether there was secondary liability, to reduce damages.

[26] More specifically, it proposed making permanent the six temporary exemptions to the basic ban on circumvention granted by the Register of Copyrights and the Librarian of Congress from 2006 to 2009. U.S. Copyright Office, "Rulemaking on Exemptions from Prohibition on Circumvention of Technological Measures that Control Access to Copyrighted Works," 2006, http://www.copyright.gov/1201/2006/index.html.

This proposal would have had no impact on the vast majority of would-be noninfringing users. Even more significantly, the bill did not touch the bans on the development and marketing of circumvention devices. Despite this very limited reach, the bill died in committee with little fanfare. Boucher introduced no similar bill in the next Congress.

This end to Boucher's efforts was made even more likely by the shake-up resulting from the 2006 election. Democrats won a majority in the House for the first time since 1994, bringing an end to Joe Barton's time as Chair of the House Committee on Energy and Commerce. In his place, long-serving Representative John Dingell became Chair from early 2007 to late 2008. Before Dingell could serve to guide the committee on many issues, though, he was bounced in an intracaucus coup by which Henry A. Waxman took his place on a narrow 137-to-122 vote.[27] Waxman served in that role until the Republicans retook the House in the 2010 elections. Although Dingell does not have a clear copyright agenda, Waxman predictably leans toward the SC coalition. To a large extent, this is a natural result of his constituency, as his California district includes all or part of the Los Angeles suburbs most clearly associated with the entertainment industry: Hollywood, West Hollywood, Santa Monica, Malibu, Bel Air, and Beverly Hills. Waxman was one of just eight co-sponsors of the Audio Broadcast Flag Licensing Act of 2006.[28] Waxman is perhaps not a clear-cut member of the SC coalition, though; his participation in relevant hearings has been modest, and he was not a co-sponsor of other landmark SC-advocated bills before and after his tenure as Chair – for instance, neither the 1998 DMCA nor the Stop Online Piracy Act (SOPA).[29] Still, his allegiance is more with the SC coalition, and thus his tenure as Chair was hardly marked by the same sort of pro-SFU agenda that found a home in the committee under Barton's leadership.

EXPORTING THE DIGITAL MILLENNIUM COPYRIGHT ACT'S MISTAKES

Although this study is about the U.S. experience, it is also worth noting here that the SC coalition's continued support for anticircumvention provisions has also extended to other countries. Canada is the clearest example of several other countries that have approached or adopted

---

[27] John M. Broder, "Democrats Oust Longtime Leader of House Panel," *New York Times*, November 21, 2008, A1.

[28] H.R. 4861, Audio Broadcast Flag Licensing Act of 2006 (2006).

[29] Stop Online Piracy Act (SOPA), H.R. 3261, 112th Cong. (2011).

DMCA-like provisions, although much of the action is increasingly taking place in ad hoc multilateral negotiations.

Canada Nearing DMCA-like Regulations

At the urging of the content industry, the Canadian government has spent the last several years considering bills that would effect a major copyright overhaul. The bill under consideration at the time of this writing, C-11, would legislate much of the content industry's wish list. Among other provisions, the bill would implement DMCA-like anticircumvention provisions – banning circumvention of DRM and the tools that facilitate circumvention – albeit in a slightly less severe form than does the DMCA.[30] At the time of this writing, the bill is on the brink of passage.[31] Unfortunately for ordinary Canadians, the lessons of the U.S. experience have not stopped the content industry from pushing similar restrictions.[32]

As if the largely U.S.-based entertainment industries' advocacy were not enough of a threat to Canadian sovereignty, C-11 is being advanced under intense pressure from the U.S. administration. The U.S. Trade Representative (USTR) has placed Canada on its "Priority Watch List" for what it describes as inadequate enforcement of copyright and other intellectual property (IP) rights; this select list of the allegedly worst-of-the-worst is just twelve countries long and is mostly populated with more obvious candidates such as China and Russia.[33] It is nothing short of appalling that the U.S. government has essentially accused Canada of being an IP pariah; Canada's IP laws and enforcement are roughly as sound as those in the United States.[34] In a key part of its short explanation for this categorization, the USTR urged Canada "to make the enactment of copyright legislation that addresses the challenges of piracy over the internet, including by fully implementing the WIPO Internet Treaties, a

---

[30] Bill C-11, §41, House of Commons (2011) (Can.), http://www.parl.gc.ca/House Publications/Publication.aspx?Docid=5144516&file=4.

[31] Michael Geist, "Does Bill C-11 Create Barriers to Network PVRs and Cloud Services in Canada?," March 21, 2012, http://www.michaelgeist.ca/content/view/6385/125/.

[32] Gwen Hinze and Maira Sutton, "Canada's C-11 Bill and the Hazards of Digital Locks Provisions," *EFF Deeplinks Blog*, February 10, 2012, https://www.eff.org/deeplinks/2012/02/canadas-c-11-bill-and-hazards-digital-locks-provisions.

[33] U.S. Trade Representative, "2011 Special 301 Report," 2011, http://www.ustr.gov/webfm_send/2841 ("USTR Report").

[34] Rashmi Rangnath, "Public Knowledge Hearing Statement, 2012 Special 301 Hearing," *Public Knowledge*, February 23, 2012, http://publicknowledge.org/files/PK%20statement%202012%20Special%20301-as%20delivered.pdf.

priority for its new government."[35] It is widely understood that Canada being named as a Priority Watch List country is in large part motivated by the desire to push them into passing anticircumvention provisions; the USTR is not explicit about this, but industry lobbyists are.[36] The United States has tried with varying degrees of success to use similar methods to push other countries into passing strong anticircumvention provisions, but it is especially stark that it would declare Canada an IP scofflaw as a means to push our most essential trade partner into implementing an ineffective anticircumvention strategy.

Anti-Counterfeiting Trade Agreement

Similarly, the SC coalition has advanced several bilateral and multilateral agreements between the United States and other countries that would commit all parties to anticircumvention provisions. The SC coalition and its allies in the last two administrations are no longer content with pursuing these agreements in either of the major established international bodies for negotiating IP rights – the WIPO, a specialized United Nations (UN) agency, and the World Trade Organization's (WTO) Council on Trade-Related Aspects of Intellectual Property Rights (TRIPS). Instead, they have been pursuing ad hoc agreements outside these structures.

The most widely discussed of these ad hoc treaties is the Anti-Counterfeiting Trade Agreement (ACTA). The agreement was and remains widely criticized, as much for process as substance. One troubling point from the U.S. perspective is that it has been negotiated as an "executive agreement," meaning that it could come into effect without Senate ratification.[37] Another problem, which angered citizens in virtually all participating countries, was the utter secrecy of the process.[38] Critics fought for greater transparency, only to be rebuffed by negotiators who claimed that such secrecy was both normal and necessary. This response, however, does not stand up to scrutiny. As SFU-allied nongovernmental organization (NGO) Knowledge Ecology International (KEI) points

---

[35] USTR Report, 27.

[36] International Intellectual Property Alliance, "Letter to Mr. Stanford McCoy, Assistant U.S. Trade Representative for Intellectual Property and Innovation, Office of the U.S. Trade Representative, Docket No. USTR–2011–0021," February 10, 2012, p. 8, http://www.regulations.gov/#!documentDetail;D=USTR-2011-0021-0011.

[37] Sara Jerome, "Critics Deride ACTA Secrecy," *National Journal: Tech Daily Dose*, January 11, 2010, http://techdailydose.nationaljournal.com/2010/01/critics-deride-acta-secrecy.php.

[38] Ibid.

out, trade-related treaty negotiation processes in UN- and WTO-affiliated bodies are quite accessible to the public.[39] It has not been the norm that international IP treaties are negotiated in secret. In particular, the 1996 WIPO treaties discussed in Chapter 3 are the closest historical analog to ACTA, and they were very much negotiated in public:

> The two WIPO Internet Treaties (WCT and WPPT) were negotiated in a completely open meeting at the Geneva Convention Center. The public was allowed to attend without accreditation. The draft texts for the WCT and the WPPT were public, and the U.S. government requested comments on the draft texts, which were available, among other places, from the U.S. Copyright Office.[40]

The secrecy of the ACTA process represented "a major shift toward greater secrecy in the negotiation of international treaties on intellectual property in an obvious attempt to avoid public participation and scrutiny."[41] Given the sharp increase in public participation in the copyright debate, and the strong degree to which greater public participation helps the SFU coalition, such secrecy is a rational – if highly questionable – strategy on behalf of SC-allied state negotiators.

In addition to the critique of its process, ACTA has also been widely panned for its substance. Thankfully for critics and those who have tried to study the process, several draft proposals and revisions for ACTA were leaked before the official release of the final version. Importantly for this study, U.S. negotiators initially sought strict, DMCA-like anticircumvention provisions. By 2010, however, the objections to such strong language from the delegations of many other countries won the day, and the U.S. delegation accepted a much more modest, WIPO Copyright Treaty-like provision that signatory countries "shall provide adequate legal protection and effective legal remedies" against circumvention.[42] Despite the final treaty having been scaled back on this and other counts, however, ACTA has encountered strong public opposition in Europe,

---

[39] Knowledge Ecology International, "Attachment 1: ACTA is Secret. How Transparent Are Other Other (*sic*) Global Norm Setting Exercises?," July 21, 2009, http://www .keionline.org/misc-docs/4/attachment1_transparency_ustr.pdf.

[40] Ibid., 2.

[41] Michael Geist, "Why The Lack of ACTA Transparency Is Not Standard," November 19, 2009, http://www.michaelgeist.ca/content/view/4549/125/.

[42] Anti-Counterfeiting Trade Agreement, Ch. 2, § 5, http://www.international.gc.ca/trade-agreements-accords-commerciaux/fo/acta-acrc.aspx?lang=eng&view=d; see Michael Geist, "U.S. Caves on Anti-Circumvention Rules in ACTA," July 19, 2010, at http:// www.michaelgeist.ca/content/view/5210/125/.

leading thousands to march against the agreement in February 2012.[43] In addition to the United States, signatories include Australia, Canada, Japan, Morocco, New Zealand, Singapore, South Korea (all in October 2011), and twenty-two of the twenty-seven European Union (EU) countries (in January 2012).[44] As of this writing, however, none have ratified it through their domestic legislatures, surely due at least in part to the public outcry. The EU delegation also signed the treaty, but the European Parliament would also need to ratify it, as would the legislature in a single country, and the first EU committee to consider the treaty recommended unequivocally against ratification.[45] This is the most dramatic of several indicators that the European Parliament seems increasingly likely to vote against the treaty; if that happens, it would effectively kill ACTA.[46]

Trans-Pacific Partnership

Another proposed international agreement, the Trans-Pacific Partnership (TPP), leans even more strongly toward the SC position – so much so that SFU ally Cory Doctorow described it as "ACTA's nastier, more secret little brother."[47] Nine countries are participating in the TPP process: Australia, Brunei Darussalam, Chile, Malaysia, New Zealand, Peru, Singapore, Vietnam, and the United States.[48] The TPP agreement is still in the drafting stage, so it may undergo a watering-down process similar to what happened with ACTA. As happened with the ACTA negotiations,

[43] Dave Lee, "Acta [sic] Protests: Thousands Take to Streets Across Europe," *BBC News*, February 11, 2012, http://www.bbc.co.uk/news/technology-16999497.

[44] Jason Walsh, "Europe's Internet Revolt: Protesters See Threats in Antipiracy Treaty," *Christian Science Monitor*, February 11, 2012, http://www.csmonitor.com/World/Europe/2012/0211/Europe-s-Internet-revolt-protesters-see-threats-in-antipiracy-treaty.

[45] Committee on Industry, Research and Energy for the Committee on International Trade (European Union), Draft Opinion, 2011/167(NLE), March 29, 2012, http://www.europarl.europa.eu/sides/getDoc.do?pubRef=-%2f%2fEP%2f%2fNONSGML%2bCOMPARL%2bPE-483.518%2b01%2bDOC%2bPDF%2bV0%2f%2fEN; see also Rick Falkvinge, "ACTA Moves to First Europarliament Committee: Rejection Proposed," April 5, 2012, http://falkvinge.net/2012/04/05/acta-moves-to-first-europarliament-committee-rejection-proposed/.

[46] Jennifer Baker, "EU Parliament to Vote on ACTA Without Waiting for a Court Decision," *PC World*, March 27, 2012, http://www.pcworld.com/businesscenter/article/252657/eu_parliament_to_vote_on_acta_without_waiting_for_a_court_decision.html.

[47] Cory Doctorow, "Understanding TPP, ACTA's Nastier, More Secret Little Brother," *BoingBoing*, April 6, 2012, boingboing.net/2012/04/06/understanding-tpp-actas-nas.html.

[48] United States Trade Representative, "Trans-Pacific Partnership" (n.d.), at http://www.ustr.gov/tpp (last visited April 11, 2012).

the public is learning about proposed TPP language via leaked draft proposals – and, even compared with the process for ACTA, the TPP process has been exceptionally and unnecessarily secretive.[49] Although the TPP could have wide-ranging impacts on domestic areas of law, U.S. participation is occurring under the guise of the U.S. trade advisory regime:

> This system allows 700-plus official industry trade advisors to have full access to negotiating texts while the public, press and most in Congress are denied equal information. It is worth noting that fewer than 40 representatives in the entire U.S. trade advisory system represent non-industry interests, many of whom are the union representatives concentrated on one committee.[50]

In this way, TPP is subject to less vocal but more profound criticism over process. The lack of transparency also makes it hard to discuss its contents – all discussion about its contents is based on leaked draft proposals – but at least as based on the newest available leaked U.S. proposal,[51] the TPP has the potential to be even more strongly pro-SC than current U.S. law.

There are many strongly argued critiques of TPP. One, authored by a group of legal scholars, concluded:

> The U.S. proposals, if adopted, would upset the current international framework balancing the minimum standards for exclusive rights for media and technology owners, on the one hand, and the access rights of the public, competitors, innovators and creators, on the other. The proposed U.S. IP chapter greatly exceeds the imperfect, but more balanced provisions codified in the 1994 WTO [TRIPS] Agreement... [52]

The authors also express concerns about the secrecy of the process and point out that it is an extension of the strategy of ad hoc international negotiations on IP rights with virtually no public accountability. They

---

[49] AFL-CIO et al., "Letter to Ron Kirk, United States Trade Representative," October 18, 2011, http://infojustice.org/download/tpp/tpp-civil-society/us-transparency-letter-2011.pdf.

[50] Ibid.

[51] Office of the United States Trade Representative, "Trans-Pacific Partnership, Intellectual Property Rights Chapter, Draft," February 10, 2011 (document leaked February 2012), http://infojustice.org/download/tpp/tpp-texts/U.S.%20Proposed%20Text,%20leaked%20February%202011.pdf ("TPP IPR Chapter").

[52] Sean Flynn, Margot Kaminski, Brook Baker, and Jimmy Koo, "Public Interest Analysis of the US TPP Proposal for an IP Chapter," *Program on Information Justice and Intellectual Property, American University Washington College of Law*, December 6, 2011, http://infojustice.org/wp-content/uploads/2011/12/TPP-Analysis-12062011.pdf.

cite ACTA as an example, as well as "the maximalist and controversial standards of the Korea-U.S. Free Trade Agreement (KORUS)."[53] Even though KORUS is another problematic example of secretive ad hoc negotiations involving IP rights, that agreement – signed in 2007 and having gone into effect in March 2012 – has received little scrutiny.

Because it is the closest analog in procedure, ACTA has been the yardstick against which TPP has been measured. To help the public understand the overlap and divergences between ACTA and the U.S. proposal for TPP, fellows at the Program on Information Justice and Intellectual Property (American University Washington College of Law) have produced a table with a comprehensive point-by-point comparison of all provisions, as well as a helpful summary.[54] For instance, the U.S.-proposed TPP text contains much stronger anticircumvention provisions. "TPP goes beyond ACTA by applying provisions on technological protection where circumvention is carried out unknowingly or without reasonable grounds to know."[55] Unlike ACTA, TPP also requires criminal penalties for circumvention for profit, and it explicitly restricts the limitations and exclusions countries can apply to this ban – meaning that the ban would apply in more circumstances.[56] The TPP also contains a notice-and-takedown provision that is structured on the U.S. system, as encoded in Title II of the DMCA.[57] Additionally, "[u]nder ACTA, a country *may* give its authorities the power to force an ISP to identify an infringer to rightholders, subject to certain conditions. Under TPP, a country *shall* establish administrative or judicial procedures for forcing an ISP to identify an infringer to rightholders, without ACTA's conditions."[58]

The lesson from the policy laundering process that turned the WIPO treaties into the overbroad DMCA has not been lost on either the SC or the SFU coalition. On the SFU side, several actors have expressed concern about a new wave of international IP policy laundering. For instance, Rashmi Rangnath of Public Knowledge draws on the history of the DMCA as an illustrative example of policy laundering in copyright

---

[53] Ibid., 3 (citing Free Trade Agreement between the United States of America and the Republic of Korea, June 30, 2007, http://www.ustr.gov/trade-agreements/free-trade-agreements/korus-fta/final-text).

[54] Carrie Ellen Sager, "TPP v. ACTA – Line by Line," *InfoJustice*, March 27, 2012, http://infojustice.org/archives/9256; Program on Information Justice and Intellectual Property Dean's Fellows and Staff (PIJIP), "TPP – ACTA Comparison Table, v. 1," March, 2012, http://infojustice.org/wp-content/uploads/2012/03/table-03222012.pdf; ibid., "TPP–ACTA Comparison: Highlights," March, 2012, http://infojustice.org/wp-content/uploads/2012/03/summary-03262012.pdf.

[55] PIJIP, "Summary," 1.   [56] Ibid., 1.

[57] PIJIP, "Table," 4–8.   [58] PIJIP, "Summary," 1.

law, then expresses concerns that TPP is just the latest and most drastic in a wave of more than a dozen treaties that have been used for policy laundering purposes.[59] The TPP "may be substantively inconsistent with U.S. law," she argues, but that is part of the motivation; by advancing widely unpopular positions in secretive international negotiations, governments can commit to policy choices that would not be nearly as easy to pass via ordinary domestic legislative channels.[60] Even when these agreements are consistent with U.S. law, they can prevent the Congress from making changes that may be warranted, such as tempering the anticircumvention provisions of the DMCA. For these reasons, the battle over domestic copyright law is increasingly being fought in secretive, unaccountable international forums – a remarkably antidemocratic development that is unfortunately not limited to the copyright debate.

AN END TO THE DOMESTIC STALEMATE?

On the domestic front, the period from 2007 to 2010 had all the markings of a time of potential transition. In the previous period, from 2003 to 2006, the copyright debate was marked by a stalemate between the SC and SFU coalitions; each coalition had enough political capital to be able to stop the other's agenda. This was a real boon for the SFU coalition, but some of the conditions that made it possible would not last. Representative Boucher gave up on DMCA reform, and then the voters sent him home. Although Boucher had earned tremendous credibility as one of the few members of Congress who understood technology well enough to write good laws, there was no clear heir to his role as a trusted voice for new technologies. For instance, Representative Barton did not have the same knowledge or credibility on technology issues; thus, once Barton lost his committee, he no longer had much capacity to shape the direction of digital copyright. Thus, the debate over DRM regulations – which was and remains a successful coalition-building topic for the SFU coalition – had basically drawn to a close in Congress. The debate over digital copyright was about to head in a different direction. By 2010, the SC coalition was gaining traction on a set of ideas with the lofty promise of reconstructing the internet to its liking. The results of that effort, however, differed from what it had hoped.

[59] Rashmi Rangnath, "The TPP and Policy Laundering," *Public Knowledge Policy Blog*, March 30, 2012, http://www.publicknowledge.org/blog/tpp-and-policy-laundering.
[60] Ibid.

11

New Strategies and a Historic Uprising

Events in the past decade have shown the folly of a digital rights management (DRM)-centric copyright strategy. Despite inconveniences to legitimate users, serious infringers proceed undaunted. In contrast, Title II
of the Digital Millennium Copyright Act (DMCA) has provided a more
meaningful set of tools for addressing online infringement. As of this
writing, in the past month, Google alone got takedown requests for
1.67 million unique URLs, with requests coming from 1,502 separate
copyright owners.[1] Obviously, this is also another sign that large-scale
copyright infringement continues online, and the notice-and-takedown
process has become an ongoing game of Whack-a-Mole. On the other
hand, online companies like Google are effectively compelled to process
millions of takedown requests per month – a situation that has led many
to implement, on a voluntary basis, the kinds of filters that have been
proposed by copyright industries as mandatory. It has also led many civil
liberties advocates to worry about the noninfringing innocent bystanders
who have been caught up in the largely automated content industry takedown requests.[2] The point here is not to defend or critique Title II as a
good or bad compromise between competing interests and values, but to
highlight that it has probably done a great deal more good for copyright
holders' attempts at enforcement than has Title I. This is beyond ironic,
as the strong copyright (SC) coalition pushed hard for Title I, fought hard
against Title II, and only accepted the latter as a necessary price to get
the former.

---

[1] Google, "Transparency Report: Copyright Removal Requests," June 12, 2012, http:
//www.google.com/transparencyreport/removals/copyright/.
[2] E.g., Seltzer, "Free Speech Unmoored."

From the perspective of the SC coalition, however, the DMCA is a failure because Title II makes it too easy for members of the internet ecosystem to escape legal liability for their users' infringement. Thus, they have sought to bring a much stricter regime to the internet, effectively or literally compelling other actors in the internet ecosystem to act as copyright holders' enforcers. As was the case leading up to the DMCA, there are clear and foreseeable holes in the strategy's ability to stop infringement, not to mention the obvious negative effects on legitimate activity. Unlike the case leading up to the DMCA, however, the strong fair use (SFU) coalition was organized and ready for combat – and more remarkably, as of this writing, won a clear and decisive victory in this debate. This story begins with a remarkably ambitious set of proposals – as well as decisions by SC advocates inside and outside Congress to disregard substantial opposition. It ends with the SFU coalition sparking the largest online protest in history.

MAKING A (BLACK)LIST OF ONLINE INFRINGERS

The SC coalition has grown increasingly frustrated with the diverse, diffuse, and international nature of the internet. Even were it feasible to track down all of the domestic infringing sites and online sources for circumvention software – and it decidedly is not feasible – foreign websites present an additional obstacle that is not easily addressed via domestic law. Thus, SC advocates have sought new powers to make it more difficult for domestic users to reach websites with allegedly infringing content, as well as to slow these sites' access to financial services and networks of advertisers. Although SC advocates bristle at the term, the simplest way to describe this strategy is as the creation of an internet blacklist. Once a site gets on the list, other members of the internet ecosystem would be prohibited (or, in some variants, very strongly discouraged) from having business relations or providing internet connections with that site.

To better understand how these blacklist proposals might look in practice, imagine a video hosting website, AllYourVideosHere.com.[3] Further, imagine that this site hosts a substantial amount of content that is

---

[3] I have chosen not to accuse specific sites of infringement. Granted, sites that traffic primarily in infringing content are numerous – and, in some cases, not only easily identified as infringers but proud of it. Especially as a nonlawyer, though, I am more comfortable discussing a hypothetical infringing site. This address, which certainly sounds like a host of infringing content, was available until I purchased it.

allegedly[4] infringing, drawing the ire of copyright holders. Some copyright holders would like to do everything possible to make this site disappear, whether the site is based in the U.S. or abroad. This could include forcing businesses with domestic ties to cease doing business with this site; in particular, payment processors and advertisers (including networks that serve ads from multiple advertisers) could be forced to stop handling finances for and serving advertising business to AllYourVideosHere. Depending on the specifics of the implementation, these proposals might be agreed to as relatively uncontroversial. It was allies of the SFU coalition – not the SC coalition – that advanced a bill consisting of these proposals in the 112th Congress, as I discuss in more detail later in this chapter.

More controversially, SC advocates have also advanced proposals that would prevent internet service providers (ISPs) and search engines from connecting users to infringing sites. Such an order could be imposed based on any level of proof of infringing activity, ranging from mere allegation by copyright holders, to a preponderance of evidence as shown in an adversarial hearing. Although not straightforward to implement at the technical level, the concept behind ISP and search engine restrictions is fairly clear. Once a site is blacklisted, ISPs or search engines would be legally barred from helping users connect to any of the sites on the list.

Another controversial proposal, which is more complicated at the conceptual level, is the strategy of seizing the domain names of allegedly infringing sites. To understand this, one must know a bit about the domain name system (DNS). A domain name is an easily remembered web address, such as AllYourVideosHere.com or Google.com. Each of these names is registered to an owner, and the owner determines which computer serves the content on that site. Behind each of these website names is an internet protocol (IP) address – a number that identifies the specific computers hosting the content. For instance, when I type Google.com into my browser, my computer is actually connecting to a computer with the IP address 74.125.115.105.[5] I can also get to the

---

[4] The SC coalition's proposals discussed herein would not withhold action until after an accused infringer has been found to have committed infringement in an adversarial proceeding in a court of law. Thus, the caveat of "alleged" infringement is not only appropriate but important. In a nod to readability, however, I often drop the caveat; even in these instances, it is implicit.

[5] This is true for me, as of this writing, in my specific location. Because Google is the world's largest website, they actually use many IP addresses, and they use the user's location and other factors to determine which IP address to use to serve a given user's search query.

Google search page by typing that same string of numbers and periods into my browser's address bar, but it is far easier to remember and type Google.com. The SC coalition would like to stop users who enter the easy-to-remember web address of an infringing site from getting to the infringing web host's computer. Thus, a user who types the domain for our hypothetical infringing site, AllYourVideosHere.com, into his or her web browser would not find the site with the infringing videos. Even better for copyright holders, that domain could be redirected to a different IP address entirely, one with a message to encourage users not to visit sites with infringing content.

The SC coalition-supported policies and proposals that build on this strategy compel (or would compel) the cooperation of any U.S.-based entity that serves any DNS-related role. This means any entity that does anything to translate a user's request in the form of an easy-to-remember domain name into the numeric IP address of that website's host computer. The most obvious example of such an entity that could be compelled to seize and redirect a website is the site's domain registrar. For about $10 per year per site, a website operator pays a domain name registrar to tell the whole internet where to send requests for the site owner's website. These domain name registrars serve an important role; they help users find their desired web destinations with plain-language domain names rather than hard-to-remember sets of numbers. With a change in U.S. code, U.S.-based registrars could be compelled to break the connection between the domain name of an allegedly infringing site and the computer hosting the allegedly infringing content. Again, this site could then be redirected to a different computer with a site explaining that the domain has been seized for allegedly trafficking in infringing content. This could apply whether the site's owners are in the U.S. or abroad.

Many companies around the world serve as registrars, so policy changes affecting U.S.-based registrars might drive website owners to use registrars based in other countries, in an attempt to escape these policies' reach. This might not be enough to avoid being affected, however, as there are still other DNS functions carried out by companies or other entities that may also be U.S.-based. In particular, this includes top-level domain (TLD) registries. Each TLD, such as .com or .org, is handled by a single registry that coordinates with the various registrars. For instance, the .com TLD is handled by the U.S.-based company Verisign. Thus, although a user who wants to register a domain with a .com ending is free to work with any approved registrar to do so, those registrars must then communicate that ownership (and pay the majority of the registration fee) to

Verisign. For this TLD – and several others, such as .net – Verisign serves as the authoritative online voice about who owns which domains. Thus, whether registered with a registrar that is based in the United States or abroad, U.S. jurisdiction could also be used to compel Verisign to seize the domain name of AllYourVideosHere.com by pointing it away from the infringing server and toward one with an anti-infringement message.

In addition to official registrars and TLD registries, a much larger, distributed set of computers serve as the equivalent of the web's phone books; these are *name servers*. Rather than needing to dial the operator (Verisign) every time an end user needs to connect with Google, many thousands of local network operators also use their own local name servers to keep cached, local versions of the list of domain names and their associated IP addresses. These informal name servers ask the authoritative name servers for updates on a periodic basis rather than contacting them specifically for each website request by each end user, thus greatly improving efficiency. This presents another potential opportunity for copyright holders to use domestic jurisdiction to interrupt a user's request for an infringing website. Even if the website's owner, the computers that serve the site's content, the registrar, and the TLD registry are based overseas, a new law could compel everyone who operates a name server to redirect requests for allegedly infringing sites. This would affect every entity that runs a local name server – that is, a local, cached list of the IP addresses of domain names – which "includes hundreds of thousands of small and medium-sized businesses, colleges, universities, nonprofit organizations, and the like."[6] In other words, a blacklist of domain names would affect nearly every entity with a computer network larger than that found in a home or small business.

Although these ideas represent several potentially independent proposals, they were advanced as a legislative package, with the intent of making it possible to erase many infringing sites from the internet – either making life so difficult for the website operator that it goes out of business, or making the sites much less accessible to local users. Without revenue from advertisers and payment processors, the sites could be starved to death. Further, if users cannot use the domain name to access the site, many could be discouraged from visiting the site. Even though the numeric IP address might still resolve to the website in question, some users do not know this or know how it works, and others might know but be

---

[6] Lemley, Levine, and Post, "Don't Break the Internet," 34.

unable to locate that IP address. If search engines are regulated, it could be even harder for users to locate affected sites. Finally, even visiting the site via the numeric IP address may not be possible if ISPs are forbidden from connecting users with such sites. These are extraordinary measures aimed at combatting infringement, but the story of their fate is even more extraordinary.

COMBATTING ONLINE INFRINGEMENT AND COUNTERFEITS ACT

In late 2010, Senator Patrick Leahy advanced a bill, the Combating Online Infringement and Counterfeits Act (COICA),[7] which embodies all of the website-targeting proposals just described.[8] If passed, it would have authorized the U.S. Attorney General to seek court action against a domain that is "primarily designed, has no demonstrable, commercially significant purpose or use other than, or is marketed by its operator, or by a person acting in concert with the operator, to offer" content that infringes copyrights or trademarks.[9] For websites that are registered domestically, the bill would have given courts and the Attorney General the power to serve notice on internet domain registrars, compelling them to "suspend operation of, and lock, the domain name."[10] For those websites registered abroad, a court order could be used to compel ISPs to block users from reaching those domains, to prevent financial services providers from processing their transactions, and to prevent internet advertisers from serving ads to these sites.[11] As envisioned by the bill, these outcomes would happen without an adversarial hearing during which a site's operator could defend its right to continue about its business

---

[7] Combating Online Infringement and Counterfeits Act (COICA), S. 3048, 111th Cong. (2010).

[8] The bill's language targets "service provider[s], as that term is defined in section 512(k)(1) of title 17, United States Code ... " § 2324(e)(2)(B)(i). The cited statute, 17 U.S.C. § 512(k)(1), is not especially clear or easy to read, but it includes both providers of raw connectivity (what most people would call ISPs) and many online businesses, including search engines. As one court contends, "A plain reading of [17 U.S.C. § 512(k)] reveals that 'service provider' is defined so broadly that we have trouble imagining the existence of an online service that would not fall under the definitions.... " *In re Aimster Copyright Litig.*, 252 F.Supp.2d 634, 658 (N.D. Ill. 2002), aff'd, 334 F.3d 643 (7th Cir. 2003). See also Electronic Frontier Foundation, "Copyright: Digital Millennium Copyright Act," March 24, 2010, § 1.4, http://ilt.eff.org/index.php/Copyright:_Digital_Millennium_Copyright_Act#Prerequisites_and_Disqualifiers.

[9] COICA § 2324(a)(2)(A).   [10] Ibid., § 2324(e)(1).

[11] Ibid., § 2324(e)(2).

without being shuttered.[12] The bill passed the Senate Judiciary Committee in November 2010 – leaving its supporters too little time to pass it through the full Senate and House during the 111th Congress, but setting up a replay of the debate in the 112th Congress.

Although COICA had too little time to become law, it served as a galvanizing force for the SFU coalition. The Electronic Frontier Foundation (EFF) and Public Knowledge sites both featured several statements opposing the bill. They also helped mobilize and bring attention to opposition from other corners. This included an open letter from nearly 100 internet engineers and another statement of opposition by the Net Coalition, an internet industry trade group.[13] They also helped publicize another letter from forty-three professors of law; it described the act as "an unconstitutional abridgment of the freedom of speech" and warned that it "would fundamentally alter U.S. policy towards internet speech, and would set a dangerous precedent with potentially serious consequences for free expression and global internet freedom."[14]

IMMIGRATION AND CUSTOMS ENFORCEMENT STARTS SEIZING DOMAINS

In a process dubbed "Operation in Our Sites," in 2010, the Department of Immigration and Customs Enforcement (ICE), a division of Homeland Security, started seizing the domain names of websites allegedly used for facilitating illegal activities. These actions have come amid accusations of many kinds of illegal activities – including trafficking in illegal drugs, child pornography, or goods that infringe trademarks – though the seizures most of interest for this study involve those of sites related to

---

[12] An operator of such a site could later petition the court to undo its orders "based on evidence that the Internet site associated with the domain name subject to the order is no longer dedicated to infringing activities; or the interests of justice require that the order be modified, suspended, or vacated." Ibid., § 2324(h)(1)(B). That such a court appearance would come only after a website's operators had lost their domain name, advertisers, links from ISPs, or ability to process transactions is, in this author's estimation, a profound affront to both due process and the First Amendment.

[13] Peter Eckersley, "An Open Letter From Internet Engineers to the Senate Judiciary Committee," *EFF Deeplinks Blog*, September 28, 2010, https://www.eff.org/deeplinks/2010/09/open-letter; Markham C. Erickson, "Letter from Net Coalition Opposing COICA," *Public Knowledge*, November 15, 2010, http://www.publicknowledge.org/letter-net-coalition-opposing-coica.

[14] Zoe Argento et al., "Law Professors' Letter in Opposition to S. 3804," (n.d.), 3, https://www.eff.org/files/filenode/coica_files/Professors'%20Letter%20re%20COICA%20and%20Signatories.pdf.

accusations of copyright infringement.[15] These efforts are still active at the time of this writing.[16] It is curious that ICE is proceeding in the name of copyright enforcement even as legislative proposals that would effect a similar outcome are actively under consideration; if new legislation is required, the legal basis for ICE seizures would by implication seem to be questionable. Although the administration has said little on the legal justifications for the authority to seize such sites, it seems most clearly to rest in the newly expanded civil forfeiture provisions of the 2008 Prioritizing Resources and Organization for Intellectual Property Act (PRO-IP Act).[17] In cases of criminal copyright infringement, these provisions give the government powers to seize infringing works, as well as "property used, or intended to be used, in any manner or part to commit or facilitate the commission" of copyright infringement, whenever the infringement happens on a large enough scale to make it a criminal offense.[18] This sounds like it would only apply to the worst infringers, but the standard for what constitutes criminal (as opposed to civil) copyright infringement is surprisingly low; any infringement becomes criminal if it is done willfully and the total retail value of copies distributed exceeds $1,000.[19] Further, to effect domain seizures, the state only need meet the burden of proof that applies to civil forfeiture – that is, they only need "to prove by a preponderance of evidence that the crime was committed and that property derived from such crime."[20] This is in stark contrast to criminal forfeiture, which only happens "once the defendant has been found

---

[15] U.S. Immigration and Customs Enforcement, "News Release: 'Operation in Our Sites' Targets Internet Movie Pirates: ICE, Manhattan U.S. Attorney Seize Multiple Web Sites for Criminal Copyright Violations," June 30, 2010, at http://www.ice.gov/news/releases/1006/100630losangeles.htm.

[16] U.S. Immigration and Customs Enforcement, "News Releases – Intellectual Property Rights," http://www.ice.gov/news/releases/index.htm?top25=no&year=all&month=all&state=all&topic=12 (last visited November 2, 2012).

[17] Prioritizing Resources and Organization for Intellectual Property Act of 2008, Pub. L. No: 110–403 (2008).

[18] 18 U.S.C. § 2323(a)(1)(B).   [19] 17 U.S.C. § 506(a).

[20] Pyun, "The 2008 PRO-IP Act," 386. Pyun cites the U.S. Department of Justice, *Prosecuting Intellectual Property Crimes Manual* (3rd ed., 2006), 295, available at http://www.justice.gov/criminal/cybercrime/docs/ipma2006.pdf. The portion of the Department of Justice manual that Pyun cites reads:

> Whereas criminal forfeiture is an *in personam* action against the defendant, civil forfeiture is an *in rem* action against the property itself. This means that civil forfeiture proceedings can reach property regardless of who owns it, if the government can prove that the property was derived from or used to commit a crime. Civil forfeiture proceedings are not part of a criminal case at all. The burden of proof is a preponderance of the evidence, and civil forfeiture proceedings

guilty . . . beyond a reasonable doubt."[21] ICE seizures have been occurring without adversarial hearings, so a copyright holder need merely accuse a website of criminal infringement for the state to claim that the preponderance of evidence shows criminal infringement and thus to seize the site. The whole process usually happens before the operator of the site even knows an accusation has been made.

Opponents argue that the on-the-ground outcomes of these seizure operations show the inherently problematic nature of a domain seizure–based enforcement strategy. One major problem is the inherent difficulty of trying to decide which websites are, on the whole, primarily dedicated to infringement. Several of the seizures have affected domains with little or no infringing content. Many of the sites have been taken down merely for linking to sites with infringing content,[22] which is not in itself a violation of copyright – at least, not without actual knowledge that the linked content is indeed infringing.[23]

Mistaken or disputed assessments of whether a site is infringing appear to be a major factor as well. Several of the music sites that have been taken down were apparently targeted because they posted files that were given to them by record label or artist representatives.[24] This highlights an internal tension and miscommunication that can happen in large media

> can dispose of property even without a criminal conviction or the filing of any criminal charges.
>
> If used as guidance for domain seizures, this seems to give a pass to the government to silence (or at least muffle) speakers whom the state has no intention of prosecuting. Except when used against those who are not in the U.S. and thus not subject to criminal prosecution, if the state is accusing the operator of a website of crimes serious enough to warrant state censorship, one might hope that these crimes should also warrant at least a good-faith effort at prosecution for said crimes. In other words, if the state does not believe strongly enough in the seriousness and provability of the alleged crime that the state is willing to pursue prosecution – either before or after the domains have been seized – it is unsettling for the state to use such a half-hearted accusation of criminality as a vehicle for censoring the accused.

[21] Pyun, "The 2008 PRO-IP Act," 386.

[22] Abigail Phillips, "What Congress Can Learn from the Recent ICE Seizures," *Electronic Frontier Foundation*, February 15, 2011, https://www.eff.org/deeplinks/2011/02/what-congress-can-learn-recent-ice-seizures.

[23] 17 U.S.C. § 512(d). The question of whether and how First Amendment scrutiny would apply to hyperlinks is still unsettled in the case law, although there are powerful arguments for applying strict scrutiny to any such regulations. See Dalal, "Protecting Hyperlinks and Preserving First Amendment Values on the Internet."

[24] Sherwin Siy, "More Domain Seizures from DOJ/ICE: Spanish Website Seized Despite Legal Status in Spain," *Public Knowledge*, February 1, 2011, http://www.publicknowledge.org/blog/more-domain-seizures-dojice-spanish-website-s; Mike Masnick, "Senator Wyden Asks WTF Is Up with Homeland Security Domain Seizures,"

companies: Marketing departments will promote copyrighted works online – or, even if not placing the works there themselves, want illicitly posted works to stay online – but legal departments will see those same copies as a problem and try to have them removed. For instance, YouTube claims to have been subjected to these kinds of conflicting messages from media company Viacom.[25] When this results in a media company's legal department contacting a site directly and asking for the materials to be taken down – for instance, via a DMCA takedown request – this can at least open a direct dialog between the affected website and the conflicting sectors of the media company. It is far more disturbing, though, that this has apparently led to the complete shutdown of entire websites, the operators of which were making good-faith efforts to obey the law.

One site, music blog Dajaz1.com, was seized by ICE for posting copies of several songs. As part of an action that collected the domains of five separate hip hop sites, ICE seized the domain of *Dajaz1*, which is run by Queens, NY, resident Andre Nasib.[26] The site's domain was seized for

Techdirt, February 3, 2011, http://www.techdirt.com/articles/20110202/23363812934/senator-wyden-asks-wtf-is-up-with-homeland-security-domain-seizures.shtml.

[25] One very well-known instance – at least, according to YouTube – was internal disagreement at Viacom about videos, some of which were uploaded by users, others by Viacom itself. Zahavah Levine, "Broadcast Yourself," *Broadcasting Ourselves: The Official YouTube Blog*, March 18, 2010, http://youtube-global.blogspot.com/2010/03/broadcast-yourself.html. Levine writes:

> For years, Viacom continuously and secretly uploaded its content to YouTube, even while publicly complaining about its presence there. It hired no fewer than eighteen different marketing agencies to upload its content to the site. It deliberately "roughed up" the videos to make them look stolen or leaked. It opened YouTube accounts using phony e-mail addresses. It even sent employees to Kinko's to upload clips from computers that couldn't be traced to Viacom. And, in an effort to promote its own shows, as a matter of company policy, Viacom routinely left up clips from shows that had been uploaded to YouTube by ordinary users. Executives as high up as the president of Comedy Central and the head of MTV Networks felt "very strongly" that clips from shows like The Daily Show and The Colbert Report should remain on YouTube.
>
> Viacom's efforts to disguise its promotional use of YouTube worked so well that even its own employees could not keep track of everything it was posting or leaving up on the site. As a result, on countless occasions Viacom demanded the removal of clips that it had uploaded to YouTube, only to return later to sheepishly ask for their reinstatement. In fact, some of the very clips that Viacom is suing us over were actually uploaded by Viacom itself.

[26] Ben Sisario, "Hip-Hop Copyright Case Had Little Explanation," *New York Times*, May 6, 2012, http://www.nytimes.com/2012/05/07/business/media/hip-hop-site-dajaz1s-copyright-case-ends-in-confusion.html?_r=0.

over a year – from November 2010 to December 2011 – while the music blogger and his attorneys fought merely to get a chance to contest the allegations in court. As the *Times* reports, Nasib "said that artists and record companies had sent him the songs for promotional purposes," and to my knowledge, music industry representatives have never made a public rebuttal of this claim.[27] After the initial seizure, Nasib filed repeated motions in federal court to get the domain back. The government not only filed counter-motions to halt these efforts, they did so through a series of requests for extensions that were sealed by the court at the government's request. After the case's documents were unsealed, the public learned that the government filed its motions for extension while waiting for the Recording Industry Association of America (RIAA) to provide requested evidence in support of the government's case. Once the state realized that no such support was forthcoming, prosecutors unceremoniously gave up and allowed the site to return to the owner's control.[28] Mike Masnick of *Techdirt* explains his concerns about the government's handling of the case by way of analogy:

> Imagine if the US government, with no notice or warning, raided a small but popular magazine's offices over a Thanksgiving weekend, seized the company's printing presses, and told the world that the magazine was a criminal enterprise with a giant banner on their building. Then imagine that it never arrested anyone, never let a trial happen, and filed everything about the case under seal, not even letting the magazine's lawyers talk to the judge presiding over the case. And it continued to deny any due process at all for over a year, before finally just handing everything back to the magazine and pretending nothing happened. I expect most people would be outraged. I expect that nearly all of you would say that's a classic case of prior restraint, a massive First Amendment violation, and exactly the kind of thing that does not, or should not, happen in the United States.
>
> But... this is exactly the scenario that has played out over the past year – with the only difference being that, rather than "a printing press" and a "magazine," the story involved "a domain" and a "blog."[29]

Andrew P. Bridges, the lawyer for Dajaz1, was even harsher in his condemnation of the process. In an e-mail to the *Times*, he said his client was grateful for the exoneration, unceremonious or otherwise. "That

---

[27] Ibid.   [28] Ibid.

[29] Mike Masnick, "Breaking News: Feds Falsely Censor Popular Blog For Over A Year, Deny All Due Process, Hide All Details...," *Techdirt*, December 8, 2011, http://www.techdirt.com/articles/20111208/08225217010/breaking-news-feds-falsely-censor-popular-blog-over-year-deny-all-due-process-hide-all-details.shtml.

exoneration, however, did not remedy the harms caused by a full year of censorship and secret proceedings – a form of 'digital Guantánamo' – that knocked out an important and popular blog devoted to hip-hop music and has nearly killed it."[30] As this case illustrates, there are clear reasons for concern the ICE domain seizures may compromise the First Amendment and due process in the agency's effort to buttress online copyright protection.

The *Dajaz1* case is not the only one that has highlighted concerns about the ICE domain seizure process. Another site, *Rojadirecta*, had two URLs (Rojadirecta.com and Rojadirecta.org), both of which directed users to the same page, seized in January 2011. This was even after a court in Spain – where the site is based – found the site not to be infringing.[31] *Rojadirecta*, run by a company called Puerto 80, is a sports blog and message board where users can and often do identify links to websites with streaming sports content. Many of these streams are infringing. Were the site U.S.-based, one could certainly argue that *Rojadirecta*'s practice of hosting user-submitted links to infringing content is of sufficient culpability to constitute inducement under the standard set out in *MGM v. Grokster*. This raises the problem of applying U.S. law to a foreign company that operates in a country where the company's behavior is legal, based on the rather ambitious reasoning that the site's TLD registry is based in the U.S. Such reasoning amounts to the claim that the U.S. government can veto any site address with domain name ending in .com or .org, based merely on whether that site's content adheres to U.S. law.[32]

---

[30] Sisario, "Hip-Hop Copyright Case."

[31] Ernesto, "Sports Streaming/Torrent Links Site Victorious in Court," *Torrent Freak*, May 10, 2010, http://torrentfreak.com/sports-streaming-torrent-links-site-victorious-in-court-100510/.

[32] John A. Greer addresses this argument in the context of the internationalization of U.S. trademark law via the Anticybersquatting Consumer Protection Act (ACPA):

> The aggressive assertion of *in rem* jurisdiction over extraterritorial defendants effectively makes U.S. trademark law the law of Internet domain names, which raises questions of comity and conflict of laws.... [B]ecause a domain name exists simultaneously everywhere and nowhere, its 'location' is at best indeterminate and arbitrary. Thus, Congress's declaration in the form of the ACPA that domain names are 'located' wherever their TLD registry is located [lacks] a clear justification...

> Greer, "If the Shoe Fits," 1885, 1886–7. While this is damning enough, the ICE domain seizures lack even this level of internal coherence, since ICE claims the right to enact such seizures whether U.S. jurisdiction applies to the TLD registry in question or to the domain name registrar – the latter being the company with whom the website operator has a direct relationship. Thus, through its system of domain seizures, ICE effectively claims that an offending domain is located wherever the U.S. has jurisdiction. Even without this conflict,

Puerto 80 retained American attorneys and petitioned in U.S. federal court to get the domain names back; the case ultimately wound up before the 2nd Circuit.[33] Lest the world think the government is accusing Puerto 80 merely of secondary infringement, the government explicitly accused Puerto 80 not only of contributing to criminal infringement but also of committing it themselves.[34] Even setting aside the question of extraterritoriality, the accusation of criminality in this case is strained, to put it mildly. *Rojadirecta* is a site where users (not Puerto 80) often submit links to other sites, and on some of these other sites, another party (neither Puerto 80 nor *Rojadirecta*'s users) is often committing infringement. Being doubly removed from the infringement in question places Puerto 80 arguably out of the realm of secondary liability. Unless the company had the intent to induce infringement, it would probably have no liability whatsoever; the 7th Circuit implies as much in a 2012 decision authored by Judge Richard Posner, *Flava Works v. Gunter*.[35] Yet even if one were to grant that Puerto 80 is a contributory infringer, making the leap to accusations of criminality is an argument that, to put it charitably, strains the case law on secondary liability.[36] Still, after fighting for about eighteen months,

> but especially in light of it, *in rem* personal jurisdiction provides barely a fig leaf of coverage for what is otherwise a naked power grab – namely, an extraterritorial exertion of U.S. law upon the citizens of other countries, but without the due process that would be accorded domestically in an offline context. The U.S. government and U.S. companies would not tolerate such behavior from other countries, and there is no just reason why those abroad should have to tolerate it from us.

[33] *Puerto 80 Projects, S.L.U. v. United States.* See also, Electronic Frontier Foundation, "*Puerto 80 v. US,*" https://www.eff.org/cases/puerto-80-v-us (last visited November 3, 2012). For a First Amendment critique, see, e.g., "Government Violates Free Speech Rights with Domain Name Seizure," *Electronic Frontier Foundation*, September 23, 2011, https://www.eff.org/press/archives/2011/09/23.

[34] The government argued in part, "in operating the Rojadirecta website, Puerto 80 has engaged in (and aided and abetted) flagrant criminal copyright infringement." Government's Response Brief at 17, *Puerto 80 Projects v. United States*, available at http://www.citmedialaw.org/sites/citmedialaw.org/files/2011-07-11-United%20States%20Memorandum%20in%20Opposition.pdf.

[35] *Flava Works v. Gunter*, 758. The court held in part, "As the record stands . . . myVidster is not an infringer, at least in the form of copying or distributing copies of copyrighted work. The infringers are the uploaders of copyrighted work. There is no evidence that myVidster is encouraging them, which would make it a contributory infringer." The site in question, myVidster, is a site that allows users to bookmark links to videos, some of which are infringing. The parallels to the Puerto 80 case are notable.

[36] Less charitably, see Mike Masnick, "Did Homeland Security Make Up A Non-Existent Criminal Contributory Infringement Rule In Seizing Domain Names?," *Techdirt*, January 6, 2011, http://www.techdirt.com/articles/20110104/12324012513/

the government gave up the case in August 2012 and allowed Puerto 80 to regain control of the domains; this came just weeks after the *Flava Works* case, and the government's letter strongly implied that the 7th Circuit case led directly to their decision in *Puerto 80*.[37] As in the *Dajaz1* case, the state held the domains in legal limbo for over a year, made it as difficult as possible for the website to do business, and abandoned the case once it looked hopeless – without apology or even much explanation.

There are other constitutional critiques as well. That ICE would undertake such a venture while Congress is actively trying to create such a procedure through legislative means suggests major administrative overreach; Senator Ron Wyden has said as much.[38] Adding to these concerns is the off-the-record observation of several of those who have been affected that, even as they have tried to contact every government agency that might help out, the administration has been shockingly nonresponsive.[39] Even if ICE seizures were working flawlessly, there would be concerns about escalating the strategy of domain seizures via something like COICA. The major concerns about how the ICE seizures have proceeded have thus only added to the technology community's white-knuckled fear of the passage of a domain seizures bill through Congress.

---

did-homeland-security-make-up-non-existent-criminal-contributory-infringement-rule-seizing-domain-names.shtml. Masnick certainly thinks so, and though I am not a lawyer, my reading of the case law supports this interpretation. There is no explicit statutory basis for liability based on secondary infringement, and while it does have a long tradition in the case law, the key cases – and, to my admittedly nonauthoritative knowledge, all cases dealing with secondary infringement – are all civil cases. For an accessible tour, see LaFrance, *Copyright Law in a Nutshell*, § 9.4.

[37] Mike Masnick, "Oops: After Seizing & Censoring Rojadirecta For 18 Months, Feds Give Up & Drop Case," *Techdirt* (August 29th, 2012), http://www.techdirt.com/articles/20120829/12370820209/oops-after-seizing-censoring-rojadirecta-18-months-feds-give-up-drop-case.shtml.
   To illustrate the central role that the *Flava Works* case likely played in the government's thinking, Masnick shares the government's letter accepting a dismissal, which cites "certain recent judicial authority involving issues germane to the above-captioned action" as motivation. Government's Letter Seeking Dismissal 1, *United States v. Rojadirecta.org*, available at http://docstoc.com/docs/127844863.

[38] Mike Masnick, "Senator Wyden Asks WTF Is Up with Homeland Security Domain Seizures," *Techdirt* (February 3, 2011), http://www.techdirt.com/articles/20110202/23363812934/senator-wyden-asks-wtf-is-up-with-homeland-security-domain-seizures.shtml.

[39] Mike Masnick, "Why We Haven't Seen Any Lawsuits Filed Against the Government Over Domain Seizures: Justice Department Stalling," *Techdirt*, May 24, 2011, at http://www.techdirt.com/articles/20110521/15125114374/why-we-havent-seen-any-lawsuits-filed-against-government-over-domain-seizures-justice-department-stalling.shtml.

THE STOP ONLINE PIRACY ACT AND PROTECT-IP ACT

In 2011, Senator Patrick Leahy introduced the Preventing Real Online Threats to Economic Creativity and Theft of Intellectual Property (PROTECT-IP) Act of 2011 (also abbreviated as PIPA),[40] and Representative Lamar Smith introduced the Stop Online Piracy Act (SOPA).[41] Both PIPA and SOPA are variants on the strategies first introduced in COICA – although, unlike COICA, which included domestic sites, SOPA and PIPA target only foreign websites. Both SOPA and PIPA would authorize the Attorney General to take action against foreign websites that are accused of being primarily dedicated to infringing activity. Each builds on the assumed legality of ICE seizures of domain names, where feasible – that is, where domain name registrars or TLD registries are subject to U.S. jurisdiction. From there, the bills both provide means for requiring service providers not to direct users who type in the domain name of infringing sites to the site they are seeking, and the language in SOPA would seem to prevent ISPs from serving traffic to foreign infringing sites via the numeric IP address.[42] Both bills also create a mechanism for requiring search engines to stop linking to these sites,[43] as well as means to cut off these sites' access to advertisers[44] and financial services.[45]

Senator Leahy introduced PIPA to the Senate Committee on the Judiciary on May 12, 2011, and the Committee passed the bill on May 26 without having held a hearing in the interim.[46] The last hearing on the

---

[40] Preventing Real Online Threats to Economic Creativity and Theft of Intellectual Property Act of 2011 (PIPA), S. 968, 112th Cong. (2011).

[41] Stop Online Piracy Act (SOPA), H.R. 3261, 112th Cong. (2011).

[42] SOPA, § 102(c)(2)(A); PIPA, § 3(d)(2)(A). Every ISP keeps local copies of DNS directory information so that website requests can be processed more efficiently. These local, cached directories are then updated regularly to include updates from the authoritative DNS directories maintained by domain name registries. Both bills would require that, upon court order, service providers change their nonauthoritative domain server infrastructure so that users who type in the domain name of an infringing site would not be taken to the numeric IP address of the site they requested. The language in SOPA, though, is much broader; upon receiving a court order, an ISP would be required to "take technically feasible and reasonable measures designed to prevent access by its subscribers located within the United States to the foreign infringing site (or portion thereof) that is subject to the order, including measures designed to prevent the domain name of the foreign infringing site (or portion thereof) from resolving to that domain name's Internet Protocol address." SOPA, §102(c)(2)(A)(i).

[43] SOPA, § 102(c)(2)(B); PIPA, § 3(d)(2)(D).

[44] SOPA, § 102(c)(2)(D); PIPA, § 3(d)(2)(C).

[45] SOPA, § 102(c)(2)(C); PIPA, § 3(d)(2)(B).

[46] See S. Rep. No. 112-39, 11-13 (2011), at http://www.gpo.gov/fdsys/pkg/CRPT-112srpt39/pdf/CRPT-112srpt39.pdf.

matter, held on February 16, 2011 – when PIPA was still not on the table and the proposal was still being described as COICA – had five witnesses but no substantive opposition.[47] Acting as an unabashed SC ally, Leahy essentially ignored written opposition from groups including the Computer and Communications Industry Association, the Consumer Electronics Association, the Center for Democracy and Technology, and Public Knowledge,[48] none of whom were invited to testify on the proposal. On November 16, 2011, the House Committee on the Judiciary also held a hearing[49] that was heavily stacked in favor of the bill's passage,[50] and the committee's website describing the hearing expresses clear enthusiasm about the bill.[51] At the very start of the hearing, Judiciary Chair Lamar Smith accused Google – the only substantive opponents at the hearing table – of obstructionism; he also accused the company of supporting "rogue" websites.[52] This is consistent with both judiciary committees' longstanding support for the SC coalition.

---

[47] The Committee had held a hearing on the general idea on February 16, 2011. *Targeting Websites Dedicated to Stealing American Intellectual Property: Hearing Before the Senate Judiciary Committee*, 112th Cong. (2011). This hardly counts as dedicated consideration of PIPA per se, as the bill still had not been introduced and witnesses who referred to the bill called it COICA.

 This hearing had five witnesses. Two – Tom Adams of Rosetta Stone and Scott Turow of the Authors Guild – were clear members of the SC coalition who expressed enthusiastic and urgent support for the bill, and no clear member of the SFU coalition was invited to testify. The other three witnesses – Christine N. Jones of GoDaddy, Thomas M. Daley of Verizon, and Denise Yee of Visa – expressed general support for additional legal mechanisms for rights holders, although they expressed various concerns and (especially in Daley's case) proposed changes. Jones in particular bragged about how GoDaddy is already especially aggressive about working with rights holders and removing infringing sites and content, and she lamented that their competitors do not do the same.

[48] S. Rep. No. 112–39, 12–13.

[49] H.R. 3261, *the Stop Online Piracy Act: Hearing Before the House Committee on the Judiciary*, 112th Cong. (2011).

[50] Nate Anderson, "At Web Censorship Hearing, Congress Guns for 'Pro-Pirate' Google," *Ars Technica*, November 16, 2011, http://arstechnica.com/tech-policy/news/2011/11/at-web-censorship-hearing-congress-guns-for-pro-pirate-google.ars.

[51] The site describing the hearing says: "The bill modernizes our criminal and civil statutes to meet new IP enforcement challenges and protect American jobs. The proposal reflects a bipartisan and bicameral commitment toward ensuring that law enforcement and job creators have the necessary tools to protect American intellectual property from counterfeiting and piracy." "Hearing Information: Hearing on: H.R. 3261, the Stop Online Piracy Act'," House Committee on the Judiciary, accessed July 6, 2012, http://judiciary.house.gov/hearings/hear_1116201 1.html.

[52] Anderson, "At Web Censorship Hearing." He quotes Rep. Smith: "One of the companies represented here today has sought to obstruct the Committee's consideration of bipartisan legislation. Perhaps this should come as no surprise given that Google just

The same groups that spoke out against COICA quickly mobilized to oppose PIPA and SOPA in 2011, although, this time, much of the persuadable technology division also put its weight into opposing the bills.[53] In advance of the House Committee on the Judiciary hearing held on November 16, 2011, a veritable who's who of internet companies signed a letter of opposition; signatories included Google, Facebook, Twitter, Yahoo!, Mozilla, and eBay.[54] Collectively, these voices have also won sympathy from several members of Congress, who themselves sent a letter to Smith opposing SOPA.[55]

At this point – specifically, through mid-November 2011 – the conventional political analysis would have cast the odds of something like SOPA passing as very strong. Even with the internet industry ramping up its lobbying expenditures in recent years, SOPA's opponents are still badly outspent on Capitol Hill; groups that support SOPA spent more than ten times as much as the bill's opponents in 2010 and over six times as much through the third quarter of 2011 – spending $280 million in less than two years.[56] As the persuadable technology division has more revenue and a bigger impact on the economy,[57] this imbalance means that SC groups spend a far greater share of their revenue on lobbying. Additionally, the SC coalition's much longer history of working with Congress – and its much better-connected roster of lobbyists (including, most notably, Motion Picture Association of America [MPAA] chief and former Connecticut Senator Chris Dodd) – means it would have a substantial advantage even if the SFU coalition had matched its lobbying expenditures dollar-for-dollar in 2011. Further, as the rest of this study shows, the technology industry has previously established a track record of going along with expansions of copyright, as long as those expansions are perceived as likely and are tempered so that the technology sector's financial interests are not substantially harmed. Senator Ron Wyden threatened to filibuster the bill if it came to the Senate floor, which gave the SFU coalition some hope, but Senate Majority Leader Harry Reid was

---

settled a federal criminal investigation into the company's active promotion of rogue websites that pushed illegal prescription and counterfeit drugs on American consumers."
[53] Declan McCullagh, "Google, Facebook, Zynga Oppose New SOPA Copyright Bill," *CNet News,* November 15, 2011, http://news.cnet.com/8301-31921-3-57325134-281/ google-facebook-zynga-oppose-new-sopa-copyright-bill/.
[54] Ibid.   [55] Ibid.
[56] Jennifer Martinez, "Shootout at the Digital Corral," *Politico,* November 16, 2011, http://www.politico.com/news/stories/1111/68448.html.
[57] See ch. 4, n. 23 (teasing apart some of the data from Gilmore, Morgan, and Osborne, "Annual Industry Accounts").

at least close to the sixty votes required to end it.[58] For all of these reasons, one of two outcomes for SOPA and PIPA looked fairly likely: either the bills would pass with few changes, or the technology sector would extract some degree of watering down of the bills before passage. Another outcome was a distant third in probability: that the core SFU advocates would provide just enough friction to keep the bills from passing at all.

What happened instead was nothing short of game changing. The internet – already the bogeyman of the SC coalition for its capacity to facilitate infringement – became the means for mobilizing millions of citizens who spoke out against SOPA and PIPA. The first action was on November 16, 2011, which was the date of the heavily stacked hearing in the House Committee on the Judiciary to consider SOPA. To mobilize opposition, hundreds of websites engaged in a coordinated information campaign, hosting banners urging users to learn more about the arguments against the act and to contact Congress to express opposition.[59] The group hosting the site, Fight for the Future, was founded in late 2011 and is "aligned with groups like EFF and Public Knowledge but [is] campaign-focused and public-facing."[60] Other groups also played key roles in spreading awareness about this campaign. Other campaign sponsors included core SFU advocates – not only EFF and Public Knowledge, but also groups such as the Free Software Foundation, Creative Commons, and Mozilla.[61] Other sponsors, as of November 17, included Demand Progress and the Participatory Politics Foundation (PPF).[62] Fight for the Future and Demand Progress brought a campaign-focused, netroots mindset that probably provided the tipping point in driving many other participants into action – although these very new SFU groups are the first to credit longstanding allies like EFF and Public Knowledge for building the movement to be in such a position in the first place. With the blackout idea in place and given a substantial behind-the-scenes push, links to the website and its calls to action were widely publicized

---

[58] Larry Downes, "Who Really Stopped SOPA, and Why?," *Forbes*, January 25, 2012, http://www.forbes.com/sites/larrydownes/2012/01/25/who-really-stopped-sopa-and-why/.

[59] Fight for the Future, "American Censorship Day November 16 – Join the Fight To Stop SOPA," *American Censorship Day*, http://americancensorship.org (last visited November 17, 2011).

[60] Fight for the Future, "Campaign Coordinator," http://fightforthefuture.org/jobs/campaign-director (last visited February 23, 2012).

[61] Fight for the Future, "American Censorship Day."

[62] Ibid.

on some of the web's most visible sites, including Tumblr, *Reddit*, and Mozilla.[63]

The effort did a great deal to create awareness about and motivate constituent calls against SOPA and PROTECT-IP.[64] The American Censorship Day website claimed to have generated over a million e-mails and four calls *per second* to Congress that day.[65] This was an extension of the SFU coalition's longstanding strategy of heavy internet advocacy, and it was a remarkably successful mobilization for an issue that previously had little visibility in the eyes of the public. Although the proposal's potential negative effects were a substantial force motivating so much online action, this explosion of constituent action is also probably due in part to the issue's clarity relative to the DRM debate. Despite having tried to explain this issue to perhaps thousands of previously uninitiated people, I still have difficulty explaining briefly what DRM is, how it is regulated, and why that is important. In contrast, a great number of internet users were quickly able to understand – and fear – the proposal that infringing sites' domain names would be seized and then redirected to government-sponsored antipiracy sites. The issue had a clarity that gave these technology enthusiasts the chance to take a specific political action in defense of the internet – not to mention an expression of their visceral dislike for the content industry, growing over the past decade of SC coalition missteps.

The congressional response to the November action was, unfortunately for SFU actors, muted. A few additional members of Congress joined the opposition, but the bills still seemed fairly likely to pass. PIPA was to be put to a vote in the full Senate on January 24, 2012, and passage in the House seemed not too far behind.[66] By the end of 2011, SOPA had attracted thirty-one House co-sponsors, and PIPA's list of co-sponsors included a remarkable forty Senators.[67]

---

[63] Kirsten Salyer, "'American Censorship Day' Makes an Online Statement," *The Ticker: Bloomberg News*, November 16, 2011, http://www.bloomberg.com/news/2011-11-16/-american-censorship-day-makes-an-online-statement-the-ticker.html.

[64] Mike Masnick, "Why the Public Is Willing to Rally Against SOPA/PIPA, But Not for It," *Techdirt*, November 23, 2011, http://www.techdirt.com/articles/20111123/00002616879/why-public-is-willing-to-rally-against-sopapipa-not-it.shtml.

[65] Fight for the Future, "American Censorship Day."

[66] Senate Majority Leader Harry Reid had scheduled a cloture vote on the bill. Jennifer Martinez, "SOPA and PIPA Dead For Now," *Politico*, January 20, 2012, http://www.politico.com/news/stories/0112/71720.html. Although technically a procedural vote, cloture requires sixty votes of support, making it the largest obstacle to final passage.

[67] Library of Congress, "Bill Summary & Status, 112th Congress (2011–2012), H.R.3261, Cosponsors," *Thomas*, http://thomas.loc.gov/cgi-bin/bdquery/z?d112:HR03261:@@@

Undeterred, SFU actors doubled down on the strategy of reaching out to sympathetic websites and engaging in a coordinated day of action; they scheduled a second day of internet action for January 18, 2012. This action drew many thousands more sites to participate – more than 115,000 in all – and more of the web's top sites participated.[68] Many sites in the January action chose the even more dramatic step of blacking out their pages to varying degrees – an illustration of the censorship that they accused the bill of threatening. The most noteworthy site to go dark was Wikipedia, the sixth most-visited website in the world,[69] and many more sites with very high visibility went dark (e.g., Mozilla, *Reddit*), made prominent changes on their home pages (e.g., Google, *Wired*, *Drudge Report*), successfully encouraged thousands of users to turn their personal pages dark (e.g., Tumblr, WordPress), or became vehicles by which millions spread anti-SOPA/PIPA messages (e.g., Twitter, Facebook).[70] This became the "largest online protest in history."[71]

The coordinated action worked beyond anyone's hopes. According to Fight for the Future, more than ten million people signed the group's petition against SOPA and PIPA, and there were more than eight million attempts to call Congress.[72] Four million people sent e-mails to Congress through EFF, Fight for the Future, and Demand Progress, and "Wikipedia wasn't even counting."[73] So many constituents tried to contact Congress that the phone lines were flooded and many members' sites crashed.[74] This made an immediate impact on the balance of congressional opinion on the bills. As of the morning of January 18, 2012, the bills had eighty supporters and thirty-one opponents in the House and Senate; by the next day, it had shifted radically to sixty-three supporters and 122

P; Library of Congress, "Bill Summary & Status, 112th Congress (2011 – 2012), S.968, Cosponsors," *Thomas*, http://thomas.gov/cgi-bin/bdquery/z?d112:SN00968:@@@P.

[68] Fight for the Future, "The January 18 Blackout/Strike in Numbers," *SOPA Strike*, http://sopastrike.com/numbers (last visited February 24, 2012).

[69] "Top Sites," *Alexa*, http://www.alexa.com/topsites (last visited June 12, 2012).

[70] Participation by millions of Twitter users was well-documented because of the site's default that all posts are public. Fight for the Future, "Strike in Numbers." I am also certain that millions of Facebook users also posted in opposition, but I found no sources that could verify this.

[71] Boonsri Dickinson, "The Largest Online Protest in History Started Here," *Business Insider*, January 19, 2012, http://www.businessinsider.com/largest-protest-in-history-started-here-more-than-a-billion-people-will-see-anti-sopa-messages-2012-1.

[72] Fight for the Future, "Strike In Numbers."

[73] Ibid.

[74] The Daily Caller, "SOPA Protests Caused Panic, Crashed Government Websites," *Yahoo! News*, January 19, 2012, http://news.yahoo.com/sopa-protests-caused-panic-crashed-government-websites-214506713.html.

opponents.[75] Just over a month later, the balance had become fifty-five supporters and 205 opponents.[76] Those who jumped into the opposition included eight former sponsors in the House and nine in the Senate (according to the Library of Congress Thomas database), but the bills were effectively dead even before the additional opponents piled on. On January 20, Senate Majority Leader Harry Reid cancelled the scheduled cloture vote, and Representative Lamar Smith said that the Judiciary Committee he chairs would cancel consideration of the bill that had been scheduled for February.[77]

OPEN TO AN ALTERNATIVE?

With a presidential and congressional election looming, nothing like SOPA and PIPA is likely to be considered until after the election, if ever. This is ironic, as something much more modest likely would have passed without many in the public even noticing. As a more modest goal, SC advocates could have seized on to the Online Protection and Enforcement of Digital Trade (OPEN) Act that was submitted in both the House and Senate as an alternative to SOPA and PIPA.[78] This session or next, a far more likely outcome is that a much more limited bill targeting foreign infringing sites will pass. As one such bill, the OPEN Act targets sites that are primarily dedicated to committing criminal copyright infringement, violating the DMCA's anticircumvention provisions, and/or infringing trademark.[79] The bill does so by treating the matter as a trade issue

---

[75] Josh Constine, "SOPA Protests Sway Congress: 31 Opponents Yesterday, 122 Now," *TechCrunch*, January 19, 2012, http://techcrunch.com/2012/01/19/sopa-opponents-supporters/.

[76] Dan Nguyen, "SOPA Opera: Where Do Your Members of Congress Stand on SOPA and PIPA?," *ProPublica*, February 23, 2012, http://projects.propublica.org/sopa/.

[77] Martinez, "SOPA and PIPA Dead for Now."

[78] Online Protection and Enforcement of Digital Trade Act, H.R. 3782 (OPEN Act, House), 112th Cong. (2012); Online Protection and Enforcement of Digital Trade Act, S. 2029 (OPEN Act, Senate), 112th Cong. (2011); Julie Samuels, "An Alternative to SOPA: An Open Process Befitting an Open Internet," *EFF Deeplinks Blog*, December 8, 2011, https://www.eff.org/deeplinks/2011/12/alternative-sopa-open-process-befitting-open-internet.

[79] OPEN Act House, §2(a); OPEN Act Senate, §2(a) (adding 19 U.S.C §337A; see §337A(a)(4)). Cited provisions in House and Senate versions are identical unless noted otherwise. The bill refers to §337A, keeping with the number in the Tariff Act of 1930, although the sections in the contemporary bill had a "1" placed before them. Thus, were OPEN to pass, it would actually create a new section at 19 U.S.C. 1337A.

subject to action by the International Trade Commission (ITC).[80] Rather than targeting sites' online presence via domain name registries, search engines, and so on, the OPEN Act would target only payment processors and advertising affiliates.[81]

Under the OPEN Act, ITC actions would be transparent and adversarial. This is in stark contrast to the ongoing domain seizures by ICE – and in less stark but still nontrivial contrast to those envisioned for the Department of Justice under SOPA and PIPA. The ITC would file a notice in the *Federal Register* for every action it undertakes.[82] Additionally, although affected owners of a copyright or trademark could initiate an action with the ITC, they would be required simultaneously to notify site owners and other affected parties.[83] Before issuing even a temporary order, the ITC would have to grant an opportunity to be heard to the operator of an affected site.[84] Affected third parties – payment processors and advertisers – would also have the opportunity to participate in the proceedings.[85]

The opponents of SOPA and PIPA in Congress advanced OPEN as a more balanced alternative. Senator Wyden sponsored the Senate version (which drew two co-sponsors), and Representative Darrell Issa sponsored the House bill (24 co-sponsors). Issa's office went so far as to set up a website touting OPEN's advantages over SOPA and PIPA, featuring video testimony from OPEN Act co-sponsors in the House.[86] The site argues that, like SOPA and PIPA, the OPEN Act "protects the rights of artists," but unlike the other two acts, it "protects against new internet police powers," "secures safe harbors for legitimate internet businesses," and "targets actual criminals."[87] SFU advocates outside Congress have also expressed their tremendous preference for OPEN – as opposed to SOPA or PIPA – ranging from some of the world's largest Internet

[80] Ibid. With one exception (§5, "Regulations"), the bill refers to "the Commission" throughout; in the context of 19 U.S.C §§ 1330–1341, this means the International Trade Commission. 19 U.S.C. §1330(a).
[81] OPEN Act §337A(f).
[82] OPEN Act §337A(c)(2) [requiring the ITC to follow the same procedures laid out in 19 U.S.C. §1337(b)(1)].
[83] OPEN Act §337A(d).   [84] OPEN Act §337A(f)(2)(C).
[85] OPEN Act §§337A(d)(3)(C), 337A(f)(5).
[86] "OPEN: Online Protection & Enforcement of Digital Trade Act," *Keep the Web Open* (n.d., retrieved February 24, 2012), http://keepthewebopen.com/.
[87] "SOPA vs PIPA vs OPEN," *Keep the Web Open* (n.d., retrieved February 24, 2012), http://keepthewebopen.com/sopa-vs-open.

companies[88] to the EFF.[89] Had the backers of SOPA and PIPA been more open to discussion and compromise with the technology sector and civil society groups, something like OPEN almost certainly could have been passed with little fanfare. Although there would have been more resistance, something between OPEN and SOPA also would have had a great shot at passage. Instead, SC actors refused to meet with SFU actors.[90] The result was an explosion of citizen outrage at their tone-deaf attempt to alter the architecture of the internet despite months of well-thought opposition from the engineers who built it, the companies and nonprofits that have made it such an interesting and lucrative place, and the citizens who are its most avid users.

The process and outcome of the efforts at domain seizures show an astonishing reversal of course in Congressional process – a reversal that may never be repeated in light of the historic backlash that occurred this time. Although there were opponents to the AHRA and DMCA, very few members of the electorate knew about the bills, and opponents had little political capital. Thus, these bills were passed virtually unopposed. Thanks to the growth of a permanent SFU coalition, the broadcast flag enjoyed no such fate. Rather than following this trajectory, however, SC-allied members of Congress tried to ram SOPA and PIPA through despite opposition from dozens of the nation's most prominent internet engineers, more than a hundred legal scholars, dozens of civil society groups, most major internet companies, and more than a million citizens.

---

[88] "Letter from AOL et al. to Rep. Darrell Issa and Sen. Ron Wyden," December 13, 2011, http://keepthewebopen.com/assets/pdfs/12-13-11%20Big%20Web%20Companies%20OPEN%20Endorsement%20Letter.pdf.

[89] Julie Samuels, "The OPEN Act: The Good, the Bad, and a Practice in Participatory Government," *Electronic Frontier Foundation*, December 14, 2011, https://www.eff.org/deeplinks/2011/12/open-act-good-bad-and-practice-participatory-government. Samuels' criticism includes many important areas of potential improvement that stand as valid criticisms. For instance, she points out that the bill includes the DMCA's anticircumvention provisions as a basis for action, even though "Plaintiffs often misuse § 1201, the circumvention statute, in effort[s] to prohibit competition and consumer choice without having to show any underlying copyright infringement."

[90] Mike Masnick, "Disney Refused Invitation from Senator Feinstein to Meet with Tech Companies over PIPA/SOPA," *Techdirt*, January 18, 2012, http://www.techdirt.com/articles/20120118/01464317448/disney-refused-invitation-senator-feinstein-to-meet-with-tech-companies-over-pipasopa.shtml.
When Public Knowledge Legal Director Harold Feld posted this on Facebook, the head of the Consumer Electronics Association, Gary Shapiro, bemoaned in a comment, "Valenti and Glickman would always pick up the phone....I can't even get a hello lunch with Dodd." When I asked if I could quote him, he said, "Just factual!" (On file with the author.)

In short, they tried to turn back the clock on copyright politics – all the way to 1998, when the DMCA passed with relative ease. The SC coalition failed to see the tectonic shifts in copyright politics that happened in the intervening years, and it blew up in its face.

CONCLUSION: WHAT THE SOPA RESPONSE SAYS ABOUT COPYRIGHT POLITICS

The events surrounding SOPA and PIPA are the best possible evidence of the profound shift in the politics of copyright – an exclamation point on the internet-fueled SFU coalition growth identified in this study. In the 1990s, the SC coalition was able to advance their legislative agenda with little resistance. Thus, the AHRA and DMCA primarily – if not exclusively – reflect that coalition's views. By the early 2000s, it was becoming clear that the SFU coalition was providing just enough of a counterweight to the SC coalition that the latter's ability to advance its agenda was substantially reduced. Rather than understanding and working in light of this trajectory, however, SC allies sought to proceed as if their agenda continued to have no real political opposition. They were not only surprised by the online uprising; they refused to accept the overwhelming public verdict as a legitimate expression of public opinion. Most prominently, the RIAA and MPAA chiefs reacted by accusing Google and Wikipedia of engaging in dirty tricks and spreading misinformation.[91] Coming from a political movement that was doggedly insistent on shutting out participation by those with concerns about the bills, these critiques ring hollow. But they show that – at least in the immediate aftermath of the blackout – the SC's core lobbyists do not really understand these events in anywhere near the same way as the general public.

The SOPA blackout and its aftermath have left several key legacies in the politics of copyright in the future. First and most obviously, the internet community and the general public have now mobilized around this issue to a previously unimaginable degree. This study's story of the building of the SFU coalition provides an important context for understanding the intellectual and logistical backing of the uprising. The efforts

---

[91] Cary H. Sherman, "What Wikipedia Won't Tell You," *New York Times*, February 7, 2012, http://www.nytimes.com/2012/02/08/opinion/what-wikipedia-wont-tell-you. html; Chris Dodd, "Senator Dodd On Irresponsible Developments of 'Blackout Day'," *MPAA Blog*, January 17, 2012, http://blog.mpaa.org/BlogOS/post/2012/01/17/ Senator-Dodd-On-Troubling-Developments-of-Blackout-Day-.aspx.

begun by Peter Jaszi and company helped create a network of dedicated activists – and, before long, many of them professional – who could represent the voices of ordinary citizens on copyright. Likewise, beginning with the anti-RIAA backlash in the Napster era and the wide dissemination of pro-SFU messages by public intellectuals and advocates, the broad internet-using public had long since begun to distrust the content industry – to put it charitably. Yet these potent forces had not yet come together in a large-scale political action until SOPA seemed certain of passage. The proposal was so objectionable, and the process by which it had advanced so willfully designed to avoid the frantic critical input by the technology sector and the public, that millions of voters had a "Howard Beale moment – [Internet] users were mad as hell, and they weren't going to take it anymore."[92]

No matter how strong their opinions, millions of people rarely act in concert unless there is substantial coordination. The SOPA protests "were a combination of independent decisions by websites including Wikipedia and *Reddit* to go black on Jan. 18, behind-the-scenes organization by a number of groups, and grassroots response to the blackout and other online efforts.... "[93] Unfortunately, most of the reporting on the backlash has credited the technology industry, failing to understand the far more significant roles played by the collective decisions of thousands of power users – including those who pushed group-created sites Wikipedia and *Reddit* to action – as nudged along by core SFU allies including NGOs, public intellectuals, and journalists. It is understandable that reporters have seized on Google in particular as a perceived epicenter of the movement. Without the historic context of the broader copyright debate, and without an understanding of how online movements are built – such as the fact that they rarely if ever follow the dictates of corporations – it seems natural that a movement involving the world's most important website must be *of* that website. Yet, although Google did work behind the scenes in supporting the move toward a blackout, the idea and nearly all of the momentum came from outside the corporate world. It is also not true, as some have alleged (despite a dearth of evidence), that these NGOs are really just fronts for the technology

---

[92] Downes, "Who Really Stopped SOPA."

[93] Grant Gross, "Who Really Was Behind the SOPA Protests?," *PC World*, February 3, 2012, http://www.pcworld.com/businesscenter/article/249270/who_really_was_behind_the_sopa_protests.html.

industry.[94] SFU-allied NGOs do get some corporate funding, but groups like EFF and Public Knowledge were founded and still mostly run on contributions from foundations or individuals. Crediting (or blaming) technology giants for the blackout misses the point of what happened. Public resentment against the SC coalition has been building for years. In this context, when the bills were so easily demonized – and being advanced in such an unsavory manner – the time was ripe for a people-powered outcry. That is exactly what happened.

The technology industry also pushed back against SOPA and PIPA, and their response worked synergistically with public outcry – helping to fuel the understanding that something bad was in the works, then helping to draw constituents to contact Congress. Yet, in the months before the public outcry, when the best hope for stopping Hollywood actually was the technology sector (via lobbying on the Hill), SOPA and PIPA were en route to easy passage.[95] Even though its website was a key driver in the January action, the "response was not organized by Google or any tech money at all (except perhaps the meager salaries that tech-policy writers tend to receive)."[96] The technology industry used mostly inside-the-Beltway politics up until the last minute, when it became clear that these strategies would not stop the bills – and that several nonprofits and the broader technology community were going to try a far more public strategy. It was only then that technology industry heavyweights decided to join the online action, and they were nearly as surprised by the outcome as was the content industry.

[94] As just one example, see David C. Lowery, "Letter to Emily White at NPR All Songs Considered," *The Trichordist*, June 18, 2012, http://thetrichordist.wordpress.com/2012/06/18/letter-to-emily-white-at-npr-all-songs-considered/. Throughout a brutally long post, Lowery repeatedly decries the free culture movement – and along the way, essentially claims they are a front for the technology sector.

For a detailed rebuttal, see Bill D. Herman, "Dear David Lowery: Thanks for the Slander and Bad Metaphors," *Shouting Loudly*, June 20, 2012, http://www.shoutingloudly.com/2012/06/20/dear-david-lowery-thanks-for-the-slander-and-bad-metaphors/.

[95] Mike Godwin, "Guest Blogger: Sunlight Got It Wrong," *Sunlight Foundation*, February 7, 2012, http://sunlightfoundation.com/blog/2012/02/07/guest-blogger-sunlight-got-it-wrong/.

[96] Ibid.

12

The Future of Digital Rights – and Digital Fights

The future of copyright in the digital era is far from certain. What is clear, however, is that the first twenty-plus years of the debate over digital copyright has already been a remarkable roller coaster ride. This is commonly understood to be because new digital technologies increase the ease of making and transmitting copies, but that is only half the story; the other half is the rise of a potent group of political actors who seek to defend those technologies against encroachment by copyright law. The political part of the story – a story largely of political messages communicated through new media – was far from expected, even at the turn of the century. And, in many ways, it has been the more remarkable and far-reaching share of the tale. Yet it has largely gone untold. Hopefully, this study will bring a bit more attention to the transformations in political organization and communication that shape copyright outcomes specifically and policy outcomes more generally.

With my study's focus on the birth of the strong fair use (SFU) coalition, combined with fairly precise measures of the degree to which that coalition has made disproportionate use of the internet, I hope to have given a better understanding of both the history of copyright advocacy and the potential value of online communication. I also think this study suggests broader meaning for issue advocacy and for the study of political communication more generally.

THE BIRTH AND STRENGTH OF THE STRONG FAIR USE MOVEMENT

Beginning with opposition to what would become the Digital Millennium Copyright Act (DMCA), and growing rapidly in the years since the DMCA's passage, SFU advocates have built a powerful multisite organizational infrastructure. They have also spread the SFU message to millions of citizens. Especially as illustrated by the downfall of the Stop Online Piracy Act (SOPA) and the Preventing Real Online Threats to Economic Creativity and Theft of Intellectual Property (PROTECT-IP or PIPA), it is now much harder to pass strong copyright (SC) legislation. The debate over digital rights management (DRM) was a key part of the rallying cry of the SFU coalition from the 1990s through the mid-2000s, although related debates have also been significant. In the years since 2006, as the debate has evolved and the SC coalition's strategies have evolved from new DRM regulations to new internet regulations, the SFU coalition has also evolved to keep up with the debate. More remarkably, the SFU coalition has become even more relevant.

This is a sharp change from the policy dynamics of copyright during the twentieth century. The Audio Home Recording Act (AHRA) became law with little substantial resistance. Although the anticircumvention provisions of the DMCA attracted more pushback, opponents did not have time to organize a coherent coalition until after the passage of Bruce Lehman's White Paper proposal was nearly a foregone conclusion. Between 1999 and 2002, however, several events led to radical changes in the politics of copyright. The publicity around peer-to-peer trading, the threat of Hollings' bill, and the sharp rise in participation by nongovernmental organizations (NGOs) and public intellectuals reshaped the playing field. By 2003, the SFU coalition had grown powerful enough that it had to be accounted for by the SC coalition. The SFU coalition played a central role in killing the broadcast flag proposals, and it made a credible push to reform the DMCA.

This study is largely a story about the SFU coalition's substantial successes at building and deploying organizations and ideas. In the decade after the DMCA's passage, countless SFU-allied groups were started, including advocacy- and litigation-focused NGOs, academic centers, and student law clinics.[1] Along with library groups – perhaps the longest-standing voices for copyright moderation, although among the quieter voices today – these NGOs and scholars are at the core of a significant, permanent, organized coalition that exists where there was none before, and the results have spoken for themselves.

The changing tenor of the offline debate about digital copyright, especially as that debate happened in Congress, showed the impressive growth of the SFU coalition in a remarkably short time. In a very short

[1] Boyle, *The Public Domain*, 243.

period – between 1995 and 2003 – the SFU coalition rose from literal nonexistence to real political capital. The few years at the start of the millennium saw a particularly sharp change, from a coalition with no permanent, professional organizations involved to one with dogged, savvy NGOs taking on the SC coalition on a consistent basis. It also saw the reverberation of pro-SFU messages in countless other venues, from newly founded research centers at top law schools to the rapidly growing cadre of technology sites. It was becoming clear that principled opposition to the SC agenda was a major force, both in Washington, D.C., and in the broader public's understanding of the issue. The difference in the policy process before and after this period was stark, giving tangible proof that the SFU coalition's mobilization efforts had made a real difference.

From 2007 to 2010, the DRM debate largely wound down in importance, and the fight over digital copyright evolved in a more directly internet-specific direction. Even as the SC coalition has been fighting to export DMCA-like DRM regulations abroad, it has rolled back its emphasis on this strategy domestically. Instead, it has sought to bring virtually all members of the internet ecosystem into the regulatory purview of copyright; this includes advertising networks, payment processors, search engines, internet service providers, and domain name registrars and registries. The Recording Industry Association of America's (RIAA) lawsuits against thousands of end users proved to be such an unmitigated financial and public relations catastrophe that one can hardly blame the SC coalition for looking elsewhere. For domestic sites, the notice-and-takedown process has been reasonably successful at removing copyrighted materials; if anything, the incentives of the law (not to mention compliance costs) have pushed large sites into much stronger copyright enforcement tactics than necessary. YouTube's rollout of an automatic content identification system in 2007[2] is only the most obvious of countless examples. Unsatisfied with the notice-and-takedown system, however, SC advocates have sought far more drastic measures, especially in pursuit of foreign sites not subject to domestic law. This led them to pursue the Combating Online Infringement and Counterfeits Act (COICA), then SOPA and PIPA, proposals that eventually drew the coordinated actions of more than one hundred thousand websites, pushing over eight millions citizens to contact Congress in opposition.

---

[2] Ellen Lee, "YouTube Introduces New Copyright Filter," *San Francisco Chronicle*, October 16, 2007.

For those who knew little about the history of copyright advocacy, the SOPA strike seemed to come out of nowhere, and it was perceived as a telling blow in a contest between large corporations. For those who have watched these debates unfold over the years, however, it was clear that the birth and growth of the SFU coalition had already made a substantial change in the political dynamics around the issue. It was also clear that core members of the SFU coalition, especially NGOs and allied scholars, had done most of the groundwork to make the strike happen, with the technology companies that joined the fight generally participating only toward the end. It is the NGOs, public intellectuals, and, particularly, dedicated members of the online technology press – Mike Masnick of *Techdirt*, Cory Doctorow of *BoingBoing*, and so on – who will continue to hold down the SFU fort.

Had SOPA and PIPA been pursued in the late 1990s, they would have stood a great chance at passage with little organized resistance. The years in between, however, saw the mobilization of a substantial political movement dedicated to preserving the right to digital communication, and adherents of that movement almost universally see the SC agenda as a threat to that right. Although the SFU coalition still does not have the kind of gold-plated Washington lobbying operation that the SC coalition enjoys, it has proven surprisingly adept at slowing down new proposals to expand the reach of digital copyright over roughly the last decade.

The birth, growth, and against-the-odds successes of the SFU coalition are among the most important developments in the history of copyright. The SFU's success is the result of a number of important developments, each of which has not gotten its due in the broader understanding of copyright history – a broader understanding that is too focused on technological, courtroom, and industry developments and too little interested in changes in policymaking and in public opinion. The founding of Public Knowledge and the Electronic Frontier Foundation (EFF)'s entrée into copyright litigation and advocacy, both in 2001, should be in the pantheon of central historical developments in copyright law. (Because of their work in the courtroom, EFF does get more credit for shaping copyright history, but even this is undoubtedly too little.) The entry of these groups to the debate should be listed alongside the founding of the American Society of Composers, Authors, and Publishers (ASCAP) in 1914; the 1984 *Sony v. Universal* ruling, in which the Supreme Court held – on a 5–4 vote, nonetheless – that the video cassette recorder (VCR) is legal; and the invention of Napster in 1999. Peter Jaszi deserves to be as well-known in copyright history as Bruce Lehman – not least because, even as Lehman has moved on to other pursuits, Jaszi and his fellow American University professor Pat Aufderheide have unleashed a movement empowering various communities to make much fuller use of fair use.[3] Far more people may read the *New York Times*, but technology websites such as *Wired*, *BoingBoing*, *Slashdot*, *Reddit*, and *Techdirt* have made a more direct impact on the copyright debate.

Core SFU coalition members are not all well-known by the general public, but this does not necessarily mean they are not having an impact. For instance, regular readers of technology news are more likely to be opinion leaders on the subject, so, even though their social networks do not consume this information, many are undoubtedly getting the SFU message indirectly. Thus, while the *Times'* balanced but light coverage has a broader direct audience, technology sites' drumbeat of highly one-sided coverage probably has a much stronger effect, especially as those messages reverberate outward. Behind much of this coverage, of course, is the steady flow of information provided by SFU-aligned nonprofits and scholarly groups. Yet because of the focus on cases, technologies, and products, much of the SFU coalition's work is underestimated, even by scholars. I hope that one result of this study is an end to this omission, and copyright comes to be seen as a highly contested political issue, with the issue's movement from barely to highly contested being credited in much larger part to the core SFU actors and their unofficial allies in the technology press and among the technorati more generally.

Because the birth and growth of the SFU coalition is a story unknown to the general public, the general level of understanding of the machinations behind the SOPA strike was sadly lacking. When asked about who was behind the action, surely most people would say, "Google and Wikipedia did it." Although these were the most visible participants, this action would not have been possible without the previous build-up of more long-standing organizations and an SFU-aligned understanding of the issue. If the SFU movement had arisen in opposition to SOPA and PIPA, instead of years earlier, it would have been very difficult to persuade two of the world's most important sites to take such dramatic action. Even in the context of a decade of SFU coalition buildup, it took coordination among several core coalition members to reach out to the countless sites – more than 115,000 – that participated. On top of this, it took the injection of brand-new coalition members, especially Fight for

---

[3] American University Center for Social Media, "Fair Use," 2012, http://www.centerfor socialmedia.org/fair-use. See also Aufderheide and Jaszi, *Reclaiming Fair Use.*

the Future and Demand Progress, to move toward such a radical online action. Even the founders of these new groups acknowledge, though, that they could not have become involved in 2011 and found such success without the groundwork laid by long-standing SFU allies – from groups such as Public Knowledge and EFF to technology sites like *Techdirt* and *Reddit*. The new netroots techniques grew so well because the SFU coalition had already been tending the farm of internet advocacy for so many years.

Technology companies, especially Google, also deserve credit for helping spread the message – and, again, especially in Google's case, for helping fund SFU organizations. Yet these organizations are far from being technology industry front groups; they often criticize technology companies for being too passive on some issues and for being on the wrong side of other issues. The founding of Public Knowledge and the entry of other groups, such as EFF and the Center for Democracy and Technology, into the debate over copyright were organic decisions by dedicated activists, thinkers, and board members. Substantial corporate funding for these groups only came after they had established themselves and, even then, other funding sources, such as individual donors and foundations, have been far more significant.[4] Further, off-the-record conversations with several participants have confirmed that, to the extent that these sectors coordinate on political strategies, it is almost always the NGOs pushing technology companies into action rather than the other way around.

The copyright debate has not been "Silicon Valley versus Hollywood" so much as it has been Hollywood versus a diffuse coalition of underfunded nonprofits, public intellectuals, and technology writers. Silicon

---

[4] The EFF started out with personal donations by three successful Silicon Valley entrepreneurs: Mitch Kapor, the founder of Lotus; Apple co-founder Steve Wozniak; and a third Silicon Valley entrepreneur who donated anonymously. Electronic Frontier Foundation, "Formation Documents and Mission Statement for the EFF," July 10, 1990, https://w2.eff.org/legal/cases/SJG/?f=eff_creation.html.

The EFF still gets roughly half of its support from individual donors, and foundation support accounts for about another third. Electronic Frontier Foundation, "2009–2010 Annual Report," 14, https://www.eff.org/files/eff-2009-2010-annual-report.pdf.

Public Knowledge has been funded primarily by foundations. For instance, its major donor list in its 2010 Annual Report is composed exclusively of foundations. Public Knowledge, "2010 Annual Report," 3, http://www.publicknowledge.org/files/docs/AnnReport2010PK.pdf.

In short, although corporate contributions are now part of each group's funding mix, they are far more closely aligned with individuals and foundations that see their work as important to the broader public good.

Valley corporations have not played a central role in coordinating the coalition's advocacy, starting allied groups, or spreading the coalition's message to policymakers or the broader public. They have sought to avoid the reach of copyright into their core business models, but they have not made a firm commitment to SFU membership. They have been persuadable on these issues, and the most persuasive political message for a business is the relationship between policy outcome and their bottom line. Because of this inexact alignment of interests, SFU actors have not been able to count on the technology industry to be full coalition members, even if they do generally lean in that direction. This may have changed with the process surrounding SOPA and PIPA. Ironically, the content industries and their congressional allies may have convinced technology companies that their best bet is permanent, prominent advocacy on the SFU side of the debate. Leading up to and during that process, however, nonprofits, scholars, and allied online journalists did far, far more of the heavy lifting to make something like the SOPA strike possible.

The future of copyright is still very much in flux. Allies of each coalition are still dissatisfied with the scope and reach of copyright, although each side's proposed solutions would only exacerbate what the other side sees as the problem. To a large extent, this future will be the result of continued struggles between these coalitions, with each trying to bring in allies, especially the persuadable actors in the technology sector. On a day-to-day basis, this will largely continue in venues that favor the still better funded SC coalition – especially in the formal and informal face-to-face discussions and debates in Washington. Yet the lessons of the SOPA strike, in which millions of constituents jammed congressional phone lines and inboxes, will not soon be forgotten, and this will continue to color the debate going forward. Once the 2012 elections are over, some members of Congress may again try to push through related legislation, but those who are not clearly allied with the SC coalition will be far more skeptical of claims that no substantial opposition exists or that opponents only want to take part in, legitimize, or profit from piracy. As far back as 2006, I thought it was fairly clear that the days of easy passage for major SC coalition-backed bills were over, but apparently not everyone agreed. Today, however, any honest observer must admit that the dynamics of the debate have changed profoundly. SC coalition denial on this count led to one of the most resounding public defeats of a legislative proposal in the history of the republic. At the center of this SFU coalition success, of course, was a crafty internet strategy. This is why the story of digital copyright policy is also a story about digital advocacy.

AN IMPORTANT ROLE FOR INTERNET ADVOCACY

The SFU coalition has long been engaged in vociferous online communications. This all-out effort to reach the broader public via the web has been a nice complement to its dedicated and consistent offline communication, and the combination has helped counterbalance its extreme funding disadvantage relative to the SC coalition's old-fashioned lobbying muscle. Even before the SOPA blackout, there was a very strong case to be made that, based at least on the circumstantial evidence, internet mobilization has helped shape policy outcomes in copyright. Now, such qualifiers are no longer necessary. Online advocacy has profoundly changed the policy dynamics around copyright, including policy outcomes. Going forward, it is much less likely that copyright will be expanded, and internet advocacy turned SOPA and PIPA from nearly certain passage to a rapid demise. The content industry still shows every willingness to use the existing statutory and case law to its strategic advantage, and the SC coalition is still almost certainly strong enough to block any roll-back of copyright. Yet SC coalition members must now rethink their understanding about if and how it may still be possible to make further significant gains in Congress.

Although the historical methods in this study have helped enlighten the twists and turns of this specific policy issue, the quantitative methods are designed so that they can be used in future research on a diverse range of policy issues. Although SFU advocates are particularly fond of and skilled with these new technologies, and while this helps explain why they were the first to score such an enormous public reaction almost exclusively through internet advocacy, the SFU coalition is not the only group trying to leverage the internet to counterbalance a disadvantage in funding and other traditional political resources. Quite the contrary, the SOPA strike is now in many ways a model outcome for every funding-disadvantaged, self-styled netroots coalition on any policy issue. By focusing on copyright, an area that draws in those who are ahead of the curve on technology, this study has allowed a glimpse into the future of how other issues are going to be debated. When asked if this outcome is unique because the issue is so near and dear to the hearts of internet enthusiasts – or whether something similar could work for advocacy on other issues – Yochai Benkler responded:

> So, there's a short answer and a long answer . . . The short answer is Susan G. Komen. I haven't done the study yet. We are. . . . That said, when I started writing about free and open source software thirteen, fourteen

years ago, the core response from all the economists was, "Software's a really weird piece of production thing, and software programmers are a really quirky tribe, so you can't learn anything from that." And my sense was, actually, no, they just live five to ten years ahead in the future of everybody else, which turns out to be true. I think you're right that a lot of what drove this, both the capabilities and the interest and the media, had a lot to do with the fact that this is about the net. My own sense is that, what it does is it gives us a way of looking 5–10 years into the future rather than that it's a dead end. Because these capabilities, these structures, the ways in which they work, are generalized.[5]

This study's focus on copyright is fortuitous – and not merely because of what just happened, but because it is a glimpse into the future of advocacy more generally.

Although the tools and strategies will undoubtedly continue to evolve at breakneck speed, people will continue to have more ways to express more opinions about more policy issues. Whether, why, and how it shapes any given policy outcome is another question. Getting a charitable foundation to change its policy in light of a public relations catastrophe, as the Susan G. Komen Foundation did, is one thing. It is another entirely to stop a bill that is backed by powerful special interests and policymakers who are used to a certain amount of criticism and scorn. Such people-powered triumphs in the face of well-heeled lobbying are especially difficult in the insular and highly donation-dependent U.S. political system.[6] On this count, the copyright story is somewhat disheartening; in November 2011, roughly a million constituents contacted Congress, leading just a handful of members to change their positions on the bills.[7] It was only in January, when untold millions called and e-mailed, that the bills were definitively shelved. It may not be realistic to expect a political group or advocacy coalition to mobilize several million people to have their voices heard on a given issue. Yet, if that is the new standard, it will only be viewed as realistic because the internet now makes it so. Across virtually all issues, new media tools will undoubtedly continue to work their way deeper into the issue advocacy process; this change, and the potential shifts in policy outcomes it creates, is a topic worthy of the attention it is now drawing from many scholars.

[5] Benkler, "The Networked Public Sphere."
[6] Lessig, *Republic, Lost.*
[7] Fight for the Future, "SOPA Timeline," http://sopastrike.com/timeline (last visited June 12, 2012).

STUDYING THE FUTURE

Political communication is undergoing rapid transformation. The time between presidential election cycles is hardly enough for the earliest effects of most major policy initiatives, yet the same period is plenty for major changes in communications technologies and practices. As is the case for politicians and issue advocates, this presents both problems and opportunities. One problem is the comparatively slow turnaround for academic studies; by the time a study is being read by an audience, the technologies under investigation may have become passé, replaced entirely, or used in very different ways. This is difficult enough for practitioners of digital advocacy, who can require months to relearn and adapt to new developments. It is even harder for academics, who face a multistep production process, each step of which (research design, human subjects approval, grant application and funding, data collection, data analysis, write-up, submission, peer review, revisions) can take months all by itself. In about as much time as it takes a large research project to go from conception to completion, the smartphone went from a niche product to a must-have device. Facebook went from "Harvard only" to hundreds of millions of users in less time. Several of the steps in the research process can be (and, in some cases, are being) substantially shortened, but any study of new media will always be conducted amid the danger of being outdated before it is even completed.

Another challenge is the increasing difficulty of merely keeping up with new developments. In decades past, new technologies arrived at a slow enough pace – and were sufficiently discrete from one another – that scholars could pontificate on their likely meaning while they were still being developed or adopted. Now, the industrialized world is drowned in a barrage of digital devices, features, and services, with many reaching spectacular success or miserable failure before many people even understand what they are for. In this whirlwind, building a scholarly agenda around studying a specific way of using media may be career suicide – yet we must adopt and understand at least some relatively new media habits and try to help the world understand where things have been and where they are headed. Thus, researchers have to walk a careful route, studying new ways of communicating, yet not doing so in such a way that is only relevant for that specific moment. Scholars must seek to make their research relatively future-proof, seeking insights that will still enlighten us as we process still-to-come developments, while making relevant observations about the world we live in today.

Despite the challenges of studying new media technologies, such study also offers many opportunities for researchers. Most obviously, there are now far more things to study, far more ways to study them, and far more access than ever before. The amount of data available to researchers is positively astounding. The never-ending flow of content on political websites – or websites in any other major category, for that matter – is far more than any team of researchers could ever study. Supplementing this torrent is a whole cottage industry of freely available data about websites, from data about audience share (even *country-specific* rankings) to which other sites link. Social media have only accelerated the amount of available data. With modest technical skill or reasonable amounts of money, researchers can now get direct access to the communication messages sent and received by millions of people every day. Just twenty years ago, such access was inconceivable. Now, researchers and marketers alike are drowning in data, trying to figure out how to make use of it all. This presents a new set of problems, but the problem of how to deal with this embarrassment of riches should be one we are more than happy to embrace.

New communication technologies are also changing the organizational ecosystem around issue advocacy, and this study hints at how some of these changes have played out in the copyright debate. As Andrew Chadwick points out, the internet is creating conditions that have led to the blurring of the traditional lines between political parties, advocacy groups, and social movements, with each category drawing on the organizational repertoires of the others.[8] While the issue of copyright law does not break cleanly along party lines, the issue features organizations that blur the lines between advocacy groups and social movements. The organizations that straddle this line most deliberately include Fight for the Future and Demand Progress. Still other types of organizations have also joined the fray. The mass community-created blogs such as *Slashdot* and *Reddit* are themselves hybrid entities that fuse the functions of journalistic outlet, virtual community, and professional society. Within these flexible repertoires, these sites' organizers and users have also shown their capacity to act like social movements and political organizations – at least in the face of perceived threats.

In *The MoveOn Effect*, David Karpf gives a more detailed treatment to questions of the changing organizational ecology of political advocacy in the digital era. In addition to organizational hybridity, Karpf identifies

[8] Chadwick, "Digital Network Repertoires and Organizational Hybridity."

the increasingly difficult fundraising environment for legacy issue advocacy groups with top-heavy professional bureaucracies to support. In an era featuring increasingly diverse ways in which citizens can be members of groups and participate in activism, and in which issue generalists like MoveOn soak up a great deal of the enthusiasm, bureaucratically organized issue specialist groups may need to reorganize. On this count, the Electronic Frontier Foundation and Public Knowledge are almost certainly better positioned than most legacy issue specialists because their subject specialization gives them a fundamentally sound understanding of internet communication. (Some legacy groups may still have leaders who are not even especially comfortable with basic internet technologies like e-mail – let alone blogs, wikis, mobile applications, and so on.) It is also helpful that they organized and rose to prominence during rather than before the internet era, so they have no history of funding their organizations via bulk mail appeals to armchair activists. Their organizations are thus leaner and better configured for today's environment.

Finally, new developments in media and technology give us an opportunity to rethink how we perceive the social world and how we study it. There are many ways in which new communication tools jar us into seeing things that were there all along but have suddenly become much clearer. For instance, I view this study as part of a small but growing focus on the communication at the core of the policymaking process. This was easy to overlook when communication was relatively expensive; if it takes money to reach policymakers or the masses, it is relatively easy to look at the money and not the communication it buys. Yet even theories that depend on communication to explain the points where disadvantaged coalitions can find success – Baumgartner and Jones's theory of punctuated equilibriums comes to mind – have not been grounded in the theories and study of communication processes. Historically, scholars of political communication have returned the favor, studying campaign communication in depth while spending relatively little energy investigating advocacy communication, let alone in a way grounded in the theories and study of the policymaking process. As new communication tools are reshaping what is possible for policy advocates, though, this space between the study of policymaking and the study of political communication is becoming increasingly problematic.

Money does not buy policy outcomes, but it does buy tools with which to communicate one's message to policymakers. This ranges from a telephone, to a $2,500 seat at a fund-raising event, to a large office on K Street with hundreds of well-trained staffers – and everything in between.

Some communicators are given much more preferential access to make their pitch, and some have much more finely tuned messages to deliver; both of these advantages are highly correlated with financial resources. Yet policymakers generally view themselves as open to persuasion, and most generally are. One of the most powerful messages elected officials can receive is, "If you want to keep your job, you will do this," and that message can be conveyed effectively by the coordinated actions of thousands of voters. The same message can be conveyed to appointed officials as well via pressure from elected officials.

Although a policymaker's job security is the ultimate trump card, even less stark messages can have an effect. One appointed official explained to me that bureaucrats are quite open to well-crafted arguments made by anybody, submitted as part of a rulemaking process, whether or not the author has serious financial backing. Here, internet participation makes it possible for even total outsiders to follow a debate, make a submission on time and in the correct format, and potentially have an impact – although such an outcome will be most likely among outsiders who are nonetheless experts in a relevant field. Members of Congress – or, more often, their staffs – are also open to more rational persuasion on many issues. Yet the process is also different for elected versus appointed officials. The same official explained to me that it is unhelpful to one's case to have thousands of similar comments from constituents mobilized to participate in a rulemaking; unless constituents will have specific stories that can help policymakers see specific examples of a broader point, the resources used urging public action would be better spent on improving an organization's own submission. For elected officials, however, the opposite is often true; a thousand short (unique) e-mails from nonexpert constituents are probably more persuasive than one very well-crafted, detailed e-mail from an expert. Here, the SOPA/PIPA debate is a fantastic example; in 2011, separate letters by technical and legal experts – crafted and signed by some of the greatest minds studying these issues – warned Congress about the bills' pitfalls, to little effect. Yet when ordinary constituents starting flooding the phone lines, members' positions changed quickly.

This study does not give definitive answers on the future of issue advocacy, but it is a start. Hopefully, it will be just one contribution to an area of increasing focus – one that draws political communication scholars to focus more on the policy process, as well as drawing scholars in other fields – not only law and policy studies, but also fields such as computer and information science – to focus more on political communication. This is at least one case study that explores which types of advocates tend to go online under which circumstances, as well as a bit of an exploration of how they do so and how this has shaped the policy environment. We still need more detailed explorations of specific strategies, the audiences those campaigns reach, how those messages reach audiences, what effects they have on audiences, and how those translate (or do not translate) into policy outcomes. Those scholars who are exploring how changes in communication are reshaping the policy process are doing work at an exciting time. On this count, I am humbled to be among some distinguished company, and I am excited that scholars across many fields are showing increasing interest in this area. In both the rapidly evolving communication environment, and the burgeoning research studying it, I look forward to seeing what the future will hold.

Bibliography

321 *Studios v. Metro Goldwyn Mayer Studios.* 307 F.Supp.2d 1085 (N.D. *Cal.* 2004).

A&M Records, Inc. v. Napster, Inc. 239 F.3d 1004 (9th Cir. 2001).

Akester, Patrícia. "Technological Accommodation of Conflicts between Freedom of Expression and DRM: The First Empirical Assessment." *University of Cambridge: Faculty Resources.* July 7, 2009. http://www.law.cam.ac.uk/ faculty-resources/download/technological-accommodation-of-conflicts-betwe en-freedom-of-expression-and-drm-the-first-empirical-assessment/6286/pdf.

Alderman, Jonathan. *Sonic Boom: Napster, MP3, and the New Pioneers of Music.* Cambridge, MA: Perseus Publishing, 2001.

American Library Association v. FCC. 406 F.3d 689 (D.C. Cir. 2005).

Anderson, Cassondra C. "'We Can Work It Out': A Chance to Level the Playing Field for Radio Broadcasters," *North Carolina Journal of Law & Technology* 11 (2011): 72–98.

Anderson, Chris. "The Long Tail." *Wired*, October, 2004. http://www.wired .com/wired/archive/12.10/tail.html.

Audio Home Recording Act. 17 U.S.C. §§ 1001–1010. Pub. L. No. 102–563 (1992).

Aufderheide, Patricia, and Peter Jaszi. *Reclaiming Fair Use: How to Put Balance Back in Copyright.* Chicago: University of Chicago Press, 2011.

Barabási, Albert-László. *Linked: How Everything Is Connected to Everything Else and What It Means for Business, Science, and Everyday Life.* New York: Plume, 2003.

Baumgartner, Frank R., and Bryan D. Jones. *Agendas and Instability in American Politics*, 2nd ed. Chicago: University of Chicago Press, 2009.

Benkler, Yochai. "'The networked public sphere': framing the public discourse of the SOPA/PIPA debate." Presentation at Guardian Activate New York, May 3, 2012. http://www.guardian.co.uk/media-network/video/2012/may/15/ yochai-benkler-networked-public-sphere-sopa-pipa.

_____. *The Wealth of Networks: How Social Production Transforms Markets and Freedom.* New Haven, CT: Yale University Press, 2006.

Bennett, W. Lance. "Toward a Theory of Press-State Relations in the United States." *Journal of Communication* 40 (1990): 103–25.

Bimber, Bruce A. *Information and American Democracy: Technology in the Evolution of Political Power.* New York: Cambridge University Press, 2003.

Bimber, Bruce A., Andrew J. Flanagin, and Cynthia Stohl. *Collective Action in Organizations: Interaction and Engagement in an Era of Technological Change.* New York: Cambridge University Press, 2012.

———. "Reconceptualizing Collective Action in the Contemporary Media Environment." *Communication Theory* 15 (2005): 365–88.

boyd, danah m., and Nicole B. Ellison. "Social Network Sites: Definition, History, and Scholarship." *Journal of Computer-Mediated Communication* 13, no. 1 (2007). http://jcmc.indiana.edu/vol13/issue1/boyd.ellison.html.

Boyle, James. *The Public Domain: Enclosing the Commons of the Mind.* New Haven, CT: Yale University Press, 2008.

Bruns, Axel. "Methodologies for Mapping the Political Blogosphere: An Exploration Using the Issuecrawler Research Tool." *First Monday* 12, no. 5 (May 7, 2007).

Cahn v. Sony Corp. No. 90 Civ. 4537 (S.D.N.Y. filed July 9, 1990).

Chadwick, Andrew. "Digital Network Repertoires and Organizational Hybridity." *Political Communication* 24, no. 3 (July 2007): 283–301.

Chinn, Susan. "A Simple Method for Converting an Odds Ratio to Effect Size for Use in Meta-Analysis." *Statistics in Medicine* 19 (2000): 3127–31.

Coe, Robert. "It's the Effect Size, Stupid: What Effect Size Is and Why It Is Important." Paper presented at the Annual Conference of the British Educational Research Association, University of Exeter, England, September 2002. http://www.leeds.ac.uk/educol/documents/00002182.htm.

Cohen, Jacob. "A Power Primer." *Psychological Bulletin* 112, no. 1 (1992): 155–9.

Copyright Act of 1976. 17 U.S.C. §§101 et seq. Pub L. No. 94–553 (1976).

Dalal, Anjali. "Protecting Hyperlinks and Preserving First Amendment Values on the Internet." *University of Pennsylvania Journal of Constitutional Law* 13 (2011): 1017–78.

Davis, Aeron. *Public Relations Democracy: Public Relations, Politics and the Mass Media in Britain.* New York: Manchester University Press, 2002.

Decherney, Peter. *Hollywood's Copyright Wars: From Edison to the Internet.* New York: Columbia University Press, 2012.

———. "From Fair Use to Exemption." *Cinema Journal* 46, no. 2 (2007): 120–7.

Diermeier, Daniel, and Timothy J. Feddersen. "Information and Congressional Hearings." *American Journal of Political Science* 44, no. 1 (2000): 51–65.

Digital Audio Tape Recorder Act of 1990. S. 2358, 101st Cong. (1990).

Digital Millennium Copyright Act. Pub. L. No. 105–304 (1998).

Doctorow, Cory. *Content: Selected Essays on Technology, Creativity, Copyright, and the Future of the Future.* San Francisco: Tachyon Publications, 2008. http://craphound.com/content/download/.

Eldred v. Ashcroft. 537 U.S. 186 (2003).

Electronic Frontier Foundation (EFF). "RIAA v. The People: Five Years Later." 2008. https://www.eff.org/files/eff-riaa-whitepaper.pdf.

Engage and Demand Progress, eds. *Hacking Politics.* Accessed June 14, 2012. http://hackingpolitics.com/.

Farrall, Kenneth N., and Michael X. Delli Carpini. "Cyberspace, the Web Graph and Political Deliberation on the Internet." *International Conference on Politics and Information Systems: Technologies and Applications.* Orlando, Florida Publishers, 2004.

Fight for the Future. "The January 18 Blackout/Strike in Numbers." Accessed June 14, 2012. http://sopastrike.com/numbers.

Flava Works, Inc. v. Gunter, 689 F.3d 754 (7th Circuit, 2012).

Gillespie, Tarleton. *Wired Shut: Copyright and the Shape of Digital Culture.* Cambridge, MA: MIT Press, 2007.

Gilmore, Teresa L., Edward T. Morgan, and Sarah B. Osborne. "Annual Industry Accounts: Advance Statistics on GDP by Industry for 2010." *Survey of Current Business* 8 (May 2011), 17. http://www.bea.gov/scb/pdf/2011/05%20May/0511_indy_accts.pdf.

Goldsmith, Jack, and Tim Wu. *Who Controls the Internet?: Illusions of a Borderless World.* New York: Oxford University Press, 2006.

Greer, John A. "If the Shoe Fits: Reconciling the International Shoe Minimum Contacts Test with the Anticybersquatting Consumer Protection Act." *Vanderbilt Law Review* 61 (2008): 1861–1902.

Hacker, Jacob S., and Paul Pierson. *Winner-Take-All Politics: How Washington Made the Rich Richer – and Turned Its Back on the Middle Class.* New York: Simon & Schuster, 2010.

Hart, Jeffrey A. "The Net Neutrality Debate in the United States." *Journal of Information Technology and Politics* 8 (2011): 418–43.

Herman, Bill D. "The Battle over Digital Rights Management: A Multi-Method Study of the Politics of Copyright Management Technologies." Dissertation, University of Pennsylvania, 2009.

———. "Breaking and Entering My Own Computer: The Contest of Copyright Metaphors." *Communication Law and Policy* 13, no. 2 (April 2008): 231–74.

———. "A Political History of DRM and Related Copyright Debates, 1987–2012." *Yale Journal of Law & Technology* 14 (2012): 162–225.

———. "Taking the Copyfight Online: Comparing the Copyright Debate in Congressional Hearings, in Newspapers, and on the Web." *Journal of Computer-Mediated Communication* 17 (2012): 354–68. doi: 10.1111/j.1083-6101.2012.01575.x.

Herman, Bill D., and Oscar H. Gandy. "Catch 1201: A Legislative History and Content Analysis of the DMCA Exemption Proceedings." *Cardozo Arts & Entertainment Law Journal* 24 (2006): 121–90.

Hindman, Matthew Scott. *The Myth of Digital Democracy.* Princeton, NJ: Princeton University Press, 2009.

Hindman, Matthew Scott, Kostas Tsioutsiouliklis, and Judy A. Johnson. "'Googlearchy': How a Few Heavily-Linked Sites Dominate Politics on the Web." Paper presented at the annual meeting of the Midwest Political Science Association, Chicago, April 2003.

Hosein, Ian. "The Sources of Laws: Policy Dynamics in a Digital and Terrorized World." *The Information Society* 20 (2004): 187–99.

Jamieson, Kathleen Hall, and Paul Waldman. *The Press Effect: Politicians, Journalists, and the Stories That Shape the Political World.* New York: Oxford University Press, 2002.

Jenkins-Smith, Hank C., Gilbert K. St. Clair, and Brian Woods. "Explaining Change in Policy Subsystems: Analysis of Coalition Stability and Defection over Time." *American Journal of Political Science* 35 (1991): 851–80.

Jones, Bryan D., and Frank R. Baumgartner. *The Politics of Attention: How Government Prioritizes Problems.* Chicago: University of Chicago Press, 2005.

Karpf, David. *The MoveOn Effect: The Unexpected Transformation of American Political Advocacy.* New York: Oxford University Press, 2012.

Katz, Elihu. "The Two-Step Flow of Communication: An Up-to-Date Report on a Hypothesis." *Public Opinion Quarterly* 21 (1957): 61–78.

Katz, Elihu, and Paul Felix Lazarsfeld. *Personal Influence: The Part Played by People in the Flow of Mass Communications,* 2nd ed. New Brunswick, NJ: Transaction Publishers, 2006.

Kelty, Christopher M. *Two Bits: The Cultural Significance of Free Software.* Durham, NC: Duke University Press, 2008.

Kingdon, John W. *Agendas, Alternatives, and Public Policies,* 2nd ed. New York: Longman, 2002.

Knopper, Steve. *Appetite for Self-Destruction: The Spectacular Crash of the Record Industry in the Digital Age.* New York: Free Press, 2009.

Kolff, Pieter Kleve Feyo. "MP3: The End Of Copyright As We Know It?" *Proceedings of the IASTED International Conference Law and Technology (Lawtech'99) August 9–12, 1999, Honolulu, Hawaii,* 32–7. http://papers.ssrn.com/sol3/papers.cfm?abstract_id=1138651.

Koss, Jordan. "Protecting Free Speech for Unequivocal Fair Users: Rethinking Our Interpretation of the § 512(f) Misrepresentation Clause." *Cardozo Arts & Entertainment Law Journal* 28 (2010): 149–74.

Krippendorff, Klaus. *Content Analysis: An Introduction to Its Methodology,* 2nd ed. Thousand Oaks, CA: Sage, 2004.

LaFrance, Mary. *Copyright Law in a Nutshell,* 2nd ed. St. Paul, MN: West, 2011.

Landes, William M., and Richard A. Posner. *The Political Economy of Intellectual Property Law.* Washington, DC: AEI Press, 2004.

Lee, Hyangsun. "The Audio Broadcast Flag System: Can It Be a Solution?" *Communication Law and Policy* 12 (2007): 405–76.

Lemley, Mark, David S. Levine, and David G. Post. "Don't Break the Internet." *Stanford Law Review* 64 (2011): 34–8.

Lessig, Lawrence. *Free Culture: How Big Media Uses Technology and the Law to Lock Down Culture and Control Creativity.* New York: Penguin Press, 2004.

———. *Republic, Lost: How Money Corrupts Congress – and a Plan to Stop It,* 1st ed. New York: Twelve, 2011.

Leyden, Kevin M. "Interest Group Resources and Testimony at Congressional Hearings." *Legislative Studies Quarterly* 20, no. 3 (1995): 431–9.

Litman, Jessica. *Digital Copyright: Protecting Intellectual Property on the Internet.* Amherst, NY: Prometheus Books, 2000.

Madden, Mary. "The State of Music Online: Ten Years after Napster." *Pew Internet & American Life Project,* http://pewinternet.org/Reports/2009/9-The-State-of-Music-Online-Ten-Years-After-Napster.aspx.

Marres, Noortje. "Net-Work Is Format Work: Issue Networks and the Sites of Civil Society Politics." In *Reformatting Politics: Information Technology and Global Civil Society*, edited by Jodi Dean, Jon W. Anderson, and Geert Lovink, 3–17. New York: Routledge, 2006.

Masnick, Michael, and Michael Ho. *The Sky is Rising: A Detailed Look at the State of the Entertainment Industry*. Sunnyvale, CA: Floor64, Inc., 2012. http://docstoc.com/docs/111579571.

McChesney, Robert Waterman. *The Problem of the Media: U.S. Communication Politics in the Twenty-First Century*. New York: Monthly Review Press, 2004.

McCombs, Maxwell E. *Setting the Agenda: The Mass Media and Public Opinion*. Cambridge, England: Polity, 2004.

McLeod, Kembrew. *Owning Culture: Authorship, Ownership, and Intellectual Property Law*. New York: Peter Lang, 2001.

Menell, Peter S., and David Nimmer. "Legal Realism in Action: Indirect Copyright Liability's Continuing Tort Framework and Sony's De Facto Demise." *UCLA Law Review* 55 (2007): 1–62.

MGM Studios, Inc. v. Grokster, Ltd., 545 U.S. 913 (2005).

Miller, Joseph M. "Fair Use Through the Lenz of § 512 of the DMCA: A Preemptive Defense to a Premature Remedy?" *Iowa Law Review* 95 (2010): 1697–1729.

Mutz, Diana Carole. *Impersonal Influence: How Perceptions of Mass Collectives Affect Political Attitudes*. Cambridge Studies in Political Psychology and Public Opinion. New York: Cambridge University Press, 1998.

Netanel, Neil Weinstock. *Copyright's Paradox*. New York: Oxford University Press, 2008.

NII Copyright Protection Act of 1995. S. 1284, 104th Cong. (1995).

NII Copyright Protection Act of 1995. H.R. 2441, 104th Cong. (1995).

Nimmer, David. "A Riff on Fair Use in the Digital Millennium Copyright Act." *University of Pennsylvania Law Review* 148 (January 2000): 673–742.

Nisbet, Matthew C., and Mike Huge. "Attention Cycles and Frames in the Plant Biotechnology Debate: Managing Power and Participation Through the Press/Policy Connection." *Press/Politics* 11 (2006): 3–40.

Nisbet, Matthew, and John E. Kotcher. "A Two-Step Flow of Influence? Opinion-Leader Campaigns on Climate Change." *Science Communication* 30 (2009): 328–54.

No Electronic Theft Act (NET Act). Pub. L. No. 105–147 (1997).

Oksanen, Ville, and Mikko Välimäki. "Theory of Deterrence and Individual Behavior: Can Lawsuits Control File Sharing on the Internet?" *Review of Law & Economics* 3 (2007): 693–714. doi: 10.2202/1555–5879.1156.

Olson, Mancur. *The Logic of Collective Action: Public Goods and the Theory of Groups*. Cambridge, MA: Harvard University Press, 1965.

Online Policy Group v. Diebold. 337 F. Supp. 2d 1195 (N.D. Cal. 2004).

Ostrom, Elinor. "Institutional Rational Choice: An Analysis of the Institutional Analysis and Development Framework." In *Theories of the Policy Process*, edited by Paul A. Sabatier. 35–71. Boulder, CO: Westview Press, 1999.

Patry, William F. *How to Fix Copyright*. New York: Oxford University Press, 2011.

Preventing Real Online Threats to Economic Creativity and Theft of Intellectual Property Act of 2011 (PROTECT-IP Act, or PIPA). S. 968, 112th Cong. (2011).

Puerto 80 Projects, S.L.U. v. United States of America. No. 11-CV-3390. (2nd Circuit, filed August 19, 2011).

Pyun, Grace. "The 2008 PRO-IP Act: The Inadequacy of the Property Paradigm in Criminal Intellectual Property Law and Its Effect on Prosecutorial Boundaries." *DePaul Journal of Art, Technology & Intellectual Property Law* 19 (2009): 355–96.

Recording Industry Association of America v. Diamond Multimedia Systems Inc., 180 F.3d 1072 (9th Cir. 1999).

Reese, R. Anthony. "The Temporal Dynamics of 'Capable of Substantial Noninfringing Uses'." *Michigan Telecommunications and Technology Law Review* 13 (2006): 197–224.

Rogers, Richard. *Information Politics on the Web.* Cambridge, MA: MIT Press, 2004.

Sabatier, Paul A., and Hank C. Jenkins-Smith. "The Advocacy Coalition Framework: An Assessment." In *Theories of the Policy Process,* edited by Paul A. Sabatier. 117–68. Boulder, CO: Westview Press, 2007.

Sabatier, Paul A., and Christopher M. Weible. "The Advocacy Coalition Framework: Innovations and Clarifications." In *Theories of the Policy Process,* edited by Paul A. Sabatier. 189–220. Boulder, CO: Westview Press, 2007.

Samuelson, Pamela. "DRM {and, or, vs.} the Law." *Communications of the ACM* 46(4) (2003): 41–5. http://people.ischool.berkeley.edu/~pam/papers/acm_v46_p41.pdf.

———. "Intellectual Property and the Digital Economy: Why the Anti-Circumvention Regulations Need to Be Revised." *Berkeley Technology Law Journal* 14 (1999): 1–49.

———. "Should Economics Play a Role in Copyright Law and Policy?" *University of Ottawa Law & Technology Journal* 1 (2004): 1–21.

Schudson, Michael. *Discovering the News: A Social History of American Newspapers.* New York: Basic Books, 1978.

Schultz, Ida. "The Journalistic Gut Feeling: Journalistic Doxa, News Habitus and Orthodox News Values." *Journalism Practice* 1 (2007): 190–207.

Scott, Allen J. "The Other Hollywood: The Organizational and Geographic Bases of Television-Program Production." *Media, Culture, & Society* 26 (2004): 183–205.

Seltzer, Wendy. "Free Speech Unmoored in Copyright's Safe Harbor: Chilling Effects of the DMCA on the First Amendment." *Harvard Journal of Law and Technology* 24 (2010): 171–232.

Sender, Katherine, and Peter Decherney. "Defending Fair Use in the Age of the Digital Millennium Copyright Act." *International Journal of Communication* 1 (2007): 136–42.

Sobel, Deana. "A Bite Out of Apple? iTunes, Interoperability, and France's Dadvsi Law." *Berkeley Technology Law Journal* 22 (2007): 267–91.

Sonny Bono Copyright Term Extension Act, Pub. L. No. 105–298, 112 Stat. 2827 (1998).

Sony Corp. of America v. Universal City Studios, Inc. 464 U.S. 417 (1984).

Stop Online Piracy Act (SOPA). H.R. 3261. 112th Cong. (2011).

Talbert, Jeffery C., Bryan D. Jones, and Frank R. Baumgartner. "Nonlegislative Hearings and Policy Change in Congress." *American Journal of Political Science* 39 (1995): 383–406.

Thierer, Adam D. *Examining the FCC's Complaint-Driven Broadcast Indecency Enforcement Process*. Washington, DC: The Progress & Freedom Foundation, 2005. http://papers.ssrn.com/sol3/papers.cfm?abstract_id=985374.

United States v. Rojadirecta et al., 11-CV-4139 (PAC) (S.D.N.Y. 2012).

Urban, Jennifer, and Laura Quilter. "Efficient Process or Chilling Effects: Takedown Notices under Section 512 of the Digital Millennium Copyright Act." *Santa Clara Computer & High Technology Law Journal* 22 (2005–2006): 621–93.

Vaidhyanathan, Siva. "Afterword: Critical Information Studies." *Cultural Studies* 20 (2006): 292–315.

———. *Copyrights and Copywrongs: The Rise of Intellectual Property and How It Threatens Creativity*. New York: NYU Press, 2001.

———. "The State of Copyright Activism." *First Monday* 9 (2004). http://firstmonday.org/htbin/cgiwrap/bin/ojs/index.php/fm/article/view/1133/1053.

Van Houweling, Molly Shaffer. "Communications' Copyright Policy." *Journal on Telecommunications Law and High Technology Policy* 4 (2005): 97–122.

Vault Corp. v. Quaid Software Ltd., 847 F.2d 255 (5th Cir. 1988).

Viacom Int'l, Inc. v. YouTube, Inc., 676 F.3d 19 (2nd Cir. 2012).

Wallsten, Kevin. "Agenda Setting and the Blogosphere: An Analysis of the Relationship between Mainstream Media and Political Blogs." *Review of Policy Research* 24 (2007): 567–87.

World Intellectual Property Organization Copyright Treaty (WCT). December 20, 1996. 36 I.L.M. 65. http://www.wipo.int/treaties/en/ip/wct/trtdocs_wo033.html.

World Intellectual Property Organization Performances and Phonograms Treaty (WPPT). December 20, 1996. 36 I.L.M. 76. http://www.wipo.int/treaties/en/ip/wppt/trtdocs_wo034.html.

Xenos, Michael, and W. Lance Bennett. "The Disconnection in Online Politics: The Youth Political Web Sphere and US Election Sites, 2002–2004." *Information, Communication & Society* 10 (August 2007): 443–64.

Index

Lightning Source UK Ltd.
Milton Keynes UK
UKOW03n0137170117
292217UK00004B/49/P